People Who Shaped the Church

20th Century

PEOPLE

WHO SHAPED THE CHURCH

Todd Temple & Kim Twitchell

TYNDALE HOUSE PUBLISHERS, INC. • WHEATON, ILLINOIS

To the men and women who may never get their own chapter
in such a book as this but whose profound influence is
written on the pages of our lives

CONTENTS

Acknowledgments

The authors would like to acknowledge the following for their significant contributions to this project:

Greg Johnson at Alive Communications, for seeing its potential from the start; Mike Yorkey, for research and writing help in some of the chapters; Frank de Jong, for research and fact checking as well as translation of Dutch and German research materials; Walt Day, for many months of encouragement; Breuer & Co., for office space; and Susan Taylor and her associates at Tyndale House, for their expertise, patience, and enthusiasm across the length of this project.

We are especially indebted to Carolyn Poirier, whose work on the project included substantial research and editing on several chapters as well as two years of coordinating the research, editing, and fact checking between two authors on opposite coasts and a publisher in the middle. Her tireless enthusiasm for the book's subjects and encouragement for its authors have carried this immense project to completion.

INTRODUCTION:
NAMING NAMES

The most difficult step in writing this book was deciding who would be included in it. Through research and surveys and our own observations we've attempted to determine who among our fellow believers have been most influential in the church and in the world in which God called them to serve. The list grew to over one hundred names, from which we have nominated the forty-six names listed in the table of contents.

We applied no formal theological test to determine our choices. Instead, we used five simple criteria:

1. *Salvation:* The person made a public confession of faith in Jesus Christ as Savior.
2. *Lordship:* His or her life shows evidence of the transforming work of Christ as Lord.
3. *Influence:* The person has had a *substantial* impact on our faith and our world. For us that meant the person has touched the lives of countless others in one or more of the following ways:

   - By revealing Christ to non-Christians
   - By leading people to faith in Christ
   - By deepening the faith of Christians
   - By developing other influential Christian leaders
   - By providing relief and a future to people in poverty, sickness, or want
   - By bringing justice or mercy to victims of war or oppression

4. *Fruit:* There is compelling evidence that the person's impact was the "fruit" God brought forth from his or her faith and not merely the result of vanity or ambition.

5. *Lifespan:* The work that led to the person's greatest impact was carried out in the twentieth century.

A sixth, more biased criterion was also used. Cognizant of the fact that most of our readers would be American and evangelical, we weighted our selection in favor of men and women whose ministries have had the greatest impact on this audience. With similar bias we sought to include people whose life stories contained lessons for our own application. If in our own research we were moved to celebrate or worship, to learn and obey, we included that person's story in the hope that God might use it to change you, too.

While those we've surveyed agree with the majority of our choices, disagreement on the remaining names ranges from mild to vehement. We've yet to find anyone who agrees with us wholeheartedly, nor have we found any two people who agree with each other. Certainly you, too, will find men and women in this book whose beliefs you don't agree with and maybe some others whose "great impact" you would dispute. In one sense we're pleased with such controversy: It is in our disagreements that we discover our true beliefs—and often find respect for those who don't share them.

It is both humbling and reassuring to note that our attempts to measure a person's true influence will always come up short. For all we know, those who had the greatest influence on the twentieth century are people we've never heard of—uncelebrated men, women, and children whose loving gestures, kind words, and simple prayers set off chain reactions that transformed our world. It may indeed be the George Baileys who come up first on God's list.

If we get to heaven and find that to be the case, we should not be surprised. God himself gives us a telling clue about how he views the rankings. When the disciples asked, "Who is the greatest in the kingdom of heaven?" Jesus responded by holding up a child. In the end, it is only God's list that counts.

Todd Temple, San Diego
Kim Twitchell, Boston

Spirit of the Times:
Events That Shaped
Those Who Shaped Us

The men and women in this book shaped great events in the twentieth century. But they were also products of these times. To better appreciate their influence on our world, it is helpful to consider the moments that made them:

The Industrial Revolution In the latter half of the nineteenth century and the early decades of the twentieth, innovations in science, transportation, and communication transformed small agricultural communities in the Western world into sprawling centers of industry. In the U.S. new factories attracted workers from the farms and immigrants from Europe, leading many into an urban life marked by low wages, deplorable working conditions, and poor health.

While many Christians looked the other way, a few saw the streets and slums as a mission field, including Salvation Army leader Evangeline Booth, social reformer Walter Rauschenbusch, and a young missionary-in-training, Amy Carmichael. Immigrants and the poor would also be among the first to embrace a new faith movement called Pentecostalism, which counted David du Plessis and Aimee Semple McPherson among its leaders.

World War I One of the greatest industrial nations was Germany, whose factories and commercial wealth fed a military machine that swept across Europe from 1914 to 1918. Those who believed in man's ability to create a new and better world saw those beliefs crushed—humanity was just as prone to evil as before

... and now could manufacture it on an assembly line. This devastating war shaped the young faith of many in this book and provided Oswald Chambers, John Mott, and Billy Sunday with a new cause for Christ.

Modernism The nineteenth century birthed Marxism, Darwinism, and a new crop of theologians who abandoned orthodox doctrines to embrace a modern, adaptable faith. The fruit of these philosophies ripened immediately after the war, feeding a new war within the church that moved many denominations to one side or the other and split some congregations and denominations in half.

Taking up the fight against modernism were theologian J. Gresham Machen for orthodoxy, Anglicans John Stott and J. I. Packer for evangelicalism and biblical inerrancy, and pastor Jerry Falwell for fundamentalism. Karl Barth embraced the middle ground of neoorthodoxy. The enduring debate regarding the relevance of Christianity in modern culture inspired the work of a diverse collection of commentators, including G. K. Chesterton, Charles Colson, James Dobson, Carl Henry, F. F. Bruce, C. S. Lewis, Dorothy L. Sayers, and Francis Schaeffer. J. B. Phillips and Ken Taylor joined in by providing modern Bible translations the English-speaking world could understand.

The Great Depression A crash in the stock market in 1929 set off a series of events that led to an economic collapse across America and around the world. Depression-weary men and women sought comfort in the ministries of radio broadcaster Charles Fuller and preachers H. A. Ironside, Peter Marshall, and A. W. Tozer. The bleak conditions of this time also prepared young leaders for the tough circumstances they would endure on mission fields overseas.

The Student Movement College ministries worldwide as well as strong evangelical schools like Wheaton College attracted bright, idealistic students to the faith and challenged many to enter Christian service. In the years between the two world wars, legions of young men and women, including Bible translators Cameron Townsend and Jim Elliot, were called into missions. Many young people were inspired to become missionaries and pastors by the student ministries of Henrietta Mears and John Mott—the latter a product of a campus ministry himself.

Student-movement leaders Bill Bright, Billy Graham, Torrey Johnson, and Bob Pierce each launched global ministries themselves: Campus Crusade for Christ, the Billy Graham Evangelical Association, Youth for Christ, and World Vision. Graham's ministry influenced another young man, Luis Palau, to global evangelistic work. More recently, youth leader Bill Hybels turned a student group into one of America's biggest churches.

World War II Within two decades of its devastating defeat, Germany had regained its industry, its economy, its military, and its desire for power. During the Nazi reign of terror, the future Pope John Paul II attended an underground seminary, Corrie ten Boom hid Jews and went to a concentration camp, and theologian Dietrich Bonhoeffer plotted Hitler's assassination and was executed.

In the aftermath, Karl Barth worked to heal the broken German church, while John Mott received a Nobel Peace Prize for his own work of healing. And when Soviet Communism replaced Nazism in Eastern Europe, Brother Andrew began smuggling Bibles behind the Iron Curtain.

Civil Rights Movement At the end of the war, the U.S. and other Western countries enjoyed a boom in the economy. The burgeoning middle class drove their new cars to their new houses in the suburbs and turned on their new television sets. Yet many were left behind. In big cities and small rural towns, the poor remained poor, the oppressed were forgotten. The cause of the forgotten masses was taken up by Christian leaders such as African Americans Martin Luther King Jr. and John Perkins and South African bishop Desmond Tutu.

Meanwhile, Joni Eareckson Tada championed the cause of another forgotten group: the disabled. And Catholics such as Pope John Paul II, Thomas Merton, and Mother Teresa would call the world's attention to other social issues: poverty, injustice, oppression, the insanities of war, and the preciousness of life.

The Lives of Our Times:

Name	Lifespan	1851–1875	1876–1900	1901–1925
Walter Rauschenbusch	1861–1918			
Billy Sunday	1862–1935			
John Mott	1865–1955			
Evangeline Booth	1865–1950			
Amy Carmichael	1867–1951			
G. K. Chesterton	1874–1936			
Oswald Chambers	1874–1917			
H. A. Ironside	1876–1951			
J. Gresham Machen	1881–1937			
Karl Barth	1886–1968			
Charles E. Fuller	1887–1968			
Henrietta Mears	1890–1963			
Aimee Semple McPherson	1890–1944			
Corrie ten Boom	1892–1983			
Dorothy L. Sayers	1893–1957			
Cameron Townsend	1896–1982			
A. W. Tozer	1897–1963			
C. S. Lewis	1898–1963			
Peter Marshall	1902–1949			
David du Plessis	1905–1987			
Dietrich Bonhoeffer	1906–1945			
J. B. Phillips	1906–1982			
Torrey Johnson	1909–			
Mother Teresa	1910–1997			
F. F. Bruce	1910–1990			
Francis Schaeffer	1912–1984			
Carl F. H. Henry	1913–			
Bob Pierce	1914–1978			
Thomas Merton	1915–1968			
Ken Taylor	1917–			
Billy Graham	1918–			
John Paul II	1920–			
John Stott	1921–			
Bill Bright	1921–			
J. I. Packer	1926–			
Jim Elliot	1927–1956			
Martin Luther King Jr.	1929–1968			
John Perkins	1930–			
Charles Colson	1931–			
Desmond Tutu	1931–			
Brother Andrew	1933–			
Jerry Falwell	1933–			
Luis Palau	1934–			
James Dobson	1936–			
Joni Eareckson Tada	1949–			
Bill Hybels	1951–			

Comparative Life Spans

1926–1950	1951–1975	1976–2000	Total Years Lived
			57
			73
			89
			85
			84
			62
			43
			75
			56
			82
			81
			73
			54
			91
			64
			86
			66
			65
			47
			82
			39
			76
			87
			80
			72
			64
			53
			29
			39

BROTHER ANDREW

STRENGTHENING THE SUFFERING CHURCH

Lord, in my luggage I have Scripture that I want to take to Your children across this border. When You were on earth, You made blind eyes see. Now, I pray, make seeing eyes blind. Do not let the guards see those things You do not want them to see.

The Prayer of God's Smuggler, from *God's Smuggler*

The prayer meeting had just ended, and Brother Andrew and his traveling companion, Hans, were waiting in the crowded vestibule of a Baptist church in Moscow for God to show them who was to receive the Russian Bibles they had smuggled into the country. Spotting a thin, balding man staring into the crowd, they approached him cautiously. When they told him who they were and why they were there, the man's eyes grew wide. His church in Siberia, two thousand miles away, had 150 secret members—and not a single Bible. He had been told in a dream to go to Moscow, where he would find a Bible.

Hans held out the big Russian Bible they had brought. Overcome with emotion, the three men hugged each other, awestruck that God would allow them to be a part of what they saw unfolding right before their eyes.

IN SHORT

In the darkest days of the Cold War, most Westerners experienced life in the "Evil Empire" through suspense films and spy novels. Brother Andrew experienced it firsthand. He was among the few who dared to venture behind the Iron Curtain. Over the course of his clandestine ministry, Brother Andrew risked life and liberty to let Christians living under communist rule know that they weren't forgotten, to hear their stories and share them with the Western world, and to give oppressed believers the most precious possession of all: God's Word.

Andrew and the organization he founded, Open Doors, expanded their efforts to other closed countries, including many in the Muslim world. Today this ministry continues to bring God's Word to forgotten believers worldwide.

FAITH

As a boy, Andrew imagined himself crawling under barbed wire and dodging bullets as they whizzed past his head. In this young Dutch boy's world of play, danger was often the theme. Born in the province of Noord Holland in the village of Sint Pancras, Andrew was one of six children in a poor Protestant family. His mother suffered from a bad heart; his blacksmith father was deaf. But despite their poverty and disabilities, the family was generous—they never turned guests away from the dinner table.

In 1939 Andrew's brother Bastian was fighting tuberculosis. Andrew decided that if his brother was going to die, then he would too. Shortly after his eleventh birthday, Andrew sneaked into Bastian's room and kissed him, hoping that the contagious disease would take his life as well. In July of that year, Bastian died, but when Andrew stayed healthy, he thought God had betrayed him.

In 1940 Nazi Germany invaded Holland. When the German soldiers appeared in his town, Andrew's imaginary war games became real. At night Andrew would sneak out to foul up the German lieutenant's gas tank or to fire cherry bombs at the enemy soldiers. The family hid Jews escaping to the coast, and Andrew and his brother and father often hid to avoid deportation.

After the war in Europe ended in 1945, Andrew joined the army and was sent to Indonesia, which was still a Dutch colony at the time. He was wounded in 1949, and during his convalescence, he picked up a Bible and began to read. He continued to read after his return to Holland in 1950. One stormy winter night in his father's home, he heard voices in the wind, asking him questions and singing songs from a tent revival he had attended. Staring at the dark ceiling above his bed, he offered a simple prayer: "Lord, if you will show me the way, I will follow you." Jesus answered his prayer, and Andrew responded by committing his life to missions.

FRUIT

Andrew found work at a local chocolate factory, where he also met his future bride, Corrie van Dam. During that time he began to investigate the requirements for becoming a missionary. Ordination appeared to be a must, but to attend college and seminary while working would take him twelve years. Discouraged, he enrolled in correspondence courses and learned English. Then he heard of an organization called Worldwide Evangelization Crusade, whose philosophy was not to rely on church missions budgets but to send out missionaries and trust God to provide the necessary funds. So in 1953 Andrew left Holland for two years of study at the Glasgow Missionary Training College in Scotland.

During his first term Andrew was sent on his first evangelism trip through Scotland with a team of five other men. Each man was given a one-pound note and told to pay for his own transportation, lodging, food, advertising, and the cost of renting meeting halls. In addition, throughout the four-week trip they were not to mention any need, and they had to tithe—within twenty-four hours—out of everything they received. At the end of the trip, they were to pay the pound back to the school.

As the trip progressed, Andrew was amazed to see God at work. Sometimes one of the men received a little money in the mail from his parents. A church they had visited weeks before would send a check. People donated fruit, vegetables, and eggs for their meals. When Andrew and his team came back to the school, they had ten pounds more than they had left with a month earlier. God had faithfully provided all that they needed.

As Andrew's two years of study in Glasgow ended, he prayed about where he should go. The week before graduation he read a magazine advertisement for a socialist youth festival to be held in Warsaw that summer. He wrote to the organizers, telling them he was a Christian missionary and wanted to exchange ideas. Could he come? He got a quick reply: Most certainly! As Andrew left school to return to Holland, he began to get a vision for ministering to the young faces he saw in the ad's photo—faces that were trapped behind the Iron Curtain.

During the three-week youth festival, Andrew often ventured out to attend churches, hand out tracts, visit a lone Bible store, and talk with soldiers and with people on the trolley and on street corners. One day he saw a parade of young people marching for their new religion, Communism. Andrew's eyes welled up as he realized that God was speaking to him through a verse he had read: "Now wake up! Strengthen what little remains, for even what is left is at the point of death" (Revelation 3:2). He knew his life's work would be behind the Iron Curtain, strengthening God's remnant church as it struggled to survive. The year 1955 saw Andrew making a series of trips to most of the countries behind the Iron Curtain.

One afternoon back in Holland, a friend knocked on Andrew's door. He told Andrew that God had impressed on him that he was to tell Andrew to learn to drive. Andrew protested—he didn't even have a car. Time passed, and when the friend saw that Andrew still had not learned to drive, he taught Andrew himself. A short time later as Andrew was preparing for a trip to Yugoslavia, another friend handed him a set of keys for a brand-new Volkswagen, saying that God had told him to give Andrew his car. Before Andrew left, another friend arrived on his doorstep holding out a stack of money. God had told her Andrew would need money for two months.

Jamil, a Christian leader in Zagreb, Yugoslavia, had often ordered Bibles in quantity from a distributor in the West. No one had heard from Jamil in years, and Andrew was asked to check on him. Andrew sent a carefully worded letter, telling Jamil that a Dutchman would be coming to visit him. Although Andrew did not know it, Jamil had moved, and it took the local post office many days to track down the new address and forward the letter. On the very day that Andrew drove into Zagreb, Jamil received the rerouted letter. Puzzled by the message from the mysterious Dutchman, Jamil boarded a train to take him to his old apartment, then stood on the sidewalk in front of it. A moment later Andrew pulled up to the curb. Seeing the Dutch license plates, Jamil seized Andrew's hands and welcomed him. Andrew's Bible ministry had begun.

In 1958, after traveling alone for three years, Andrew married Corrie van Dam. Together with a growing team of courageous followers, they smuggled dozens, then hundreds, and then thousands of Bibles into communist countries. In 1961 they completed Project Pearl, smuggling one million Bibles into China on a single night. On every mission they risked deportation, seizure of their vehicles, arrest, and imprisonment. And on each trip they trusted God to confound the authorities, to open doors into countries guarded with machine guns, to lead them to believers who were willing to risk their own lives to receive and distribute Brother Andrew's holy contraband.

The demise of the Soviet Empire did not mean the end of Brother Andrew's work. The church in that part of the world still suffers hardship, and Andrew has continued to serve. Indeed, Christians around the globe, including those in China and in much of the Middle East, face intense persecution for their beliefs. Andrew's ministry reaches believers worldwide—wherever politics, law, or culture opposes faith in Christ.

Open Doors, the ministry Andrew founded in 1955, has served persecuted Christians for half a century. Since 1956 the ministry's monthly magazine, *Open Doors,* has informed Christians about the suffering church around the world. Since Brother Andrew's book *God's Smuggler* was first published in 1958, over ten million copies have been printed, with editions in several languages. Today Brother Andrew is president emeritus of Open Doors, which now has over two hundred full-time workers in twenty countries. The ministry delivers Bibles where they are banned or restricted, supports and encourages believers who are suffering for their faith, and trains church leaders living in countries opposed to the gospel. Open Doors workers and their founder take seriously the words of Jesus, who said, "Go and make disciples of all the nations" (Matthew 28:19). To them, that little word *all* is significant. The miracles they have encountered as they have seen God open closed doors indicate that God thinks so too.

LEGACY

Long before most of us could even imagine the fall of the Iron Curtain, much less see its crash, Andrew was praying for just such a deliverance. He saw the cold war not as a clash of political and economic philosophies but as a spiritual battle in which God's children had been taken prisoner by their enemy Satan. Like Dietrich Bonhoeffer, whose faith led him into defiance of the evil Nazi regime and even to plot an assassination attempt against Hitler, Brother Andrew faithfully defied the authority of governments who declared themselves enemies of Christianity. He broke the law to spread the great news of God's grace as seen in Jesus Christ.

It is tempting to romanticize Andrew's subterfuge, to see his mission as an exciting, biblically sanctioned way to sneak around and do illegal things. But Brother Andrew's actions were and are the result of simple obedience—an answer to God's call that could just as easily have led him to become a preacher or Sunday school teacher or anything else we would consider less sensational. Andrew's faith came first. God's endless provision—from seeing Andrew's team through that first Scottish mission trip, to blinding the eyes of border guards, to providing money for Bible printing—is compelling proof that Andrew has obeyed God's orders.

Few Christians give God the chance to prove his faithfulness to such an extent. Andrew has had faith enough to trust God with what seemed impossible, and millions of people worldwide have trusted Christ because Brother Andrew dared to trust him first.

For additional information about Open Doors, see appendix A.

Now wake up! Strengthen what little remains, for even what is left is at the point of death.
Revelation 3:2

BOOKS BY BROTHER ANDREW

And God Changed His Mind (with Susan Devore Williams) (1999)
A Time for Heroes (with Dave and Neta Jackson) (out of print)
For the Love of My Brothers (with Verne Becker) (1998)
God's Smuggler (with John and Elizabeth Sherrill) (1964)
The Calling (with Verne Becker) (1996)

Karl Barth

MOVING MEN BEYOND THEMSELVES

Our church, our very own church, still
believes far too much in a good man and
far too little in the only good Master.
Too much and too little—that is why our
church is perhaps no longer the light
that lightens the darkness, which is
what the church ought to be. It is a much
too feeble church, a liberal church,
just like the German Church that was
overthrown in 1933.

From a speech given in 1937 in Basel

After meeting Karl Barth for the first time, a young Dietrich Bonhoeffer wrote that the professor was "beyond his books, a very alive person and theologian who was so overcome by the cause of theology that he could for the sake of the matter be humble and haughty, doubting and overbearing." Like Bonhoeffer, whose own theology would be tested under Hitler's reign of terror, Barth believed that God's Word was not merely a topic for study but a call to live one's faith to the limit, even when doing so might get you killed.

Bonhoeffer died proving this. Barth survived long enough to remind us that neither the dry study of ancient religion nor the active pursuit of modern humanistic theology can save us from our sins. For that we need Christ himself, as Savior and Master, Lover and Ruler, unchanging and everlasting.

In Short

The writings of neoorthodox theologian Karl Barth have influenced countless theologians, pastors, and ministry students through the greater part of this century. He opposed the liberal teachings of Germany's influential theologians and stood just as firmly against the godless ideologies of the Nazi regime. His passionate faith, tested in the heart of two world wars, shows us how to oppose evil, minister to its victims, and restore what it leaves behind.

Faith

Karl Barth (pronounced "Bart") was born in Basel, Switzerland, on May 10, 1886. His father, Fritz Barth, was a Reformed Swiss minister and a professor of New Testament studies and ancient history. Karl was an avid student who especially enjoyed history, music, and drama. He was also a voracious reader. In his later years those who knew him joked that the moment he was born he asked for an evening paper. His reading and his passions for study, research, and intellectual creativity became lifelong habits.

At age eighteen Barth began theological studies under his own father in Bern. He went on to study at German schools in Berlin, Tübingen, and Marburg under renowned teachers of progressive liberalism of the early twentieth century. Another student about this time was J. Gresham Machen, who quickly rejected modernist theology and became one of its most formidable opponents. Barth, however, accepted the liberal teachings of Wilhelm Hermann and others, which became the foundation for his own theology for the next several years.

Barth completed his studies in 1909 and entered the ministry in the Swiss German Reformed Church. He was placed in a German-speaking congregation in the predominantly French-speaking city of Geneva, where he developed a love for the French language and culture. There he met Nelly Hoffman, whose family belonged to the church. Karl and Nelly were married in 1913 and eventually had five children.

Two years before his marriage, Barth had moved from Geneva to become pastor of a church in the Swiss town of Safenwil. Most of his church members worked in factories that were springing up in this once-rural village. The factory owners were strong, the labor movement weak, and Barth took a stand for the latter, assisting in union-organizing efforts and demanding wage increases for the workers. The owners branded him a socialist. In 1915 he joined the Social Democratic Party.

Barth's liberal theology harmonized with his social activism, but it didn't offer his parishioners the spiritual food they desperately needed. This became even more clear to him when World War I broke out. Now, years after his formal studies, he reexamined his theology and began studying the Bible intensely. In the process he discovered a "strange new world," a world of faith he had not found in all his previous pursuits.

FRUIT

In 1916 he pored over the book of Romans and like Martin Luther centuries before him, found the makings of a theological revolution. Barth concluded that liberal theology attempted to reshape Christianity to fit modern culture. But because the foundational truths of the faith were incompatible with the world, this reshaping resulted in a version of Christianity that wasn't true. From his study notes he wrote a commentary on Romans, published it in 1919, and released a second and more influential edition in 1922.

The book brought to light a fundamental division in Germany's theological community. Former professors denounced him. But other Christians were eager to embrace Barth's views. They had just passed through a horrific war that was the result of putting one's faith in the power of modern man. Barth reminded them that God's Word is eternal and his kingdom is not subject to the corruptions of this world.

In 1921 Barth left Safenwil to work with the Reformed Church in Friesland, the Netherlands, then took a series of professorships at German theological schools, including Göttingen, Munster, and in 1930, Bonn. During this time he wrote some of his greatest works, including *The Word of God and the Word of Man* and *Theology and Church,* and began writing his five-volume *Church Dogmatics.*

In the 1930s Germany witnessed the rise of an Austrian immigrant named Adolph Hitler. Barth used his theology to oppose Hitler and his swelling National Socialist, or Nazi, party policies. Many in the official German Evangelical Church, including some of Barth's fellow professors, embraced the Nazi movement and its charismatic leader. Swastika-bearing flags hung in churches, Nazi songs were sung along with Martin Luther's hymns. By the end of 1933, the church's relationship with Hitler was so entrenched that Barth and others, including Dietrich Bonhoeffer, could no longer be part of it. They formed the German Confessing Church.

Barth also launched a written indictment of the compromised German Evangelical Church in the form of a periodic journal, *Theological Existence Today,* which enjoyed wide readership for two years before Hitler shut down the opposition. In May 1934 Barth and others in the new Confessing Church met in Barmen to draft what became the Barmen Confession—six articles that defined Christian opposition to Nazi ideology and practice. Before the year ended, the Nazis suspended Barth from teaching at Bonn and a few months later forced him to leave Germany altogether.

From Basel, the town of his birth, nestled between Germany and France in Switzerland's northwest corner, Barth could remain close to the Germany he had grown to love and could continue to speak out against the Nazi regime he had chosen to fight. Basel also provided a ringside seat for the war about to burst forth.

Barth began communicating with churches in countries being threatened by Nazism, and he continued to encourage believers even after they had been overrun by the German war machine. Like the apostle Paul, he wrote open letters to be read from pulpits and distributed to church members, offering words of comfort and hope. He called them to hold firm to their faith in the midst of their great trials, to reject the evil and spiritually bankrupt Nazi ideology, and if called for, to become martyrs in the name of Christ. In 1945 these letters were collected and published as *A Swiss Voice.*

Germany surrendered on May 7, 1945. Its cities had been reduced to rubble; its economic, political, and social structures were destroyed, and the Allied forces divided the country into four occupation zones. Barth, so gracious and encouraging to the victims of Nazi aggression, turned his heart to the now beaten and despised aggressors. The enemy, he pleaded, was not the German people but the Nazi regime that had ruled them. They had been Hitler's accomplices, but they had also been his first victims. In the end, it was their own country that Hitler had destroyed.

In 1946 Barth accepted an invitation to return to the university in Bonn to teach for a semester. In what remained of his old, bomb-torn school, he taught dogmatics to a new generation of young theologians eager to find solid spiritual ground among the ruins of a world built on a false foundation.

In the postwar years Barth continued to write and teach and to work to rebuild the German church. In the spring of 1948 Barth took a trip to Hungary. The country was now under communist rule, and Barth told Christians to live peacefully with a humble faith, in whatever circumstances they were in, which led many to question his political views.

But Barth was not indifferent to the persecution of Christians behind what would become known as the Iron Curtain. That Curtain ran right through the country he loved, and he spoke out for the rights of East German Christians caught on the other side. But what alarmed him as much as Communism was the fervent anticommunist feeling festering in the Western world. To him, the proper response to Communism's argument was not a war of words or weapons but a commitment to social justice rooted in living faith.

In his later years Barth continued to reevaluate his theology and to write about what he found. Just as his earlier examination had led him to reject the teachings of his liberal theology professors, later study brought conclusions that some welcomed and others found alarming. He is best known for his formation of neoorthodoxy. While orthodox theologians such as J. Gresham Machen counted the inerrancy of Scripture a foundational pillar to Reformed theology, Barth's neoorthodoxy claimed that the Bible was not the actual revelation of God but the record of that revelation. Today these two theologies—orthodoxy and neoorthodoxy—make up the vast majority of Reformed Christian thinking.

Habits from Barth's early years stayed with him throughout his life. He did not own a television set, nor did he drive a car. He read the newspaper, devoured classical literature, and enjoyed everything from fiction to detective stories to historical works, but he cherished family and friends and was always ready to set aside his study and writing to spend time with those he loved. And above all else, Barth was in love with God, and he was never ashamed to change his thinking if he discovered that it stood between him and the Lord.

LEGACY
Karl Barth's name often appears with those of Augustine, Anselm, Aquinas, Luther, and Calvin as those most influential to the

formation of Christian doctrine. While theologians continue to debate his views and their impact on the twentieth-century church, some things are above dispute. Barth offered the world a reasoned rebuttal to the liberal teachings of Germany's influential theologians, thus limiting their impact on the church.

If Barth were alive today, he would undoubtedly still be up to his lifelong habits, declaring and sharing his faith, standing against institutions and ideologies that threaten that faith, and calling Christians to live for Christ whatever the cost.

Remember your leaders who first taught you the word of God. Think of all the good that has come from their lives, and trust the Lord as they do.

Hebrews 13:7

BOOKS BY KARL BARTH

Anselm, Fides Quaerens Intellectum: Anselm's Proof of the Existence of God in the Context of His Theological Scheme (1995)
Church and State (Church Classics series) (1991)
Church Dogmatics: A Selection with Introduction by Helmut Gollweitzer (1994)
Dogmatics in Outline (1986)
Ethics (1992)
Homiletics (1991)
Humanity of God (1960)
Karl Barth: Preaching through the Christian Year (1999)
Knowledge of God and the Service of God according to the Teaching of the Reformation: Recalling the Scottish Confessions of 1560 (out of print)
The Christian Life (1999)
The Epistle to the Romans (1968)
The Göttingen Dogmatics: Instruction in the Christian Religion, vol. 1 (1991)
The Holy Spirit and the Christian Life: The Theological Basis of Ethics (1993)
The Theology of John Calvin (1995)
The Theology of Schleiermacher (1999)
Wolfgang Amadeus Mozart (1986)

1906–1945

DIETRICH BONHOEFFER

DOING THE RIGHT THING, NO MATTER WHAT THE COST

One man asks: What is to come? The other: What is right? And that is the difference between the free man and the slave.

Ethics

August 1936
Olympics at Berlin.
Dietrich preaches
at Olympic Village
the same year in
which, much to
Hitler's chagrin,
African-American
Jesse Owens
medaled in track.

Dietrich Bonhoeffer stood on the deck of a ship bound for England. He had fled to America to escape the Nazi atrocities in Germany, but now, just months later, he had decided that was not to be. The year was 1939, and Dietrich knew he must return to his homeland. In a letter to Reinhold Niebuhr, the man who had offered him safety in the United States, he wrote: "I have come to the conclusion that I made a mistake in coming to America. . . . I shall have no right to take part in the restoration of Christian life in Germany after the war unless I share the trials of this time with my people."

Five years after his return to Germany, he climbed the gallows steps of Flössenberg concentration camp and was executed. Just twenty-nine days later the Nazis surrendered.

In Short

In his short life of thirty-nine years, pastor, theologian, and writer Dietrich Bonhoeffer led three congregations and taught hundreds of university and seminary students in Europe and America. He played a vital role in the German Resistance, rescued his sister's family, and saved the lives of fourteen Jews. But the greatest legacy of his faith is what he left behind. His books, numerous articles, and a collection of prison letters have influenced tens of thousands of Bible students, seminarians, and ordinary, everyday Christians. Many have found in his writings the wonder of faith, the purpose of life.

FAITH

Dietrich, the sixth child of Karl and Paula Bonhoeffer, was born ten minutes before his twin sister, Sabine, on February 4, 1906. His father was a professor of psychiatry and neurology in Berlin; his mother was a member of the German aristocracy. The society Dietrich entered was convinced of its enlightenment and natural superiority. By age ten Dietrich knew he wanted to be a theologian.

Years later he studied in Berlin, taught systematic theology, and was awarded his doctorate. He served as an assistant pastor in Barcelona, Spain, and then in 1930 sailed to New York to spend a postgraduate year at Union Theological Seminary.

New York changed Dietrich. He absorbed everything around him, considering and evaluating it and then dismissing it or integrating it into his life. At the seminary, Dietrich became close friends with Frank Fisher, an African American. They were thrown out of a restaurant together simply because one of them was black. The encounter angered Dietrich and forced him to grapple with bigotry face-to-face. During his American sojourn Dietrich also became involved with the Abyssinian Baptist Church in Harlem, teaching Sunday school and listening to sermons preached in ways he had never heard in his native country. It stirred his soul and opened his eyes to a gospel rich in passion for the poor and the outcast. He would not forget these American experiences. They helped shape the faith for which he would live and die.

FRUIT

Upon Bonhoeffer's return to Germany after his year in New York, colleagues within the German evangelical church who gladly welcomed Hitler, Germany's rising star, confronted Bonhoeffer. But he saw Nazis interfering in the church, deciding on the basis of race who could join. Excluding Jews from the church, Bonhoeffer realized, was only a part of a broader campaign to exclude them from German society. The church must fight Nazi injustice, he argued. Ministry was not a privilege of race. Christians must help the victims and, if necessary, "fall into the spokes of the wheel itself" to halt the Nazi machine. When the evangelical church was swept under Nazi influence, Bonhoeffer and others formed a new church, the Confessing Church.

In October 1933 Bonhoeffer took the pastorate of a German church in London and began to write *The Cost of Discipleship*. The following year he returned to Germany to teach at Finkenwalde, the Confessing Church seminary. Three years later, in 1937, the Gestapo closed Finkenwalde's doors, and after coming under increasing Gestapo observation, Bonhoeffer was banned from Berlin in January 1938.

Bonhoeffer's brother-in-law Hans von Dohnanyi approached him. Would he join the Resistance? Bonhoeffer was uncertain. As a pastor, how could he, in good conscience, fight? That question led to more. Should he fight? leave Germany? If he stayed, he would be drafted into Hitler's army. To find answers to these questions, he continued to search his soul and to write what he found there. The result was *Life Together*, which many consider to be his greatest book.

As danger grew for Jews, Bonhoeffer escorted his sister; her husband, Gerhard Leibholz, a Jew; and their children to the border of Switzerland to flee to London for safety. In early 1939 he himself decided to leave his homeland. He was offered a position at Union Theological Seminary in New York, but only months later he returned. He knew what he had to do.

Upon his return, Bonhoeffer joined his brother-in-law Hans in a small Resistance cell in the German Foreign Office. With his ecumenical contacts, he helped to foster resistance throughout Europe. One month after returning from New York, on order of the Gestapo, Bonhoeffer was forbidden to speak in public. He began work on his book *Ethics*, exploring the questions he now faced: Could Christians in good conscience disobey the government? Could they lie? Could they kill?

The Nazis were about to force him into making such choices. They were compelling Jews to wear the Star of David, and soon after, they were deporting the Jews to concentration camps and then to the death factories. In response, Bonhoeffer's Resistance cell made plans for "Operation Seven." Seven Jews, traveling with forged papers claiming they were agents of the German Foreign Office, were to be escorted into safety in Switzerland. When the operation was complete, fourteen Jews had made the escape. Bonhoeffer led them out personally.

Soon Bonhoeffer joined others in the Resistance in a plot to destroy Hitler. On March 13, 1943, Hitler paid a visit to the battlefront. Bonhoeffer's brother-in-law Hans flew there with explosives in his briefcase. On Hitler's return flight, the bomb was on the plane. It failed. The Resistance then made a second attempt on March 21. Hitler was visiting an exhibition of captured military equipment in the Berlin arsenal. There a Resistance fighter, wired with explosives to blow up both Hitler and himself, waited. Bonhoeffer was at home with his family, celebrating a birthday. As he sat at the piano, directing the family in singing, he waited for the phone call that would signal the mission's success. The phone did not ring. Hitler had left the exhibition ten minutes earlier than planned, unknowingly avoiding his own assassination.

On April 5, 1943, fifteen days after the second attempt, Bonhoeffer and several other German resisters were arrested. The Gestapo had traced a money trail that led from the fourteen Jewish escapees back to Bonhoeffer and his cohorts. He was charged with rescuing Jews, using his travels abroad for nonintelligence matters, and misusing his intelligence position to keep Confessing Church pastors out of the military. The Gestapo report described Bonhoeffer as "completely in the opposition." Still, the Nazis had not discovered Bonhoeffer's hand in the assassination attempts.

On July 20, 1944, while Bonhoeffer was in prison, there was yet another attempt to assassinate Hitler. This time the Gestapo was able to trace a trail back to Bonhoeffer. After a meeting with Hitler himself, a high-ranking official drove to Flössenberg concentration camp carrying the important files and a candid diary of Resistance activity. Bonhoeffer was convicted of high treason and sentenced to death. On April 9, 1945, at the age of thirty-nine, Dietrich Bonhoeffer was executed.

According to Eberhard Bethge's book *Dietrich Bonhoeffer: Man of Vision, Man of Courage,* the SS doctor who witnessed Bonhoeffer's hanging later recalled a man "devout . . . brave and composed. Early in the gray dawn, Dietrich met his accusers and the other coconspirators at the gallows. His death ensued after a few seconds. . . . I have hardly ever seen a man die so entirely submissive to the will of God." Bonhoeffer sent out a final message through an English prisoner at the camp: "This is the end . . . for me, the beginning of life."

Fifty-one years after his death, Dietrich was exonerated of the charge of high treason against Germany. The Berlin Public Prosecutor's Office formally overturned the 1945 death sentence an SS tribunal had imposed. On July 8, 1998, in a ceremony in Westminster Abbey in London attended by Queen Elizabeth II, statues of ten twentieth-century martyrs were unveiled. Dietrich Bonhoeffer's statue is one of them.

LEGACY

Dietrich Bonhoeffer lived and breathed questions most of us would rather avoid because they force us to consider what we really believe. Where is the line that divides personal faith and civic duty? Is there a line? What actions are justified against an immoral regime? Can we ever justify personal safety over Christian duty? Do we believe in something so fiercely that we would die for it? Bonhoeffer's answers were and still are controversial.

While many theologians write and teach what to them has become merely academic, Dietrich Bonhoeffer dared to seek God from the depth of his own soul. The God he found there was alive, at work, shining light upon Bonhoeffer's most troubling questions and guiding him not merely to know the truth but to live it to the fullest extent of his abilities. To many, Bonhoeffer's writings are too deep, too complex, too troubling. But to those willing to wrestle with the questions of who God is and how we are to respond to him in the real world, Bonhoeffer's answers inspire humility, a sense of purpose, and overwhelming awe.

If you are suffering according to God's will, keep on doing what is right, and trust yourself to the God who made you, for he will never fail you.

1 Peter 4:19

BOOKS BY DIETRICH BONHOEFFER

A Testament to Freedom: The Essential Writings of Dietrich Bonhoeffer (1995)
Act and Being (1996)
Creation and Fall: A Theological Exposition of Genesis 1–3 (1997)
Creation and Fall/Temptation: Two Biblical Studies (1997)
Danctorun Communio: A Theological Study of the Sociology of the Church (1998)
Ethics (1995)
Fiction from Tegel Prison (1999)
Letters and Papers from Prison (1997)
Life Together (1996)
Meditations on the Cross (1998)
Spiritual Care (1985)
The Cost of Discipleship (1995)
Voices in the Night: The Prison Poems of Dietrich Bonhoeffer (1999)

1865–1950

EVANGELINE BOOTH

AT WAR WITH THE DARKNESS

O Lord . . . don't let us live
so that You will have to say
we have just done
ordinarily, or middling,
but let us live so that you
will say, "Well done! You
have done the best
that could be done!"

General Evangeline Booth of the Salvation Army

W hen Evangeline Booth was appointed U.S. commander of the Salvation Army in 1904, she became the most powerful woman in America: The commander to hundreds of officers and tens of thousands of soldiers serving in ministries that touched millions of Americans. And she took command of this giant ministry at a time when women did not even have the right to vote.

In Short

In her thirty years as commander of the Salvation Army in America, Evangeline Booth led her ministry's forces through countless assaults on poverty, hunger, sickness, and oppression, through natural disasters, a world war, and the Great Depression. Then when her service in the United States was done, she was promoted to the rank of general of the Salvation Army worldwide. In the first half of the twentieth century, no other Christian woman had a greater influence on the world.

Faith

Evangeline Cory Booth was born on Christmas Day 1865, the same year her parents, William and Catherine Booth, founded the Salvation Army. Eva's parents and their courageous followers took the gospel to the toughest parts of London, preaching and singing in the slums, marching in the streets, and renting out old theaters and halls for their nightly meetings.

Evangeline inherited her parents' ministry talents in full measure. In her teens she and her Army friends carried the gospel into the taverns, singing and speaking to the unruly crowds. She had her father's boldness and her mother's superior command of language; these qualities combined with her naturally dramatic, girlish charms to create a captivating speaker.

At age twenty-three Evangeline was placed in charge of all of the Army's evangelical centers and training homes in London, and by 1895 Evangeline commanded 350 officers (the Army's term for ministers), 200 cadets in training (ministry candidates), and 21,000 soldiers (church members).

FRUIT

Late in 1895 Evangeline was sent to New York to reconcile with her brother Ballington, who was in charge of the Army in the U.S. and was threatening to secede from the London-based organization to start his own ministry. Ballington, upstairs discussing the secession with his leading officers, refused Evangeline admittance. Undeterred, she climbed the fire escape and crawled through a window. Once inside, she took the platform and addressed the mutinous officers. Most decided to stay with the Army, and they rallied with Evangeline as she took temporary command of the U.S. ministry. The public was another matter. After witnessing years of strong, pro-American male leadership, the press was quick to characterize Evangeline as a "minion of British Despotism." Evangeline proved herself again and again; she was quick in word and action, especially in crisis, and few could outwit, outspeak, outcharm, or upstage her.

When her replacement arrived in 1896, Evangeline moved to Toronto to command the Army in Canada. In 1898 gold fever struck the continent, and many thousands of men raced across Canada to stake their claims in the Klondike. Evangeline sent a mission and nursing corps to minister to the miners and later visited them herself. Evangeline, dressed in vivid colors and with her clear and compelling voice, was a rare and welcome experience. At one meeting twenty-five thousand men sat on a mountainside and sang as she directed "Nearer My God to Thee."

In 1904, at the age of thirty-eight, Evangeline returned to New York to command the Salvation Army in the U.S., a post she would hold for thirty years. She created new ministries and expanded old ones. One of her first innovations was the school breakfast program. At that time seventy thousand children in New York City alone went to school without food. Today the Salvation Army still serves meals to needy children in schools across the country.

The great San Francisco earthquake leveled that city in 1906, and the Salvation Army, itself decimated in the quake, responded with immediate aid. It was one of the first disasters to muster the troops. Many more would follow, and disaster relief became one of the Army's most appreciated ministries. Evangeline visited the city soon after the earthquake to show support and to rally the rest of the country to send aid.

Evangeline's troops were always in need of money to carry out the many ministries in their charge. Most churches are funded by the tithes of their congregations, but Army corps ministered to the poor, the abandoned, the homeless . . . those least able to give. To fill the gap, Evangeline fostered relationships with many of America's rich and powerful, appointing them to advisory boards and fund-raising campaigns. In many ways she was their equal: Each commanded giant workforces spanning the nation; each grappled with multimillion-dollar budgets; and each managed buildings and factories, products and services. Evangeline's bold, uncompromising leadership dazzled her benefactors, and her example of faith moved more than a few to make a Christian commitment.

Her critics said that she was autocratic and at times abusive. But those who worked with her served long and well. Under Eva's leadership, the Army spread rapidly across the country and reached out to the poor wherever they found them. In 1911 the American Army distributed 1.5 million pounds of ice, 4.5 million pounds of coal, and 18,335 Thanksgiving dinners.

The Army also ran day-care centers, children's homes, summer camps, youth activities, sewing and cooking classes, laundry facilities, work shelters, homeless shelters, women's shelters, homes for unwed mothers, soup kitchens, clinics, hospitals, and prison ministries. It offered aid to immigrants and military families as well as performing dozens of other missions of mercy to those in need. Most of these ministries began or greatly expanded under Eva's leadership and continue to this day.

World War I presented new challenges for the Salvation Army. There were German corps and French corps and Salvationist officers and soldiers in every country caught in the conflict. But this didn't stop Eva. Her leading officers adopted a policy of supporting the president with humanitarian aid. After cutting through a mountain of red tape, the Salvationists finally received permission to serve in the war effort. Evangeline sent hundreds of Salvationists to France, along with food and supplies for the troops and sorely needed ambulances for the U.S. Army.

They lived as the soldiers did, in wet and snow, mud and gunfire, working long hours with little rest. The Salvation Army and its workers gained the respect and gratitude of the soldiers, their commanding officers, and their nation back home. In October 1919 President Woodrow Wilson awarded Evangeline the Distinguished Service Medal for her contribution to the American armed forces and for that of her "peace soldiers."

Evangeline and her Army's next great battle with despair began October 11, 1929, the day the stock market crashed, setting off the Great Depression. The Salvationists, long relied upon to help the needy, found themselves among them. Their bank accounts were frozen or wiped out as the banks collapsed. Their wealthy benefactors were struggling to stay afloat and had little money to contribute. And the average contributor on the street was now knocking on the Army's door, looking for help. The Army had always offered help and haven to the poor. Now it was struggling to help *everybody*.

Like their commander, the persistent officers pursued every option, no matter how unusual. They worked with the owners of shuttered buildings, converting them into shelters. They opened soup kitchens in the cities, twenty-four in New York City alone. In 1932 Evangeline opened the Democratic National Convention in prayer. Their nominee, Franklin Roosevelt, became the country's next president, and his New Deal soon had the government battling alongside the Salvationists to get the country through the depression.

In 1934 Evangeline sailed to London for the Army's High Council, which convened to choose the next general. Eva, now sixty-eight, was chosen fourth general of the Salvation Army.

Evangeline returned to London to command the Salvation Army worldwide. The depression had struck the remotest parts of the globe, and wherever the Army was established it fought the depression's effects. General Eva traveled, preached, wrote extensively, and rallied her troops in an international "World for God" campaign. But another conflict was stirring in Europe. Nazism had swept Germany, and an Austrian despot named Adolf Hitler was about to take oppression to its hellish limit.

In 1937 Hitler decided that the Salvationists could continue to work in Germany but they couldn't wear uniforms or collect money. General Eva sent him a stiff letter: "If we cannot wear uniforms, what in heaven's name are we to wear? If we cannot collect money, how can we get funds for our work? As I think you over, I have not decided whether you are a dunce or a devil." Hitler rescinded his order two weeks later but would soon make his character clear: He was bent on destroying the poor, the afflicted, and the oppressed, the very people Eva's Army ministered to.

General Eva retired in 1939 at the age of seventy-three in accordance with Army policy. There was no grand farewell; the German bombing raids over England had begun. Evangeline sailed quietly home to America.

In 1950, at the age of eighty-four, she was promoted to glory.

Legacy

Half a century after Eva's death, her story is still remarkable. To this day, it is a rare woman who rises to Eva's level of leadership in the world, much less in the church. But in Eva's lifetime, her accomplishments were unbelievable. No one could have imagined that the unmarried daughter of an English preacher would rule an international army, counsel with kings and presidents, and win the hearts of millions. It is clear that God has a much bigger imagination.

Throughout her lifetime, Evangeline traveled the globe. She

covered the North American continent and Europe and made trips to India and the Far East. At a garden party in Japan, Emperor Hirohito, who never looked in the face of "commoners," gazed at Evangeline and saluted. The king of Sweden awarded Evangeline one of his country's highest honors: the Vasa Gold Medal. And in Buckingham Palace, the little princess who would become Queen Elizabeth II was singing Eva's song, "World for God."

Her sermons and worship services were clearly ahead of the times. Churches that are just now incorporating drama, dialogue, and musical performance into their sermons might be surprised to learn that Evangeline was doing this at the turn of the century without microphones, spotlights, or video screens—and with audiences numbering in the thousands. In a single service she might interrupt the sermon with a harp performance, then don a costume for a dramatic sketch, and finally lead the congregation in singing. Those in her audiences, accustomed to long, dry sermons—or ignorant of church in any form—were spellbound.

Eva's legacy lives on through the ministry her parents founded. Chances are pretty good that the Army's ministry in your area began or expanded under Eva's national leadership. And if there's a Salvation Army women's shelter near you, it's an Evangeline Center, named in her honor. The Evangeline Center in New York is on Thirteenth Street in the building that once housed Evangeline's national offices—the same building Evangeline entered by fire escape a century ago. Wherever God led her, locked doors were no problem.

For additional information about the Salvation Army, see appendix A.

I am sending you out as sheep among wolves. Be as wary as snakes and harmless as doves. Matthew 10:16

BOOKS BY EVANGELINE BOOTH

Out of the Depths (with Clarence W. Hall) (out of print)

A thousand times a day rough voices blessed
her, and smiles of unwonted softness stole
over hard faces, as she passed; and when she
tripped fearlessly over dangerous places,
rough sooty hands were stretched involun-
tarily out to save her, and smooth her path.

Description of Eva, in Harriet Beecher Stowe's
Uncle Tom's Cabin

BILL BRIGHT

LIVING IN THE JOY OF SALVATION

I have one goal in life. . . .
And that's to take the
gospel to everybody
on planet Earth.

Christianity Today magazine, July 14, 1997

The passenger in the backseat leans forward, continuing to talk to the taxi driver long after they have reached their destination. Pointing to a small orange booklet, he tells the simple truth about humanity's sin and God's love. Jesus Christ was sent as God's only provision for man's sin, he explains. Finally he asks if the driver would like to pray a simple prayer and invite Jesus Christ into his life. The driver nods. The passenger, shy in his nature yet confident in his message, has done what he was born to do—lead yet another person to faith in Christ.

In Short

It could be argued that Bill Bright's influence on our world has been as great as that of Billy Graham or John Paul II. Yet few outside the evangelical community recognize the name of the founder of Campus Crusade for Christ, one of the largest evangelical organizations in the world, and Bill Bright seems to prefer it that way. The breadth and depth of Campus Crusade is evidence of its founder's relentless commitment: not merely to share the Good News but to raise up disciples who will pass it along.

Like the Lord he serves, Bill has poured his vision into workers who carry the ministry and message across the globe to people of all ages, in hundreds of languages and diverse cultures. These disciples have in turn multiplied themselves to reach ever further. Indeed, fulfilling the great commission has been Bill Bright's lifelong goal and his daily operating strategy, and at one level or another his name will appear in the spiritual genealogies of millions.

FAITH

Bill Bright grew up on a ranch in Coweta, Oklahoma, the sixth of seven children. His grandfather was a pioneer in the oil business, and Bright's parents and their ranch prospered. The ranch was a hub of homespun entertainment, from watermelon feasts to ice-cream socials, a gathering place for family, friends, and neighbors. In the center stood Bill's mother, Mary Lee Rohl Bright, whose strong character and deep spiritual qualities shaped the future leader in profound ways.

Bill attended a one-room schoolhouse until eighth grade. When he graduated from Coweta High School in 1939, he had already developed his own herd of registered shorthorn cattle. Bill left the ranch to study economics and sociology at Northeastern State College in Tahlequah, Oklahoma. Bill was an achiever in both high school and college, doing well not only in academics but also through his involvement in student government, drama, debate, and oratory. Before graduating with honors in 1943, he also served as president of the student body and editor of the university yearbook.

Immediately following the attack on Pearl Harbor in 1941, tens of thousands of young men marched into their local recruiting offices to enlist. Bill's three brothers and all of his fellow fraternity members were among them. Bill went too but was rejected because of a perforated eardrum. Forced to stay behind, he eventually headed out to California, hoping to find a way into the service there.

On his first evening in Los Angeles, as he drove out looking for a good time, Bright picked up a hitchhiker who turned out to be a member of the Navigators. Bill was invited to dinner with Dawson Trotman, the founder of the Navigators, and later that evening ended up at a party given by Dan Fuller, son of radio evangelist Charles Fuller, who also founded Fuller Theological Seminary. These encounters were not merely a string of coincidences. Back on the ranch, Bill's mother had been praying, and God answered.

In California, Bill's hopes of joining the military were frustrated again, so he launched his own business: Bright's California Confections. Despite his earlier encounters with influential believers, Bill expressed no interest in Christianity. But the elderly couple with whom he was living urged him to join them at First Presbyterian of Hollywood to hear their pastor, Louis Evans Sr., preach. One Sunday, after a trail ride and still smelling like a horse, Bright slipped into a service. When Bill was invited to a church-sponsored party, he concluded that he could build a good business network through the church, and he began to attend regularly.

Bill also began attending the church's college group, led by Henrietta Mears. One night in the spring of 1945 Miss Mears was speaking to the college group about Paul's conversion on the Damascus Road. When she finished, she challenged her class to go home, get down on their knees, and like the apostle Paul, ask God what he would have them do with their lives. Bill did as he was told. When he finished, he knew something had changed, and he committed his life to Christ.

After deciding that he needed to know more about the Bible, Bill left his business under the oversight of a manager and headed east in the fall of 1946 to attend Princeton Theological Seminary. But the demands of running his business from the other side of the country took their toll on his studies, so he returned home less than a year later and enrolled as a member of the first class of the fledgling Fuller Theological Seminary in Pasadena. He also joined Miss Mears's discipleship group known as The Fellowship of the Burning Heart, pledging "absolute consecration to Christ."

During this time Bill kept in touch with his hometown sweet-heart, Vonette Zachary. In spring of 1946 he returned home to propose to her. But back in California, as he continued his corre-spondence with her, he realized that not only was she not a believer in Jesus Christ, but she wasn't interested in becoming one. Soon the letters stopped, and Bill never sent her a ring.

But God wasn't finished with them yet. Vonette realized that her heart belonged to Bill, and if that meant considering the faith he was so fired up about, so be it. When she went to California for a visit, Bill introduced her to Henrietta Mears, who explained the faith to the smart and skeptical young woman in terms she could understand. One year later Bill and Vonette were married.

The newlyweds soon sat down and drew up lists outlining what they wanted out of life. As they read the lists over, they realized that most of what they wanted was material gain. So, with their new lives of faith in mind, they drew up fresh lists. This time the lists included such desires as "living holy lives," being "effective witnesses" for Christ, and "helping to fulfill the great commission" in their generation. To carry out these desires, they wrote up a contract with God. In this document, they renounced materialism in their marriage, surrendered their lives, and accepted the status of slaves to Jesus Christ.

Shortly after writing the contract, the vision of Campus Crusade for Christ began to form. The motto became "Win the campus to Christ today, win the world to Christ tomorrow." As Bill studied and spent time with those in the academic world, he realized there was a need to develop simple how-to materials for the Christian life. He promptly dropped out of seminary and sought the counsel of other Christian leaders such as Wilbur M. Smith, Henrietta Mears, Billy Graham, Richard Halverson, Dawson Trotman, Cyrus Nelson, Dan Fuller, and J. Edwin Orr. He also started a twenty-four-hour prayer vigil and targeted the University of California Los Angeles campus as the organization's first mission field.

FRUIT

Campus Crusade for Christ began humbly in 1951, with a one-on-one ministry of evangelism and Bible studies targeting campus leaders. Students made decisions to begin personal relationships with Jesus Christ, staff members joined Bill and Vonette, and ministries opened up on new campuses. In 1958 they moved their headquarters to Mound, Minnesota, where a pocket of land had been donated to them. During their first winter there, they survived thirty days of temperatures thirty degrees below zero in a town that offered them no encouragement. The Minnesota head-quarters was not conducive to this ever-expanding ministry, so Bill and Vonette set their sights once again on southern California. They packed and moved to Arrowhead Springs, a small mountain community above San Bernardino. They would remain there until 1991, when they moved their headquarters to Orlando, Florida, keeping their Arrowhead Springs property as a conference center.

By 1960 the ministry was active on forty campuses in the United States and included outreach ministries in Korea, Mexico, and Pakistan. As their campus work grew, Bill realized his staff needed a uniform, accessible approach to communicating the gospel message. The system he devised has become known as the Four Spiritual Laws, though at first he simply had his staff people memorize these general principles. They were later published when a businessman asked if he could make this presentation available to anyone, not just Crusade staff members. To date this little booklet has been printed in nearly two hundred languages, and more than 1.5 billion booklets have been distributed.

The growth and influence of Campus Crusade for Christ has not stopped, nor has the energy of its visionary founders. The scope of the ministry is staggering: Today it includes nearly thirteen thousand full-time staff members, who, like Bill and Vonette, renounce materialism and live on the gracious prayers and financial gifts of their supporters. Together with over one hundred thousand trained volunteers, they minister in 165 countries. Their college campus ministry is active on over 650 U.S. campuses and 470 schools overseas.

True to the original vision, Campus Crusade has moved beyond the college campus, with dozens of large-scale ministries under its umbrella, including Josh McDowell Ministry, André Kole Ministry, Student Venture, Here's Life, and Athletes in Action. Since its debut in 1979, Campus Crusade's feature-length *JESUS* film, which documents the life of Christ, has been released in a record 355 languages and viewed by an estimated 750 million people in 217 countries. Bright's latest projects emphasize mobilizing millions of Christians to fast and pray for worldwide spiritual revival. Two gatherings of prayer and fasting (with a combined attendance of nearly forty-three hundred Christian leaders) were held in Orlando, Florida, in 1994 and in Los Angeles, California, in 1995.

In 1999 Bright announced that he would step down as head of Campus Crusade in 2001. The identity of his successor is known only to Bill, a small team of advisors, and, of course, the person who will replace him.

LEGACY

While his organization continues to expand, Bill's message of God's grace remains simple. He has never lost his sense of wonder at his own salvation. Now in his seventies, Bill has been a Christian for over half a century, yet he tells of his first encounter with Christ as if it happened yesterday. Calling himself a "slave of the Lord Jesus Christ," Bill Bright takes very seriously his commitment to spend his life telling others how they can know God personally. With such a great love for his Savior, Bill Bright passionately shares with others what truly is good news.

One of his assistants, whose responsibility includes ushering his boss through airports and hotels and meetings and speaking engagements worldwide, says that his greatest challenge is not dealing with lost luggage, flight delays, or constant jet lag but keeping Bill on schedule. Wherever he goes, Bill takes time to talk with anyone who will listen—from CEOs to salesclerks to taxi drivers. His vision may be global, but his commission is personal. Bill Bright lets nothing stop him from what he was born to do: Share the good news of Jesus Christ.

For additional information about Campus Crusade for Christ ministries, see appendix A.

Go and make **disciples of all the nations,** baptizing them in the name of the Father and the Son and the Holy Spirit. Matthew 28:19

A FEW OF THE MINISTRIES OF CAMPUS CRUSADE FOR CHRIST

André Kole Ministry: Uses Kole's illusionist skills (likened to David Copperfield's) to stupefy audiences while weaving a gospel message into his performances

Josh McDowell Ministry: Coordinates campaigns for young people; provides the church with apologetics; provides humanitarian and evangelistic campaigns to Russia and surrounding republics

Student Venture: Follows the same blueprint in local high schools that Campus Crusade for Christ uses on college campuses

PriorityOne Associates: Develops Christ-centered business leaders through luncheons and speakers

SOLO (Singles Offering Life to Others): Networks with local churches to coordinate conferences, small groups, and outreach to singles

Here's Life, Inner City: Partners with urban centers in meeting the physical and spiritual needs of the urban poor

Athletes in Action: Equips athletes to proclaim Christ

Family Life: Provides practical, biblical tools to strengthen and build family relationships

The JESUS Video Project: Uses the *JESUS* film for effective church-based, citywide evangelism

Campus Ministry: Reaches students on campus for Christ

BOOKS BY DR. BILL BRIGHT

7 Basic Steps to Successful Fasting and Prayer (1995)
A Man without Equal: Jesus, the Man Who Changed the World (1992)
Beginning Your Journey of Joy (1997)
Come Help Change the World (1999)
God: Discover His Character (1999)
How You Can Be Sure You Are a Christian (1998)
How You Can Experience God's Love and Forgiveness (1998)
Have You Heard of the Four Spiritual Laws? (1993)
Promises: A Daily Guide to Supernatural Living (1998)

Quiet Moments with Bill Bright (1999)
Red Sky in the Morning (1998)
The Holy Spirit: The Key to Supernatural Living (1993)
Witnessing without Fear: How to Share Your Faith in Confidence (1993)
Would You Like to Know God Personally? (1988)

1910–1990

F. F. Bruce

DISCOVERING TRUTH AT ITS SOURCE

To modern man in his
frustration and despair, the
full-orbed gospel of Christ,
as Paul presents it to the
Colossians, is the one
message of hope.

The Apostolic Defense of the Gospel

S itting in his home, young Frederick Bruce would listen to his father and his father's friends converse about the Bible and its meaning. But the all-important book they discussed was written in ancient languages. How could they know that their English interpretation of those ancient texts was accurate? What if the writers of these words had meant something else entirely? There was but one way to find out: Travel back in time and discover what the ancients really said.

Frederick set out on what became a lifetime journey to the worlds of the Bible. He learned their languages, studied their cultures, read what the people wrote, and discovered that the God they worshiped was real then—and still is.

IN SHORT

Many evangelicals consider Scottish Bible scholar F. F. Bruce the leading authority on the New Testament. His life's work would fill a small library: commentaries, dictionaries, histories, archeological studies, atlases, and encyclopedias. Indeed, no serious Bible student's library would be complete without Bruce's contributions. To read his work is to take a round-trip journey with him back to the days when the Bible was written and home again to apply its truths.

FAITH

Frederick Fyvie Bruce was born October 12, 1910, in Elgin, Scotland. His father, Peter Fyvie Bruce, was a Plymouth Brethren preacher and evangelist. Raised in a devout home,

Frederick was surrounded by Christian teaching and practice. Both parents were passionate students of Scripture, and discussions between them and their twelve children, occasionally joined by fellow church members and visiting missionaries, were deep and challenging.

The written word expanded Frederick's mind too. The Bruce home was filled with books, and he devoured them throughout his childhood. He read fiction and fantasy, but he especially enjoyed adventure stories of missionaries and explorers and tales of history and archeology. What fascinated him most were histories of ancient civilizations that ruled during Bible times. He studied Latin as a child and by age thirteen had begun learning ancient Greek, which enabled him to pursue some of those histories in their original languages.

As a teenager Frederick began to personalize Christ's death on the cross, to see that Jesus had died to rescue *him*. By age seventeen, he was a baptized member of the church and an eager student and teacher of the Bible. That same year, 1928, he also began his university studies. He received his first degree from the University of Aberdeen in Scotland and his second from England's Cambridge University. From there he went to the University of Vienna, where he studied for two years. He had intended to complete his doctorate there, but when the University of Edinburgh offered him a position teaching Greek, he accepted and returned to his Scottish homeland.

Fruit

Bruce taught at Edinburgh from 1934 to 1938. Two years into his work there, he married Betty Davidson, whom he had met when the two were students at Aberdeen. They eventually had two children. In 1938 Bruce left Scotland again to teach Greek at the University of Leeds in England, where he stayed until 1947. While at Leeds, his work as a Bible scholar began. He was asked to teach New Testament Greek, even as he completed his own diploma in Hebrew and earned another degree from Cambridge.

In 1939 he received a letter from Bible expositor and theologian William E. Vine, who asked Bruce if he would help him by proofing his *Expository Dictionary of New Testament Words.* It was a great honor and an early confirmation that the young Scot from the Brethren Church was a brilliant Greek scholar. He proofread, edited, and contributed to other scholarly works that called upon his knowledge of Hebrew, Greek, and Latin, and he wrote his first book, *Are the New Testament Documents Reliable?* published in 1942.

In 1947 Bruce moved to another Yorkshire school, the University of Sheffield, where he served as a professor of biblical history and literature until 1959. Meanwhile, his reputation as a brilliant scholar, writer, and lecturer grew, resulting in invitations to speak at churches, conferences, and other schools. Among the most popular topics were the historical backgrounds of the Old and New Testament and the history of the early church.

But soon the most-requested topic became the Dead Sea Scrolls. After the initial discovery of the scrolls in 1947, archeologists and Bible scholars began the decades-long search, preservation, and translation of these ancient writings from the Qumran community. Written in Hebrew with some pieces in Aramaic and a few fragments in Greek, the scrolls immediately grabbed the attention of Bible scholars worldwide. With his command of ancient languages and an interest in archeology that began in childhood, Bruce became fascinated with the project and soon became an expert. He lectured frequently on the subject and eventually published a book titled *Second Thoughts on the Dead Sea Scrolls.*

In 1959 Bruce made one more school move. The University of Manchester invited him to take the prestigious Rylands Chair of biblical criticism and exegesis, a position he held until his retirement in 1978. During his time at Manchester and for many years afterward, Bruce continued his research and writing. He edited scholarly journals on biblical writings and archeology, lectured at universities and seminaries around the world, worked on dozens of books, and served on the editorial boards of Bible translation projects. F. F. Bruce died on September 11, 1990, bringing to a close a ministry of biblical scholarship unequaled in the twentieth century.

LEGACY

As a child reading ancient history, F. F. Bruce discovered a world filled with fascinations beyond the greatest fiction. As a young man he learned the languages that would transport him back to those times to understand how people lived, what they believed, why they wrote what they did. It was this growing expertise, not just in the words themselves, but in the cultures and people that produced the words that allowed him to enter the minds of the Bible's writers and tell us what he saw there.

Just as important, he applied his discoveries to his own life. The students of F. F. Bruce found in their professor not only an expert in ancient ideas but a man who spent a lifetime testing those ideas in his own life to see if they were still true. His excitement, evident in his lectures and writings, came from his daily discovery that they were. To those who dismiss the Bible as an inaccurate account of an ancient faith that is no longer relevant, the library-filling works of F. F. Bruce provide ample evidence to the contrary. The words are accurate, the faith they describe is real, and the Holy Spirit who inspired the ancients is still here to reveal what that means for us today.

Unfailing love and truth have met together. Righteousness and peace have kissed! Psalm 85:10

BOOKS BY F. F. BRUCE

Hard Sayings of Jesus (1983)
In Retrospect: Remembrance of Things Past (1980)
In the Steps of Our Lord (1997)
In the Steps of the Apostle Paul (1995)
Jesus Past, Present & Future: The Work of Christ (1998)
New Testament Documents: Are They Reliable? (1984)
The Acts of the Apostles: Greek Text with Introduction and Commentary (1999)
The Canon of Scripture (1988)
The History of the Bible in English: From the Earliest Versions to Today (1978)
The Illustrated Bible Atlas: With Historical Notes (1999)

[Frederick Bruce] is a man of warm and vital
faith in Christ. All who know him personally
recognize that this is supremely important
for him in his life and ministry,
including his life as a scholar.

J. D. Douglas, classical scholar and colleague of F. F. Bruce

AMY CARMICHAEL

THE ABANDONED LIFE

If the ultimate, the hardest,
cannot be asked of me;
if my fellows hesitate to ask
it and turn to someone else,
then I know nothing of
Calvary love.

If

reena was a young Hindu girl. After Preena's father died, Preena's mother had been persuaded to devote her to the gods, and she sent Preena to the Hindu temple. When the girl tried to escape, she was caught and returned to the temple women, who branded her hands with hot irons and told the seven-year-old that she was to be "married to the god," meaning that she was to be a slave in the temple—a temple prostitute. To frighten her and discourage her from escaping again, Preena's captors told her of a white woman who stole children from the temple. But instead of being frightened, Preena wanted to find this rescuer. She escaped again and found her way to Amy Carmichael.

Fifty years later Preena wrote of that encounter: "The first thing she did was to put me on her lap and kiss me. . . ." From that day forward, the little girl called her rescuer *Amma,* the Tamil word for "mother."

IN SHORT

As a young woman Amy Carmichael left her home in Britain to serve as a missionary in India. She never returned home. When she died fifty-five years later, she had written enough stories, prayers, and devotions to fill thirty-five books. And over a thousand neglected, abused, abandoned, and enslaved children like Preena called her *Amma.* Amy's life of sacrifice and unbounded love redeemed children from darkness to light and inspired legions of Christians to follow in her footsteps.

FAITH

The oldest of seven children, Amy Beatrice Carmichael was born on December 16, 1867, in Millisle, County Down, Northern Ireland. Her parents, David and Catherine, loved God, and her mother cared for the sick and elderly, modeling the kind of ministry Amy would one day provide. Amy received her education from governesses until she was twelve and then attended Marlborough House, a Wesleyan Methodist boarding school, where at age fifteen she made a commitment to Christ.

After Amy's father died when she was seventeen, she threw herself into serving her brothers and sisters, along with other children in her poor, working-class neighborhood. She taught at a night school for boys, held Bible studies and prayer meetings, and formed a class for "shawlies," girls who worked in the mills and wore shawls over their heads because they couldn't afford hats. When Amy's work with the shawlies grew beyond the capacity of the YMCA hall she was using, a woman agreed to provide funds for a five-hundred-seat hall, and the head of the largest mill in the city donated the land for it.

FRUIT

In 1887 Amy heard Hudson Taylor of the China Inland Mission speak in Belfast, where he called for workers to join the mission field to reach the millions who didn't know Christ. Later Amy wrote in *Scraps*, the family magazine, "Does it not stir up our hearts, to go forth and help them, does it not make us long to leave our luxury, our exceeding abundant light and go to them that sit in darkness?" She felt called to mission work but didn't know how or when she would answer the call. When her family's money ran out the following year, they moved to England. In 1892 Amy contacted China Inland Mission, but after making preparations and packing her trunks for China, she received word that the organization's physician had rejected her for medical reasons.

Disappointed but not defeated, Amy looked for another way to the mission field. She found it the next year when she was approved to serve in Japan with Reverend Barclay F. Buxton of the Church Missionary Society. Upon her arrival in Japan she immediately plunged into the work, studying the language and adopting the Japanese style of dress. Within a year, however, she became ill, and after brief visits to Shanghai and Ceylon, she returned to London, where she published her first book, *From Sunrise Land*, a collection of letters she had written in Japan and had illustrated with her own sketches. Again Amy applied for a missions position overseas, and again she was rejected for medical reasons.

At last she was accepted by the Church of England Zenana Missionary Society. She arrived in Bangalore, India, with a tropical fever and a temperature of 105 degrees. Some missionaries believed she would not last six months, but she recovered and stayed. After a year in Bangalore she moved to Tinnevelly, which became her home for the rest of her life. Indeed, she remained there without furloughs for fifty-five years.

Amy poured herself into Indian culture, learning the Tamil language, studying the customs, and traveling from home to home to speak with the people. She wrote about her experiences, producing a manuscript that told of the wickedness practiced in the Hindu temples and the utter indifference of most of the people when someone told them of the love of Jesus. Amy also wrote about the few who did want to hear, but the publisher rejected the manuscript as being too discouraging. After all, readers wanted to hear of great successes, of people greeting the gospel with open arms. Amy continued to write the truth and eventually found a publisher, who published *Things As They Are* in 1903. Readers questioned its accuracy—things could not possibly be as bleak as Amy had described. When a fourth edition was published, it included letters from missionaries in India, confirming in the strongest terms what Amy had written.

Amy soon discovered that the way to reach the Indian people was not through preaching but through sacrifice. She reached out to the poorest, youngest, and most despised. This included babies and children given to the Hindu temples to serve virtually as slaves—shut up in back rooms, carefully watched, and tortured if they tried to escape. Amy began rescuing these children, building a home and recruiting a staff to care for them. The ministry became known as Dohnavur Fellowship, and to the children she rescued, Amy was *Amma*.

Dohnavur Fellowship had no salaried workers and never appealed for funds. The staff served out of love for the Lord, and Amy took their needs to God, who supplied what they needed. God also provided for growth. As the rescued children grew into adulthood, most moved on, but some stayed and joined the staff, allowing the ministry to take in more children. The Dohnavur Fellowship became Amy's life work, and by the end of her life the ministry had rescued more than one thousand neglected and abused children.

In 1931 Amy stumbled into a freshly dug pit and sustained multiple injuries. The accident left her a near invalid and in constant pain. During the last twenty years of her life until her death at the age of eighty-three, she conducted her duties from her room and wrote prolifically. Fifteen of the books that bear Amy's name were written, as she put it, "out of the furnace." She died January 18, 1951.

LEGACY

With few exceptions, women in the first half of the twentieth century were not permitted to rise to leadership roles in the church. Among the few doors open to them were those leading to the most difficult and unglamorous ministry—the mission field, especially working among the poor, sick, outcast, and despised. Women carried on such labors far from the admiring eyes of other Christians, usually without hope of advancement and often without a circle of financial supporters. Given these conditions, there could be just one reason that a woman would choose such a life: an absolute commitment to serve Christ at any cost.

Amy Carmichael had such a commitment. Convinced of her call to serve, she refused to turn her back on the mission field, even when she had twice been rejected. When she finally made it to India, she refused to go home. Not once did she return to hear the praises of her friends and supporters. As Elisabeth Elliot writes in *A Chance to Die: The Life and Legacy of Amy Carmichael,* to Amy, anything that called attention to herself stole attention from the God she served. Indeed, in 1919 her name appeared on a British honors list. When she found out about it, she wrote to England, asking to have her name removed. It troubled her to "have an experience so different from His Who was despised and rejected—not kindly honoured."

Ironically, the woman who wanted no other honor than that of being Christ's servant became famous nonetheless. Tens of thousands of readers in Britain and America were moved to action by her writings, choosing for themselves the same difficult, less-traveled, glorious path. On every page Amy shouts, whispers, or weeps praise to God, yet one cannot help but be awed by the faith and work of the writer as well.

Jesus said to the disciples, "If any of you wants to be my follower, you must put aside your selfish ambition, shoulder your cross, and follow me."

Matthew 16:24

BOOKS BY AMY CARMICHAEL

Candles in the Dark (1982)
Edges of His Ways (1980)
God's Missionary (1997)
Gold by Moonlight (1995)
His Thoughts Said . . . His Father Said (1999)
If (1999)
Learning of God (1986)
Mountain Breezes: The Collected Poems of Amy Carmichael (1999)
Rose from Briar (1980)
Thou Givest . . . They Gather (1982)
Toward Jerusalem (with Alexander Carmichael) (1989)
You Are My Hiding Place (Rekindling the Inner Fire) (1991)
Whispers of His Power (1993)

There were days when the sky turned black
for me because of what I heard and knew
was true. Sometimes it was as if I saw the
Lord Jesus Christ kneeling alone, as He knelt
long ago under the olive trees. And the only
thing that one who cared could do was to go
softly and kneel down beside Him,
so that He would not be alone in His
sorrow over the little children.

Amy Carmichael, speaking of her burden
for the children of India

1874-1917

OSWALD CHAMBERS

GIVING THE UTMOST FOR GOD

Shut out every other
consideration and keep
yourself before God for
this one thing only—
My Utmost for His Highest.
I am determined to be
absolutely and entirely for
Him and Him alone.

My Utmost for His Highest

D ressed in a Scottish tartan, Oswald Chambers would creep into the kitchen in the early morning hours, fix himself a pot of tea, and then read, write, and fall to his knees in prayer. From the corner of the room his young niece would sit and watch the proceedings. She felt important in his presence, content to be with her uncle in the quietness as he sat wrapped in his plaid, happy to be spending time with the Lord.

In Short

The books of educator and mission worker Oswald Chambers are among the most popular Christian writings of the twentieth century. Ironically, this humble Scotsman wrote just one book in his lifetime, and most of his readers have never seen it. The book they *do* know about, *My Utmost for His Highest,* is a compilation of notes from his lectures and was not published until many years after his death. It has been in print for sixty-five years, showing generation after generation of readers that the Christian life is not about length of service or volume of work but about abandoning all that *seems* to matter in this world to focus only on what *truly* matters: Christ and Christ alone.

Faith

Oswald Chambers was born July 24, 1874, in Aberdeen, Scotland, the fourth son of Clarence and Hannah Chambers. Oswald's mother, like her biblical namesake, gave each of her nine children to God. Oswald's father was a Baptist minister and together with his wife raised the children to love God and to seek him in prayer.

As a young teenager Oswald accompanied his father to a church service held by the famous Baptist preacher Charles Spurgeon, the man who had ordained the senior Chambers to the ministry years earlier. As father and son walked home after the service, Oswald confessed that had there been an opportunity, he would have given himself to the Lord. His father stopped him in his tracks and encouraged him to do it at once. There on the street the young man gave himself to God. The transformation was immediate. Oswald immersed himself in study and prayer, began teaching Sunday school, and paid visits to the local Young Men's Christian Association (YMCA) to help in its ministry to former prisoners.

Throughout his childhood Chambers loved to draw and became quite skilled at it. Now, as a teenager, he determined to pursue an art education and at age eighteen obtained an art master's certificate and then entered the University of Edinburgh. While there, he sensed God's call to pursue full-time Christian service, so after completing his studies at the university, he went on to study theology at Dunoon College.

At Dunoon, Chambers's ministry began to take form. His appearance and personality were well suited for leadership. He was tall and lean with a crown of long hair; his personality was both winsome and striking. The artist in him enjoyed literature and music; the hungry student in him led to a tutoring position in logic, moral philosophy, and psychology.

After seven years of studying and teaching at Dunoon, Chambers left in 1905 and soon began a four-year stint as an itinerant Bible teacher, traveling throughout the United Kingdom, America, and Japan. These were the toughest years of his life. Answering God's call became difficult and painful and engulfed him in a cloud of depression, poverty, and spiritual loneliness. He was teaching about the joy to be found in Christ, but he found none of it for himself.

Eventually Chambers began to see why God had allowed him to get to such a desolate place. It was only there that he could discover his own utter worthlessness, his absolute inability to find value in anything other than what Christ had given him. From this discovery grew a desire to abandon everything else. The cross of

Christ took on a new dimension. It was not just the point of salvation; it was the place of self-abandonment, the grounds for total surrender to God. When his four years had ended, he was ready to begin a new life of ministry at the foot of the cross.

FRUIT

Soon after his return home, on May 25, 1910, Chambers married Gertrude Obbs. Biddy, as she was known, was a member of his brother's church. The two would have one child, Kathleen. In 1911 Chambers founded and became principal of the Bible Training College in Clapham, London. In his new surrendered life, he created not just a school for the *study* of spiritual matters but a truly spiritual place. His infectious faith permeated the school, igniting a similar passion in his students. But the Great War was about to explode on the world, and in 1915 the school was closed.

The Young Men's Christian Association then commissioned Chambers to minister to Australian and New Zealand soldiers stationed in Zeitoun, Egypt. He found himself overseas again, conducting lessons from the same Bible as before. But everything inside him had changed, and his ministry was far different as a result. His nighttime talks to the troops, who were themselves far from home and its earthly comforts, focused on the only Source of comfort, the only Lord worthy of our surrender.

Just as the war had cut short his teaching days, his health cut his life short unexpectedly at the age of forty-three. On November 15, 1917, Chambers died of a ruptured appendix. He had often told his friends, "I feel I shall be buried for a time, hidden away in obscurity; then suddenly I shall flame out, do my work, and be gone." His prophesy had been fulfilled.

Before his death Chambers had written just one book, *Baffled to Fight Better*. But he had kept a journal and had written many letters, poems, and essays. Most of all he had delivered hundreds of lectures to his students at school and to the troops in Egypt. During their seven-year marriage, Biddy, who was trained as a court stenographer, had recorded many of her husband's messages word for word in shorthand. Several years after her husband's death, Mrs. Chambers, living in an Oxford lodging house with twelve-year-old Kathleen, set about the arduous task of crafting these notes into 365 daily devotional readings, each no more than five hundred words in length.

Biddy Chambers completed the manuscript for *My Utmost for His Highest* in October 1927, ten years after her husband's death. Although she had toiled for three years on the book, her name appeared nowhere in it. In the forward she wrote: "It is because it is felt that the author is one to whose teaching men will return, that this book has been prepared, and it is sent out with the prayer that day by day the messages may continue to bring the quickening life and inspiration of the Holy Spirit." The forward is simply signed "B. C."

First published privately through the financial gifts of Mrs. Chambers's friends, *My Utmost for His Highest* was picked up by Dodd, Mead & Company in 1935 and has been in print ever since. The book remains among the top ten Christian titles sold in America and has found an eager audience of readers who are discovering that the man who spoke to students and soldiers in the century's first decades still has a lot to offer to young people in the next century.

LEGACY

Oswald Chambers taught God's Word for years before he discovered its most essential truth: The Christian life is not about rallying one's talents for great deeds. It's about surrendering those talents—and every other personal possession—to Christ. As Chambers put it, "The battle is lost or won in the secret places of the will before God. . . . That is the Great Divide in the life; from that point we either go towards a more and more dilatory and useless type of Christian life, or we become more and more ablaze for the glory of God." When he found this truth, he set about living it daily. It is most appropriate that the book by which we know Chambers best is such a practical devotional tool for helping us follow his example.

The unsung hero of Oswald Chambers's story is Biddy Chambers. For half a century following her husband's death she labored to give his words to the world. With but one exception the dozens of books that bear her husband's name would not be in print if not for her tireless dedication to him, both as a wife and as a widow. Yet neither she nor her husband would have stood much praise for their enduring work. To them, all praise must be directed at Jesus, the only one worthy of our utmost.

I live in eager expectation and hope that I will never do anything that causes me shame, but that I will always be bold for Christ, as I have been in the past, and that my life will always honor Christ, whether I live or I die. Philippians 1:20

BOOKS BY OSWALD CHAMBERS

Approved unto God: The Spiritual Life of the Christian Worker (1997)
Baffled to Fight Better (1980)
Biblical Ethics: The Moral Foundations of Life, the Philosophy of Sin (1998)
Biblical Psychology (1999)
Bringing Sons into Glory (1999)
Faith: A Holy Walk (1999)
God's Workmanship: And She Shall Glorify Me (1997)
Growing Deeper with God (1997)
The Love of God (1999)
My Utmost for His Highest (original 1935 edition with prayers)
Not Knowing Where (1999)
Our Brilliant Heritage (1999)
Quiet Moments with Oswald Chambers (1999)
Studies in the Sermon on the Mount (1999)

1874–1936

G. K.
CHESTERTON

THE UTTER SANITY OF CHRISTIANITY

The Christian faith has not
been tried and found
wanting. It has been found
difficult and left untried.

What's Wrong with the World

By the age of nine Gilbert Chesterton had grown into a boy of extreme proportions. He was as tall as most men, with a voice an octave higher than his peers. His alarmed parents sent him to a brain specialist. After examining their son, the expert, declaring the boy's brain to be the largest and most sensitive he had ever examined, stated that the boy would turn out to be either a genius or an imbecile. It took several more years before Gilbert's anxious parents discovered which was the case.

In Short

British novelist, biographer, poet, and journalist G. K. Chesterton turned his enormous brain into a writing machine, pouring out humor, paradox, verse, drama, argument, political commentary, and perspectives on faith at a rate greater than that of any other Christian writer. The result was that millions of people in the English-speaking world got their first glimpse of a God whose reign extends far beyond the bookshelf marked "Religion."

Faith

Gilbert Keith Chesterton was born on Campden Hill in Kensington, London, on May 29, 1874. His parents were a curious pair. Edward Chesterton, a real estate agent, retired early out of fear for his health and was at home throughout most of Gilbert's childhood, dabbling in various hobbies from watercolors to photography to building his own telephone. Gilbert's mother, Marie Louise Grosjean, was small, untidy, energetic, and witty. Raised in a family of twenty-three children, Marie had just three of her own: Beatrice, Gilbert, and Cecil. Beatrice died when she was eight and Gilbert was still an infant. The children's father forbade the family to speak of her and shuffled the boys indoors whenever a funeral procession passed along the street.

As a boy Gilbert went to St. Paul's, a prestigious London boarding school, attending as a day student since the school was near his home. Despite his immense size, Gilbert would wear a juvenile sailor suit, often wrinkled and dirty. At times he would arrive at school only to find the playground empty because it was Saturday. When he happened to show up on a school day, he found few friends there. His classmates considered him an oddity. They teased him and made him the brunt of practical jokes but were careful not to push the gentle giant too far. In class Gilbert sat in the back, drawing sketches on his unfinished papers. Sometimes he wandered the halls, absentminded and lonely.

Gilbert found two sources of relief from his dreary existence. The first was books. Gilbert memorized long passages of Shakespeare and Dickens and recited them to himself as he walked down the street, which made him appear even more strange. He found his second source of relief at age fifteen in a friendship that started with a fight. At the end of a furious playground scuffle with a much younger classmate, Gilbert's opponent quoted Dickens. The lively discussion that ensued launched the boys into a growing friendship that transformed Gilbert. No longer was he the strange, lonely giant. Now he was the brilliant giant, and soon he was surrounded by a small circle of brilliant younger students who respected him.

The circle around Gilbert soon became a debating club, its members always ready to argue various views on literary and political topics. The club came up with the idea of producing a small magazine to sell to other students. Gilbert contributed prose and verse to every issue of the *Debater*, often illustrating his contributions with his own scribbled sketches. The magazine's contents astonished the school's headmaster, who had considered Gilbert to be a fool. From that point on, it was Gilbert's brilliance and not his strangeness that got people's attention.

One of the debating club's members was Gilbert's younger

brother, Cecil. While Gilbert took after their moody, absent-minded father, Cecil displayed their mother's energetic, domineering nature. The two were the best of friends yet were constantly engaged in disagreements. Their longest argument, timed for future reference, lasted eighteen hours and thirteen minutes. Later neither could ever recall exactly what the disagreement was about. During their arguments the world around them disappeared. They would march around the room, making points, offering rebuttals, and ignoring anyone else in the room.

After leaving boarding school, Chesterton attended the Slade School of Art for three years to study painting. Away from his old school friends, he spent much of this time in depression, struggling with dark thoughts and self-doubt and even contemplating suicide. The crisis had passed by the time he turned twenty, but it had led him to consider the reason for living and to conclude, as he would later write, "that even mere existence . . . was extraordinary enough to be exciting."

Chesterton returned to reading, clinging to Walt Whitman and Robert Louis Stevenson. He read the Old Testament and found an empathetic voice in Job and a kindred lamenting poet in Isaiah. The young artist's notebooks became filled with more writing, fewer sketches. His words expressed his soul-searching. If existence was wonderful, then there must be someone who had created that existence. He began to embrace the idea of God and to consider religion as a possible source for finding purpose.

One decision he did make was that he didn't want to spend his life as a painter. Books were what he loved, and so he pursued them. Chesterton got a job at Redway, a publisher of books about spiritualism and the occult, where he sent out review copies of the books they published and rejection letters to the authors whose manuscripts they didn't. At age twenty-one he moved to another publisher, Fisher Unwin, where he was able to edit manuscripts and do some ghostwriting.

It was during this time that he met Frances Blogg, a secretary at the Parents' National Educational Union, which ran exclusive schools that embraced advanced teaching methods. Frances was Chesterton's first love, a love at first sight, and her opinions, often different from his own, fascinated him. He carried on much of their courtship in writing, often in verse. They were married on June 28, 1901, a month after Chesterton turned twenty-seven.

While at Fisher Unwin, Chesterton began to write for publication. When his first book, *Greybeards at Play,* was published in 1900, he dedicated it to E. C. Bentley, the boy with whom Chesterton's transforming friendship had begun in that playground scuffle. Unfortunately the book went largely unnoticed by the public. Chesterton's father, who was by now well convinced of his son's genius, provided money to publish the next book, *The Wild Knight and Other Poems.* But while it received positive reviews, it sold poorly.

Chesterton's articles were another matter. With a byline composed only of his initials, G. K. C., Chesterton's magazine pieces addressed political topics with a unique, bold style that surprised readers and attracted the attention of radical intellectuals.

For Chesterton the personal journey from discussion to practice came slowly and mostly through the influence of Frances, who encouraged him to embrace Anglicanism. Chesterton soon met another Christian who actually practiced what he preached— Conrad Noel, a minister and socialist. Noel could carry on a decent debate, which impressed Chesterton nearly as much as the man's faith and certainly increased his willingness to consider that faith.

During that time the British reading public got a unique opportunity to observe a portion of Chesterton's journey to faith. He had entered into a running debate about determinism and free will with Robert Blatchford, a popular socialist commentator. Each opponent had his own column in the *Daily News* from which he would make his case. The argument naturally moved to Christianity. Perhaps to force Chesterton to paint himself into a religious corner, Blatchford posed four questions about his opponent's religious beliefs. Chesterton's answers, published in his own column, surprised many:

1. Are you a Christian? *Certainly.*
2. What do you mean by the word *Christianity? A belief that a*

certain human being whom we call Christ stood to a certain super-human being whom we call God in a certain unique transcendental relationship which we call sonship.

3. What do you believe? *A considerable number of things. That Mr. Blatchford is an honest man, for instance. And (but less firmly) that there is a place called Japan. If he means what do I believe in religious matters, I believe the able statement (answer 2) and a large number of other mystical dogmas, ranging from the mystical dogma that man is in the image of God to the mystical dogma that all men are equal and that babies should not be strangled.*

4. Why do you believe it? *Because I perceive life to be logical and workable with these beliefs and illogical and unworkable without them.*

Although at this point Chesterton was not quite ready to accept orthodox Christianity, he would get there eventually. After his conversion he described the process as the fitting together of two seemingly incompatible, "huge and unmanageable machines"—the world and the Christian tradition. His new faith brought sense and new purpose to his life. It also made him a better writer. In the five years following his debate with Blatchford, he wrote his best works, including *Dickens, Heretics, Orthodoxy,* and the somewhat autobiographical *The Man Who Was Thursday.* A few years later he began his popular *Father Brown* detective series.

In his early successes Chesterton ate, drank, and worked himself into awful shape, which only exacerbated the health problems he would contend with for the rest of his life. In addition to his many and exhausting book projects, he committed himself to producing an endless stream of articles and essays and took over the publication of his brother's paper when Cecil passed away. There were few topics he considered beyond his ability to address. The broad scope of his work took form in many genres, from drama to poetry, commentary to fiction, political commentary to biography to nonsensical humor, all in many creative combinations.

Later in his life Chesterton took another step in his faith journey when he left the Anglican Church to become a Catholic. He had considered it for years but had postponed the change in the hope that Frances would join him. She declined, so in 1922 he converted on his own. Frances eventually did follow but not until years later. By 1936 Chesterton's chronic health problems had grown far worse. He would fall asleep in the midst of dictation and then awaken confused. On June 13, 1936, he fell into a coma and died the next morning. The great debater had finally rested his life-long case.

LEGACY

G. K. Chesterton stands among the most prolific writers of not merely the twentieth century but of all time. His writings include thousands of articles and essays, more than a hundred books, and contributions to hundreds more. The span of topics he covered is broader than any other Christian writer's, even more than that of C. S. Lewis, who himself wrote far beyond the borders of Christian subject matter. And like Lewis, Chesterton used this great breadth to reach outside Christian circles, exposing many non-Christian readers to the teachings of our faith.

It is clear that God gave Chesterton great success in life, but it is fascinating to observe how God used the most uncomfortable and tragic episodes in his life to make that success possible. The moments that *made* Chesterton were the kinds of episodes that most of us, including Chesterton, would certainly avoid if given the power. The incessant arguments with his brother became the boot camp for his legendary ability to write persuasively. A near suicidal depression triggered a search for meaning that ended at the foot of the cross. G. K. Chesterton's life is proof that God really does work even the bad things into something very good for those who belong to him. And if challenged on that fact, Chesterton would have argued in the affirmative—for eighteen hours straight.

After this time had passed, I, Nebuchadnezzar, looked up to heaven. My sanity returned, and I praised and worshiped the Most High and honored the one who lives forever. His rule is everlasting, and his kingdom is eternal. Daniel 4:34

BOOKS BY G. K. CHESTERTON

Napoleon of Notting Hill (1998)
Orthodoxy (1995)
The Annotated Innocence of Father Brown: The Innocence of Father Brown (1998)
The Ball and the Cross (1995)
The Best of Father Brown (1919)
The Club of Queer Trades (1998)
The Collected Works of G. K. Chesterton (1999)
The Everlasting Man (1993)
The Hound of Heaven and Other Poems (1978)
The Man Who Was Thursday (1998)

We do not want, as the newspapers say,

a Church that will move with the world.

We want a Church that will move the

world. . . . It is by that test that history will

really judge, of any Church,

whether it is the real Church or no.

Michael Finch, in *G. K. Chesterton, A Biography*

1 9 3 1 –

CHARLES COLSON

RELEASED FROM PRIDE

I can work for Him in prison

as well as out.

Born Again, from a statement Chuck Colson made to the press
after he was found guilty of Watergate crimes.

T he *whack* of the gavel punctuated the reading of his sentence: a five-thousand-dollar fine and up to three years in prison, the harshest among the Watergate defendants. Outside the courtroom moments later the convicted criminal gave a statement to the swarm of reporters. "What happened in court today was the court's will and the Lord's will—I have committed my life to Jesus Christ, and I can work for Him in prison as well as out." Former Nixon hatchet man Chuck Colson's political life was over, but his ministry had just begun.

In Short

Chuck Colson, who found faith before he entered prison, found release from his sinful pride only behind bars. The result has been a formidable combination: God has used Colson's intelligence, education, powerful persuasion skills, and even his treacherous past to lead thousands into Christian faith and millions to a deeper, riskier walk with Christ. In many ways, Charles Colson is the apostle Paul in a business suit.

Faith

At age eight an awed Chuck Colson watched his father, Wendell Colson, in black cap and gown, graduate from Northeastern Law School. His father had worked hard to get to this moment, which was the result of twelve long years of night school. Such dedication was the hallmark of the Colson home: pride in study, in work, in honest living. Chuck made it the theme of his valedictory address to his high school graduating class. That same pride led him to turn down a full scholarship at Harvard, choosing instead Brown University and its ROTC program, which launched him into the height of the Korean War as an officer in the Marine Corps.

After Colson's tour of duty he studied law at George Washington University. When he graduated in 1959, he turned down offers to join prestigious law firms and threw his future—and his entire savings of five thousand dollars—into a new law practice with a brilliant young lawyer he had met. With Colson's pride-driven work ethic the firm grew quickly, and so did Colson's government and political contacts. Meanwhile, Colson had married Nancy Billings. They had three children, Wendell, Christian, and Emily. But marriage and family took a backseat to politics and business, and Colson was divorced in January 1964. Later that year he married Patty Hughes, a woman who shared his passion for politics.

When Colson first met him, Richard Nixon was vice president under President Dwight Eisenhower. Years later Colson joined the former VP's 1968 presidential campaign. In November 1969, nine months after Nixon took office, Colson left his law practice to serve as special counsel to the president. Over the next four years Chuck earned a reputation in Washington as the "White House hatchet man" because he was the one Nixon counted on to carry out the "dirty work." These projects included leading investigations, compiling "enemy lists," leaking erroneous information to the press, and eventually Watergate—a plot to bug the Democratic National Committee headquarters in Washington's Watergate office complex during Nixon's 1972 re-election campaign.

Investigations of the break-in led prosecutors to members of the White House staff, Colson among them. Looking for support, Colson visited Tom Phillips, a close Massachusetts friend and a client of his law firm. Phillips challenged his friend to look at himself honestly and squarely. He read a passage from C. S. Lewis's book *Mere Christianity:* "As long as you are proud you cannot know God. A proud man is always looking down on things and people; and, of course, as long as you are looking down, you cannot see something that is above you."

As Colson left his friend's home, the emotions he had held in check all evening broke loose. Sobbing uncontrollably, he prayed a desperate first prayer: "God, I don't know how to find you, but I'm going to try. . . . Take me!" Over the next week Colson devoured *Mere Christianity,* hashing and rehashing Lewis's logical arguments. It began to dawn on him that his real problem wasn't Watergate. It was sin. He prayed a simple prayer, asking Christ to be his Lord and Savior.

FRUIT

When Colson flew back to his troubles in Washington, he found himself surrounded by Tom Phillips's Christian friends, including Doug Coe, Senator Harold Hughes, Congressman Al Quie, and Graham Purcell. These men, some of them old enemies from across party lines, became Colson's dearest friends and supported him through the most difficult period of his life.

The Watergate investigation grew as quickly as his new faith, and in 1974 Colson was indicted on a series of charges of obstruction of justice. By cooperating with prosecutors he was eventually able to plead guilty, on June 3, to a single count of obstruction of justice. He was sentenced on June 21 and entered prison on July 8.

Colson had been told that prison life would be safer and more bearable if he kept to himself. He did just the opposite: He got involved in the lives of many of the men around him, started prayer groups, conducted Bible studies, and spoke in chapel services. He began to see God using him to make a difference.

On a cold January night after several of his Watergate compatriots had been released and he alone was left in prison, Colson learned that the Virginia Supreme Court had announced his disbarment and that his son Christian had been arrested for possession of narcotics. At this darkest of moments the men from his Washington support group called, each offering to take his place in prison so he could be with his son. Their gesture overwhelmed him. He fell to his knees and completed the process that had begun in Tom Phillips's driveway a year and a half earlier, surrendering his entire life to be used in whatever way God chose. The pride that had driven Chuck Colson all his life was gone. Two days later, on January 31, 1975, Colson was released from prison after a court order reduced his sentence to time served.

But Colson was not done with prison. In 1976 he launched Prison Fellowship, a ministry to those behind bars. The organization flourished dramatically, both across the country and overseas, providing hope and help to prisoners and their families, both during their incarceration and after their release. One of the most effective programs ever attempted, it is credited with making substantial gains in breaking the cycle of crime. Prison Fellowship now ministers in more than fifty countries; its fifty thousand volunteers work in more than eight hundred state and federal prisons and reach a quarter of a million inmates each year.

In the same year that Prison Fellowship was founded, Colson delivered his book *Born Again*. It tells the tale of Watergate from his perspective, but its bigger story is that of Colson's own imprisonment by sin and his release through Christ. His first book led to many more—seventeen to date—covering a range of topics from faith to crime prevention, politics to media deceit, the role of government to the role of the church in our society. He covers a similar scope of subjects in his *BreakPoint* radio commentaries, aired daily across the country. Much like C. S. Lewis, the author who first challenged Colson's mind about God, he writes and speaks with deep insight, prophetic accuracy, and an overwhelming conviction that true faith must necessarily alter every aspect of our lives—both private and public—our thoughts, and our deeds.

LEGACY

God seems to revel in using prisoners to tell his story. The apostle Paul's incarceration became a life sentence, a period in which he wrote some of his best work. The Old Testament itself is the story of the Jewish nation's cyclical journey from freedom to captivity to freedom again. From these ancient former slaves, captives, and prisoners we have received much of our Bible. Their experiences make it clear that God indeed comforts the prisoner. But God does something more: He speaks to captives in a voice few of us hear in our freedom. He tells them that sin is the real captor, that true freedom comes only through a higher Court.

And that has been Colson's message too. To those in and out of prison, inside and ouside the beltway, across America and around the world, Chuck Colson is a voice of freedom in its truest sense.

For additional information about Prison Fellowship, see appendix A.

You will know the truth, and the truth will set you free. John 8:32

BOOKS BY CHUCK COLSON

A Dance with Deception: Revealing the Truth behind the Headlines
   (with Nancy R. Pearcey) (1993)
A Dangerous Grace (with Nancy Pearcey) (1994)
Against the Night (1989)
Born Again (1976)
Burden of Truth (1997)
Convicted: New Hope for Ending America's Crime Crisis (with Daniel Van Ness)
   (1989)
Evangelicals and Catholics Together: Working toward a Common Mission
   (with Richard John Neuhaus) (1995)
Gideon's Torch (with Ellen Santilli Vaughn) (1995)
How Now Shall We Live? (with Nancy Pearcey) (1999)
Kingdoms in Conflict (with Ellen Santilli Vaughn) (1987)
Life Sentence (1979)
Loving God (1983)
The Body: Being Light in Darkness (with Ellen Santilli Vaughn) (1992)
The God of Stones and Spiders: Letters to a Church in Exile (with Ellen Santilli Vaughn)
   (1990)
The Role of the Church in Society (1986)
Who Speaks for God: Confronting the World with Real Christianity (1985)
Why America Doesn't Work (with Jack Eckerd) (1991)

1936–

JAMES DOBSON

FOCUSING ON THE FAMILY

There are families to be
rescued—children to be
protected—babies to be saved—
teens to be comforted—widows to
be supported—single parents to
be encouraged—marriages to be
preserved—and governmental
activities to be monitored.
It's a gigantic task, but together
we can make a difference.

Focus on the Family newsletter, December 1998

J ust days before James Dobson Sr. died, he embarked on a three-day prayer vigil, asking the Lord to extend his days and his ministry. He received his answer from the Lord and shared it with his family: "I have heard your prayers. I know that you are concerned about My people and My kingdom. I know your compassion, and I'm going to answer your prayers. In fact, you're going to reach millions of people. But it is not going to be through you. It will be through your son."

More than twenty years later that son has seen the prophecy fulfilled, and God continues to keep the promise he made to Dr. James Dobson's father.

In Short

Psychologist and social commentator James Dobson reaches an audience of millions worldwide through his radio programs, books, magazines, films, and events. The name of the organization he founded summarizes his message: Focus on the Family. With wisdom, encouragement, and biblical truth, Dobson invites us to consider that the family is the fundamental unit of society. Its well-being is essential to a healthy world. Its reflection is an image of our heavenly Father's love for his children.

Faith

James Dobson Jr. was born in Shreveport, Louisiana, on April 21, 1936, the son of James and Myrtle Dobson. His father was an evangelist and pastor with the Nazarene denomination, and he watched his son walk closely with the Lord from the time the boy heeded his father's invitation at a revival meeting when he was just three years old. James Sr. was a third-generation minister, and although he had hopes that his son would carry on the tradition to a fourth generation, when the teenage James announced his desire to become a psychologist, the family wisely left the subject alone.

Dobson pursued his dream, starting at Pasadena College for his undergraduate studies and graduating in 1958. During his time there he met the homecoming queen, Shirley Deere. They were married August 27, 1960, while Jim was completing a master's program at the University of Southern California. After receiving his Ph.D. in child development from the same university in 1967, he served as assistant professor of pediatrics from 1969 to 1977 and associate clinical professor from 1978 to 1983, both positions at Children's Hospital at the University of Southern California (USC).

Early in his professorship Dobson wrote his first book, *Dare to Discipline*. Published in 1970 at the height of the social upheaval precipitated by the Vietnam War, *Dare to Discipline* swam against the cultural tide, calling for a return to old-fashioned biblical principles in the disciplining of children. The book found an eager audience nationwide and prompted hundreds of speaking invitations. Dobson spent many weekends crisscrossing the country to deliver a seminar he called "Focus on the Family," returning to Los Angeles in time to fulfill his weekday duties at USC.

Now with a young family at home Dobson realized that while he was spending many of his weekends on the road telling parents how to raise their kids, his own young children were spending these weekends without their father. To practice what he was preaching, he sought ways to reach out to parents long-distance. Dobson rented a two-room office in Los Angeles, hired a part-time secretary, and wondered if the phone would ever ring. In the meantime he arranged for the filming of his next-to-last "Focus on the Family" seminar and released it as a seven-hour training series. He also began hosting a weekly fifteen-minute radio program of the same name. The ministry of Focus on the Family had begun.

FRUIT

On film and through radio this highly educated psychologist sounded less like a clinical professor and more like a wise country doctor sitting down to share a conversation about marriage and children over a cup of tea. Christians across America embraced his homespun message. The film series would eventually be seen by over sixty million people, and his weekly fifteen-minute radio broadcast grew into a daily half-hour show, now heard by five million listeners.

As the radio network grew, Dobson's phone started to ring again, and soon it rang constantly. Postal carriers stopped slipping letters into his mailbox and started tossing sackfuls of mail on his doorstep. The calls and letters came from people across the country desperate to get the good doctor's advice on the challenges they faced: Parents asked for help with a disabled child; a pastor sought guidance for a pregnant teenage daughter; a harried mom cried for help with her two uncontrollable children; a workaholic dad wondered if it was too late to become involved in his family again.

As the ministry expanded, it outgrew one office after another and eventually moved to its own large campus in Colorado Springs, Colorado. Mike Yorkey, in his book *Turning Hearts toward Home,* says that to Dobson the ministry became a success because it offered to meet a great need. Says Dobson, "We hung out a shingle and said, 'We care about you. We don't have all the answers, but we have some correct conclusions to share with you.'"

Focus on the Family continues to grow. Its thirteen hundred employees serve in nearly eighty ministries within the organization, from radio programming to counseling, from education to the publication of eleven different magazines. Each day the office receives five thousand phone calls a day and twice that many letters and ships ten thousand letters, products, and other ministry helps. Its daily radio programs, broadcast in eight languages, are heard on twenty-nine hundred North American radio stations and thirteen hundred stations in seventy countries overseas.

Throughout Focus on the Family's history, Dobson has spoken out forcefully in the public square regarding social issues such as abortion, homosexuality, pornography, euthanasia, and moral relativism. At various times government officials have either sought his counsel or run from his conservative activism. He is not afraid to take politicians to task when they fail to uphold the sanctity of life and the importance of the traditional family.

In recent years the press has taken notice of Dobson's outspoken views, giving him an audience wider than the reach of his radio broadcasts and magazines. Aware that his mailing list includes millions of like-minded, politically conservative voters, not a few of his critics are concerned that he will throw his full weight behind certain candidates—or even throw his own hat into the arena.

But ultimately Dobson and his organization's mission is not political, or even social, but eternal. As he puts it in a Focus on the Family newsletter, "Yes, we are attempting to help families function more effectively and lovingly. But we have an even more basic motive in what we do. By helping to bond family members to one another, we hope to create an environment in which the gospel can flourish. This is our primary reason for being." For three decades that's exactly what the good doctor has been about.

LEGACY

At a time when America's culture was being rent by an unpopular war and its youth were abandoning traditions both bad and good, James Dobson rose above the clamor with a gentle call to hold firmly to what is good—the family. Not just any idea of family but the institution established by the original Father to provide life, love, and purpose to his earthly children. For a third of a century this tireless advocate of parents and children has continued to direct us with that same focus.

Much of the success Dobson has in delivering his message comes from his method. When he calls parents to love their children to obedience, he does so in a tone that reveals his own love for the people he's addressing. When he speaks against a bad social policy, it's hard not to hear behind his words the concern of a dad looking after his kids. After all, he seeks not just to encourage moral living among families but to point people to the Creator of life itself. In a world where moral debates quickly turn into hate-laced battles, Dobson offers a better way to fight: with conviction couched in love, and a message that is lived out in the home before it is spoken on the street.

For additional information about Focus on the Family, see appendix A.

Teach your children to choose the right path, and when they are older, they will remain upon it.

Proverbs 22:6

BOOKS BY JAMES DOBSON

Dr. Dobson Answers Your Questions (1992)
Emotions, Can You Trust Them? (1993)
Home with a Heart (1996)
In the Arms of God (1997)
Life on the Edge (1999)
Love for a Lifetime (1999)
Love Must Be Tough (1996)
Parenting Isn't for Cowards (1994)
Preparing for Adolescence (1989)
Romantic Love (1997)
Solid Answers (1997)
Straight Talk (1995)
The New Dare to Discipline (1996)
The New Hide or Seek (1999)
The Strong-Willed Child (1992)
When God Doesn't Make Sense (1997)

DAVID DU PLESSIS

LIFE IN THE SPIRIT

If you will take the great
truths of the gospel out of
your theological freezers
and get them on the fire of
the Holy Spirit, your
churches will yet turn the
world upside down.

A Man Called Mr. Pentecost

David du Plessis sat in his office one spring morning, ready to attack his pile of mail. He was general secretary for South Africa's Apostolic Faith Mission, a Pentecostal denomination whose continuous growth placed great demands on its leader. The door burst open, and Smith Wigglesworth entered. With a fierce expression the renowned English Pentecostal evangelist pointed at David and demanded, "Come out here!"

Wigglesworth put his hands on du Plessis's shoulders, looked straight into his eyes, and began to prophesy. "I have been sent by the Lord to tell you what he has shown me. Through the old-line denominations will come a revival that will eclipse anything we have known throughout history. . . . God is going to use you in this movement. You will have a very prominent part. . . . All he requires of you is that you be humble and faithful under all circumstances. . . ." When the messenger finished, he prayed, then turned and walked out the door without another word.

In Short

In fulfillment of a prophecy South African David du Plessis worked to show Christians that the Spirit-filled life was not a tradition to be shared only among Pentecostal churches but a gift from the Holy Spirit available to all believers. His charismatic faith and great vision won the respect of influential church leaders in many denominations, spurred the spread of the Pentecostal movement far beyond its roots, and encouraged millions to consider the role of the Holy Spirit in today's church.

FAITH

David John du Plessis was born on February 7, 1905, in Twenty-four Rivers, a Christian commune near Cape Town, South Africa. David's parents were farmers, and his father also served as a lay preacher. Prior to David's birth, his parents promised God that they would raise their child to do the Lord's work. His father strove to fulfill this promise by enforcing strict discipline and insisting that all work be carried out with excellence.

When David was a child, a Pentecostal minister came to visit, and his charismatic faith made a lasting impression on the family. But when David's father embraced the minister's teachings, he was expelled from their Dutch Reformed church. The following year a Pentecostal missionary from England arrived to establish a mission station among the native Africans. The du Plessis family, persuaded to join him, packed up and moved to Basutoland (now Lesotho), a country in southern Africa surrounded by the Republic of South Africa.

David spent the next few years in that remote place, living with his family in dirt-floor huts. He spent most of his time observing African believers who had no education but tremendous faith. David wanted to know Jesus in the same way.

One day David was asked to go to a post office in a village eleven miles away. Riding on horseback, he got to the post office, picked up the mail, and turned for home just as the sky began to darken. He thought he could outride the bad weather, but when he was not yet halfway home, a lightning bolt struck the ground in front of him, spooking the horse. David slid out of the saddle and fell to his knees, begging Jesus to save him. When he got up, he knew that Jesus had saved not only his body but also his soul.

Soon after his conversion David became aware that there was still something missing in his faith: the baptism of the Holy Spirit. Seeking to attain it through prayer and fasting, he became exhausted and frustrated until a young girl told him to confess what was on his conscience. Young David went to his parents and confessed a seven-year-old lie he had never divulged. Overwhelmed and relieved as he recalled the forgiveness Jesus had given him, he opened his mouth to give praise. Out came another language, which someone identified as Chinese. David had spoken in tongues.

Soon afterward he began giving his testimony in public. As he taught from the Bible and began to preach, he sensed a clear call into ministry. A notice in the Apostolic Faith Mission's denominational newspaper announced a publishing apprenticeship at the headquarters in Johannesburg. David applied for the position and got it, thus confirming his conviction that he was called to ministry. He was about to fulfill the promise his parents had made to God before he was born.

FRUIT

After serving his apprenticeship, du Plessis took a job in Pretoria to earn money for schooling. He attended an Apostolic Faith Mission church there and worked as a correspondence clerk in the South African Railways engineering department. There he was introduced to Anna Cornelia Jacobs, a lapsed churchgoer. He reached out to her and before long was delighted to see her heart reopening to God. So delighted, in fact, that they had a date two days later. After courting for a year and a half, David and Anna were married on August 13, 1927.

Sadly, David's father did not approve. When he heard of his son's engagement, he told him he was too young. Father and son were not reconciled until the young couple brought their new baby, the first of six children, home for a visit.

After completing two years of basic college training at Grey University, du Plessis made plans to attend the university. Again his father objected, fearing that David would turn from serving the Lord. But David was right. His education improved his preaching and won him credibility. He became the first Pentecostal in South Africa with a university degree. Meanwhile, his job with the railroad allowed him to travel inexpensively to preach.

His growing ministry talents soon attracted the attention of Apostolic Faith Mission leaders, who in 1930 offered him the position of secretary of the Orange Free State province and handed him the editorship of the denomination's struggling national newspaper. Du Plessis took over the paper, and it soon flourished.

As he maintained his pastoral and preaching duties, he also began to delve more and more into the publishing business, launching a regional paper, the first in that area. Soon he was confronted with a decision: remain in a lucrative publishing industry or do what God had called him to—ministry. In 1937, having made his decision, he moved his family to his denomination's headquarters in Johannesburg.

It was there that du Plessis received his strange visit from Smith Wigglesworth. Three weeks later he received an invitation to speak at the Assemblies of God general council in Memphis, Tennessee. By this time du Plessis's name had become known to some American Pentecostals, in part because he had sent copies of his newspaper to denominations around the world, inviting their critiques and asking for copies of their own newspapers in order to exchange ideas.

Du Plessis accepted the Assemblies' invitation and traveled throughout the U.S. and Europe, speaking, meeting with church leaders, and harvesting ideas to take back to South Africa. In 1940 he and Anna began a Bible school, living in the school alongside their first class of sixteen students.

In 1944 du Plessis handed over the school, now the Apostolic Bible College, to new leadership and began traveling again as World War II ended. One night in 1948 while in Tennessee on a visit to the U.S., he sustained serious injuries in a terrible car accident. He survived, but doctors told him that his recovery would take two years. Du Plessis sent for his family, and they made America their home.

During his long recovery, du Plessis organized the 1949 Pentecostal World Conference, seeking to bring the many Pentecostal denominations together in a common vision. Eventually the Church of God asked du Plessis to join them officially. But in his heart he carried Wigglesworth's vision: to reach *beyond* the Pentecostal traditions to attract even the leaders of the old mainline denominations to the powerful work of the Holy Spirit.

One of his first entries into mainline denominations was through John MacKay, president of Princeton Theological Seminary. After reading MacKay's description of the Pentecostal movement as the greatest blessing that had come to Christianity, du Plessis telephoned him. They met, and a few days later du Plessis spent a day with the leadership at the headquarters of the World Council of Churches (WCC).

Soon after, he went to the International Missionary Council in Willingen, Germany. Before leaving, he met with over half of the 210 delegates there, all of whom wanted him to explain Pentecostalism to them. Among the men he met with was Willem Visser 't Hooft, the first general secretary for the World Council of Churches. In 1954 the Dutchman invited du Plessis to the WCC's assembly.

Du Plessis had encountered many prejudices against mainline churches among Pentecostals, but he soon found that prejudice resided in all of the denominations. The divisiveness saddened him—and spurred him to work for reconciliation. Whenever he spoke, he first confessed his own past prejudices. He shared his testimony of God's forgiveness for his own sins and how he had discovered forgiveness and genuine love. As he told his story, listeners saw their own prejudices, sought forgiveness, and found fellowship with those whom they had resented. Du Plessis's mission to the greater church was bearing fruit.

Prominent mainline seminaries, including Princeton, Yale, and Union, invited him to address their students. He encouraged Pentecostals to reach beyond their own denominations. Others joined the Pentecostal movement as a result of his teaching. Still others took what they learned back to their mainline churches. To a great extent, the surprising interest in the charismatic gifts among mainline denominations throughout the sixties and seventies was sparked by du Plessis's ministry.

In the last fifteen years of his life until his death on January 31, 1987, du Plessis dedicated himself to reaching the Roman Catholic Church. He attended sessions in which Pentecostal scholars and theologians met with their Catholic counterparts to explore "issues of mutual concern" and also attended Vatican Council II as an observer. In Pentecostalism and Catholicism du Plessis found a powerful common thread: a desire to know the power of life in the Spirit.

LEGACY

Pentecostalism and David du Plessis grew up together. The former was a product of America's Holiness Movement in 1901; the latter arrived just four years later, half a world away. Rejected by mainline denominations, stigmatized by scoffers from without and charlatan faith healers from within, the true movement grew first among the poor, the working classes, minorities, and through missions overseas. But within a few decades Pentecostalism became the largest Christian movement of the twentieth century.

While many great leaders helped champion this movement, most did so from within their own denominations. Du Plessis stands alone in his mission to reach a much wider church with a charismatic message. God honored his diligence.

On the Day of Pentecost in the first century of the Christian church the Holy Spirit empowered the apostles to transcend cultural and religious barriers to share the Good News. The same Holy Spirit used David du Plessis to break through another set of barriers, to show the world what the power of the Holy Spirit looks like in a real live human living in the *twentieth* century.

Peter's words convicted them deeply, and they said to him and to the other apostles, "Brothers, what should we do?"

Peter replied, "Each of you must turn from your sins and turn to God, and be baptized in the name of Jesus Christ for the forgiveness of your sins. Then you will receive the gift of the Holy Spirit."

Acts 2:37-38

BOOKS BY DAVID DU PLESSIS

A Man Called Mr. Pentecost (1977)

You will live to see this work grow to such
dimensions that the Pentecostal movement
itself will be a light thing in comparison with
what God will do through the old churches.

There will be tremendous gatherings of
people, unlike anything we've seen, and great
leaders will change their attitude and accept
not only the message, but also the blessing.
All He requires of you is that you be humble
and faithful under all circumstances.

If you remain humble and faithful,
you will live to see the whole fulfilled.

Smith Wigglesworth, prophesying over
David du Plessis in 1936

JIM ELLIOT

LOSING EVERYTHING TO GAIN CHRIST

He is no fool who gives what
he cannot keep to gain
what he cannot lose.

Shadow of the Almighty

S plashing into the Curaray River with an outstretched hand and a broad, beaming smile, Jim Elliot waded toward the Indian men coming out of the jungle. He greeted them in their native tongue and motioned for them to come to his side of the river. This was the hour. This was everything he and his mission team had worked for. They were finally making contact with the Auca Indians.

Days later, a search party found the bodies of Jim Elliot, Nate Saint, Pete Fleming, Roger Youderian, and Ed McCully in the river. They had been murdered by men for whom they had prayed for six years.

In Short

The courageous, tragic story of Jim Elliot and his mission team has gripped the imaginations of countless young people, inspiring them to go to the mission field. Jim's words and actions, which reflected radical obedience despite personal risk and the overcoming of cultural, linguistic, and geographical barriers to share the love of Jesus Christ with men and women who had never heard the Good News, have evoked passionate responses to serve Christ wholeheartedly.

Faith

Philip James Elliot was born October 8, 1927, in Portland, Oregon, to Fred and Clara Elliot, joining three brothers and one sister. As a young man Jim's father had traveled with evangelist and Bible scholar Harry Ironside and had served as an itinerant evangelist in the Puget Sound area before moving to Portland to farm, preach, and raise his family. Clara conducted a chiropractic practice out of their home. When Jim was six years old, he came home from a worship meeting and informed her that Jesus could return whenever he wanted because Jim was now "saved." After that his mother would observe Jim in the yard telling his friends about his new Savior.

Jim was inspired by missionaries who frequently visited the Elliot home. He decided that he, too, wanted to serve God with his whole life. So in high school he excelled in architectural drawing and sports, figuring the latter would help him build up his body for the rigors of missionary work. In the fall of 1945 he enrolled in Wheaton College, west of Chicago. In studies and athletics, Jim was a ferocious achiever, doing everything to increase his discipline and strengthen his commitment to God. He made the varsity wrestling team in his freshman year, began speaking to youth groups in the Wheaton area, and in his junior year started a spiritual journal.

In the summer of 1947, after spending six weeks in Mexico with a missionary family, Jim sensed a call to mission work in Latin America. The next year he became president of the Foreign Mission Fellowship on campus. He also fell in love with Elisabeth Howard and told her so. Yet he believed God was calling him to be single and told her that, too. He chose Greek as his major and graduated with highest honors in 1949.

Following graduation, Jim spent a year working at home with his family, then attended Bible translator Cameron Townsend's Summer Institute of Linguistics (SIL) in Norman, Oklahoma. There he met a former missionary to the Quichua Indians of Ecuador and first heard of the remote and much-feared Waorani tribe of Auca Indians in that country. His response was immediate. After ten days of prayer for guidance, Jim wrote to a missionary in Ecuador, offering to join him in reaching these dangerous people.

During the next two years Jim built a team and prayerfully prepared for their mission, staying active in teaching, preaching, and Bible study work in Oklahoma, Indiana, and Illinois. He also renewed his correspondence with Elisabeth Howard. She had sensed God's leading to do linguistic work in Ecuador but as an independent missionary on a separate assignment.

FRUIT

After raising support and completing final preparations, Jim and team member Pete Fleming set sail for Ecuador in February 1952. Elisabeth arrived in Quito that April. In June, from the Mission Aviation Fellowship (MAF) station at Shell Mera, the men made their first aerial search over the territory where the Quichua and Auca tribes were located. The men learned that Shell Oil Company had just abandoned their jungle station in Shandia, near the hostile tribes, deeming it too dangerous—five persons had been killed. Unshaken, Jim and Pete moved to the abandoned site.

In February 1953 Jim went to Quito to meet Elisabeth and asked her to become his wife. On October 8, Jim's birthday, they were married in a civil ceremony in Quito. The newlyweds made a tent their home, setting up a school for a family of Indian children. Jim and Elisabeth's only child, Valerie, was born eighteen months later.

In September 1955, with the assistance of MAF pilot Nate Saint, Jim and Ed McCully located the first Auca huts in the jungle. The sighting lit the men's enthusiasm and determination. They would attempt contact. In October, joined by Roger Youderian and Pete Fleming, the team began making weekly flights over the village, using a battery-powered speaker to broadcast words of encouragement in the Auca language and dropping gifts such as buttons, a kettle, a machete, and tinted photographs of each man. The Aucas responded by sending back a parrot and feathered headdresses in the drop bucket.

Encouraged by the responses, the men decided to find a suitable landing strip for the plane. They selected a sandy bank on the Curaray River, naming it Palm Beach. On the second day of 1956 they made their landing. After a few trips to bring in a radio and supplies, they built a tree shelter and began shouting Auca phrases into the jungle. A few days later two Auca women and a young man came out of the jungle. They appeared to be friendly, and "George" (the name the mission team gave to the young man) accepted a brief ride in the airplane. The team spent the following day quietly and without contacts.

On Sunday, January 8, after songs, prayers, and a service, the men radioed their wives just after noon to announce that they expected contact with the Indians within hours and that they would report in again at 4:30 P.M. They were not heard from again.

Days later a search party found the bodies of Jim Elliot and his four team members; they had been killed by nine-foot hardwood spears and machetes. Pilot Nate Saint's watch had stopped at 3:12 P.M. The deaths were reported worldwide.

Remarkably, the mission carried on. In less than three years' time the Auca tribe invited Jim's widow, Elisabeth, and their young daughter, Valerie, to live among them and resume the work of the husband and father whose life they had taken. The Auca tribe had turned to God. And in turn, other neighboring Indian tribes heard the story of another man, named Jesus, who had laid down his life in love for them.

Forty years later the Aucas who had been on the beach that tragic day shared a last remembrance. After the massacre several of the Aucas saw lights above the trees—a sky "full of jungle beetles similar to fireflies with a light that was brighter and didn't blink." It was only later, when they heard recordings of gospel choirs, that they realized what they had witnessed. It was supernatural . . . something like angels.

LEGACY

Many have called Jim a hero for giving his life. His widow, Elisabeth, sees it another way. In *Shadow of the Almighty* she writes: "Is the distinction between living for Christ and dying for Him, after all, so great? Is not the second the logical conclusion of the first? Furthermore, to live for God *is* to die, 'daily.' . . . It is to lose everything that we may gain Christ. It is in thus laying down our lives that we find them."

Jim certainly saw his own life that way. As a junior at Wheaton College, he wrote in his prayer journal: "God, I pray Thee, light these idle sticks of my life and may I burn for Thee. Consume my life, my God, for it is Thine. I seek not a long life, but a full one, like you, Lord Jesus." Like his Savior's, the earthly life of Jim Elliot did not burn long, but it burned very brightly, and that light is with us still.

For to me, living is for Christ, and dying is even better. Philippians 1:21

Edæ inguipoga quëwëmo incæ botö Codito ingante entawëninque tömengä beyænque ante quëwëmopa. Wæætë wäëmo incæ tömengä beyäe botö godömenque nanguï entawenguïmo ïmopa.

Pidipenteidi 1:21 (from the Waorani language, courtesy of Wycliffe Bible Translators)

BOOKS BY JIM ELLIOT

The Journals of Jim Elliot (edited by Elisabeth Elliot) (1983)

1 9 3 3 –

JERRY FALWELL

FAITH IN THE PUBLIC FORUM

Now is the time to call
America back to God, back to
the Bible, back to morality.

Listen, America!

A young Bible college student was asked to teach a Sunday school class. It was a small class: just one boy. After three weeks the college student had managed to double the attendance. Then he tried to quit. The Sunday school superintendent told him he would never make it in ministry. Discouraged, the young man began looking for students to fill his lonely classroom. He scoured parks on Saturdays, hung out at ball fields, found boys, and joined in their games.

The teacher who went out to find students saw many of those students come to church on Sundays to find him. The class grew to fifty-five. It was the first of many crowds that would gather to hear the affectionately contentious Jerry Falwell.

IN SHORT

Pastor Jerry Falwell is one of the most recognized Christian leaders in America. His church is among the country's largest; his university is the biggest evangelical school in America. But he is best known for his very public stands on controversial moral issues. Though many are eager to debate his mixing of politics with religion, few can dispute his role in leading conservative Christians out of the safety of their churches and into the public arena.

FAITH

On August 11, 1933, in Lynchburg, Virginia, Helen Falwell gave birth to twin boys. One of the twins, Gene, followed in his father's footsteps and become a businessman. The other, Jerry, followed a far different path.

The boys' father, Carey, had a reputation for spotting new trends in the business world and met with great success in several ventures, including a bootleg whiskey operation during the era of Prohibition. He was a heavy drinker and an agnostic who hated preachers. Growing up, the Falwell children saw little of their father as he left them in the charge of their strict yet gracious mother.

As a boy Jerry loved to read and spent a great deal of time listening to the radio. He was also clever and mischievous, showing up at Sunday school at age nine long enough to answer "Present!" when the roll was called. Then he would skip out to read the Sunday newspaper comics at his uncle's house, returning to the church just before his mother came to pick him up. In the fifth grade he let a snake loose in the classroom. In high school he managed to lock his gym teacher in the basement and hide a dead rat in another teacher's desk drawer. In spite of all this, Jerry finished school with a near perfect academic record and was valedictorian of his graduating class. However, another prank kept him from delivering the speech; he sat out his high school graduation under suspension.

As a young man, Jerry lived life to the full, dated lots of girls, drove fast cars, and took in late-night parties. In the fall of 1950 the seventeen-year-old entered Lynchburg College, planning to study there for two years and then transfer to Virginia Polytechnical Institute and pursue mechanical engineering. In the meantime he began to consider the Christian faith. His mother kept the radio in his room tuned to a station that carried radio preacher Charles Fuller's *Old-Fashioned Revival Hour*. Too lazy to get up and change the station when the show came on, Falwell would sit and listen to Fuller, although he was too embarrassed to admit that the program was having an effect on him.

One Sunday night in 1952 Falwell and some friends visited Park Avenue Baptist Church to check out a rumor that it was the haunt of numerous attractive girls. They arrived late and were seated in the front row. When the pastor began to preach, Jerry heard much the same message he had been hearing from Fuller's radio sermons, and finally it took hold. He committed his life to Christ that night. The next day he went out and bought a Bible, a Bible dictionary, and *The Strong's Exhaustive Concordance of the Bible.* He joined the youth group and dragged his friends along with him. By the end of the summer he had helped bring fifty new members into the group. He also took an interest in one of the attractive young women he had originally hoped to find there. Macel Pate was the church pianist, and one day Jerry would marry her.

Soon after his conversion Falwell made another commitment: He would enter the ministry. He left the local college and went off to Baptist Bible College in Springfield, Missouri, to complete his degree and prepare for what later became his first and only pastorate.

FRUIT

After graduating from Bible college, Falwell returned to Lynchburg to start a church. On June 21, 1956, Thomas Road Baptist Church was born. It had thirty-five charter members and met in an abandoned building that had once housed the Donald Duck Bottling Company. In that same year the twenty-two-year-old pastor, a fan of radio throughout his childhood and a believer because of it, took to the airwaves himself, purchasing half-hour blocks of airtime at seven dollars per broadcast. Soon he began broadcasting his church services on television. The program, called *The Old-Time Gospel Hour,* has aired every week without fail ever since, a record for religious broadcasting.

As the church grew, its ministry expanded into education. In 1967 Falwell founded Lynchburg Christian Academy and four years after that, Lynchburg Baptist College, which eventually became Liberty Baptist College and then Liberty University. Other schools, a seminary, and a Bible institute followed. Fed by the ministry aspirations of Falwell's congregation and students, the church opened a home for unwed mothers (the Liberty Godparent

Home), a treatment center for alcoholism, a distribution center for food and clothing, a youth camp, and a broadcasting network.

It is clear that God has blessed Jerry Falwell's ministry. Thomas Road Baptist Church now has twenty-two thousand members. Liberty University, with an enrollment of fourteen thousand, is the largest evangelical Christian university in the country. But outside of his hometown, most people know of Jerry Falwell for his far more controversial endeavors.

In 1979 Falwell felt called to mobilize Christians to confront moral and social issues, and he began to encourage them to express their beliefs through the political process. This was a novel idea to the conservative believers who made up his constituency. Many fundamentalists, including Falwell himself, had long preached against the idea of Christians becoming embroiled in political issues, calling them instead to work for change in individuals. Now, to carry out this bold plan Falwell founded an organization called the Moral Majority.

At its launch Falwell pledged to commit five years of his life to awakening the conservative church in America, crusading for issues such as the support of human life and the protection of the family. Soon after he started, it was clear that he had awakened a sleeping giant. Tens of thousands of churches joined in the organization's causes; millions of voters were registered; and politicians suddenly had a substantial new block of constituents to woo: the "religious right."

The Moral Majority's loud cries against abortion and homosexuality were applauded by millions, but many Americans perceived the organization's outspoken leader as mean spirited and divisive. And many Christians who agreed with Falwell's moral beliefs disagreed with his tactics, which often bordered on arrogance and occasionally crossed over the line.

Still, the Moral Majority's influence on American politics in the 1980s was profound. When Falwell formally dissolved the organization in 1989, five years after his original commitment expired, he had traveled three million miles to speak in churches, direct voter-registration efforts, conduct demonstrations at civic centers and on the steps of state capitals, and rally concerned citizens to oppose moral decay. When it was over, many conservative Christians had emerged from the safety of their churches to express their beliefs in the ballot box as well as in the public forum, a trend that continues to this day.

Since then, Falwell has devoted most of his attention to his Lynchburg ministries, but he still finds time to land himself in the national news. Typically he gets negative coverage, the result of a careless public remark or a thoughtful statement that gets edited out of context. One thing is certain: The media will play up the words of Jerry Falwell, whether well spoken or poorly chosen, to the dismay of some and the delight of others.

Legacy

The mention of Jerry Falwell's name in any conversation is guaranteed to spark a spirited reaction. Certainly he makes for an easy target. His unapologetic stands against politically correct issues land him in hot water frequently. He's not afraid to speak out on the moral issues that alarm him, nor does he mind the debates his words generate. To him, it is far better for Christians to speak out in disagreement than to hide in a silent pretense of unity.

Many disagree with Falwell's practice of mixing religion and politics. Ironically, among these detractors are politically liberal Christians who would applaud the work of Walter Rauschenbusch, Martin Luther King Jr., and Desmond Tutu. Yet each of these believers saw politics and government as institutions of society, a society into which God has placed Christians to carry out his work. And though these critics might strenuously disagree with Jerry Falwell's political views, they would not question his conviction that the life of a Christian extends far beyond the walls of the church.

Unfortunately, in his public persona Falwell often projects an attitude that appears insensitive and unloving. But those who know him best, including hundreds of ministry leaders and the members of his own congregation, see him for who he truly is: a passionate, witty, lovable pastor who counts it an honor to serve the Lord.

For additional information about Jerry Falwell's ministries, see appendix A.

Timothy, guard what God has entrusted to you.

1 Timothy 6:20

BOOKS BY JERRY FALWELL

Capturing a Town for Christ (1973)
Champions for God (1985)
Church Aflame (1971)
Falwell: An Autobiography (1997)
Finding Inner Peace and Strength (1982)
If I Should Die before I Wake (1986)
Listen, America! (1980)
Stepping Out on Faith (1984)
Strength for the Journey (autobiography) (1987)
The Fundamentalist Phenomenon (1981)
The New American Family (1992)
When It Hurts Too Much to Cry (1984)
Wisdom for Living (1984)

1887–1968

CHARLES E. FULLER

COMPELLED TO PREACH THE GOSPEL

My burning desire is to preach
the Word; to get souls saved;
and to get believers to study
the Word. When a believer
studies the Word prayerfully
and with an obedient heart,
two things are accomplished:
He grows in grace and in
the knowledge of God,
and he goes to work.

Give the Winds a Mighty Voice: The Story of Charles E. Fuller

T his is Charles E. Fuller speaking."
Millions of men and women from coast to coast, of all
colors, creeds, classes, and backgrounds, heard Charles
Fuller's trademark greeting. Nowhere in the country could one
find such a diverse gathering of saints and sinners—except in the
virtual revival tent of Fuller's Sunday-night broadcasts. Radio
dissolved the earthly distinctions that kept people apart, and Fuller
used this technology to bring them together to hear about the
Jesus who came to save them all.

In Short

While the new phenomenon of "broadcast media" was reshaping
culture at a mind-boggling pace, many Christians shuddered at the
thought of using technology in the spread of their old-time religion.
Fuller held no such prejudice. He used new tools to deliver a timeless message, a message that originated "in the heavens" and passed
through them again as radio waves directed at the homes and hearts
of everyone with a receiver. For him the numbers of those with "ears
to hear" were not limited to the people who could fit in America's
church pews. He pioneered national radio ministry, reaching
millions of Christians and non-Christians in nearly four decades of
broadcasting. Yet now his name is better known for his other legacy:
a world-class seminary in downtown Pasadena, California.

Faith

Charles Fuller was born in the booming town of Los Angeles on
April 25, 1887. A year after Charles was born, his family moved to

Redlands, a then-rural town near San Bernardino, where his father, Henry, prospered as a fruit grower. As a boy, young Charles's responsibility was to set gopher traps in the seventy-acre grove. For every gopher tail he brought in, his father gave him a dime, insisting that he tithe to their church from his gopher earnings.

With the dimes he earned from his gopher patrols, Charles bought a telegraph set from a mail-order catalog. He learned Morse code and set up his own telegraph system by stringing wire around the farm—the start of his long connection with radio.

His high school nickname was "Chub," because by age fifteen he was six feet tall and wore size twelve double-E shoes. His exceptional size and farm-honed strength helped him excel in football. After a scrimmage a friend introduced Charles to Grace Leone Payton, whom he courted throughout high school and college. He attended Pomona College, where he majored in chemistry, excelled in his studies and in sports, became captain of the football team as well as president of his class, and graduated magna cum laude. The caption beneath his class picture in the college annual reads: "Physically the biggest man in school, mentally a fine student, morally every inch a man."

After a brief stint as a miner in northern California, Charles returned to Redlands to marry Grace Payton on October 21, 1911. The groom stuck close to his rural roots, working as a salesman for a fertilizer company, then purchasing an orange grove of his own, and later managing a fruit-packing business. He was a hardworking businessman and an energetic member of his local church. He served as a ruling elder, a Sunday school superintendent, and a leader of the young men's club. Remarkably, despite all his church activity, Charles did not know Christ. It was only at his wife's prompting to read F. W. Grant's book *The Mysteries of the Kingdom* that he finally became interested in spiritual matters.

In 1917, after hearing a powerful message at the Church of the Open Door in Los Angeles, Charles went out to his car, drove to a park, and committed his life to Christ. Charles and Grace, sharing a burden to reach people in out-of-the-way places, spent the next year traveling as missionaries to rural towns throughout the western states. The following year Charles was sitting in his manager's office in the packinghouse when the conviction to go into full-time ministry became so powerful that he left his desk, crawled behind a stack of orange crates, and began to pray. After a fitful pleading with God for direction and courage, he got up and quit his job to study for the ministry. From that day on he said he felt as the apostle Paul must have felt when he wrote: "Woe is unto me, if I preach not the gospel!" (1 Corinthians 9:16, KJV).

In the fall of 1919 Fuller entered the Bible Institute of Los Angeles (now Biola University). After graduating, he formed a new congregation, Calvary Church of Placentia, California, and served as pastor for eight years. During this time and soon thereafter Fuller began two pursuits that would become his life's work: training church leaders and preaching the gospel through radio. His call to ministry education came through his alma mater, Biola, where he served on the board of trustees. Then in 1928 he joined the faculty of the Los Angeles Baptist Seminary, teaching classes in Bible exegesis.

FRUIT

In 1929, from the sanctuary of his church in Placentia, Charles launched his radio ministry, broadcasting sermons from a radio station in nearby Santa Ana. Eventually these broadcasts evolved into a program Fuller called *The Old-Fashioned Revival Hour,* an ingenious title that suggested the familiar excitement of a tent meeting conveyed through what was then the state-of-the-art technology of radio.

The program's format gained immediate acceptance, and soon other stations around the country were broadcasting it. Three years later, in the fall of 1932, Fuller resigned as pastor of Calvary Church to devote his time to radio. The morning after his last sermon at the church, President Franklin Roosevelt closed all banks. Within a year the stock market bottomed out. Fuller's entire radio-ministry budget depended on the gifts of his listeners, who, like the rest of America, were trudging through the dark days of the Great Depression. Yet Fuller persevered, trusting that God would provide the funds. God did his part, the cash-strapped listeners continued to support the ministry, and millions of Americans heard the Good News in a time when all other news was bad. The show stayed on the air for twenty-three years, and at its peak, *The Old-Fashioned Revival Hour* was the most popular radio show on Sunday nights.

If the remarkable financial provision was proof that God wanted Fuller on the air, the constant stream of letters he received from listeners was confirmation that radio was indeed a powerful tool for the gospel. From refined words on monogrammed stationery to notes scribbled on smudgy pieces of paper bags from miner's cabins, Fuller read the stories of listeners who had committed their lives to Christ because of the broadcast.

Fuller was a man of disciplined exuberance. Where others saw crazy ideas and financial ruin, he saw opportunities to rely upon God's vision and provision. To his critics, launching a national, listener-supported broadcast in the dregs of the depression seemed a colossal act of foolishness. For Charles, it was just business as usual—business that utterly depended on God to see it through. From his first broadcast to his last he never depended on any one individual to finance the broadcast. To Charles this would have meant that he had stopped depending on God. Instead, he relied upon small gifts from his listeners, even when his show was airing on a thousand stations and costing $35,000 a week to stay on the air.

Once he had seen the remarkable result of faithful obedience in his radio venture, realizing his next wild vision was just another step of exuberant obedience. One night in November 1939 God revived Fuller's other great ministry passion, training Christian leaders, in a remarkable way. Fuller awoke from a deep sleep with a vision for "a Christ-centered, Spirit-directed training school, where Christian men and women could be trained in the things of God . . . to become steeped in the Word, in order to go out bearing the blessed news to lost men and women." That was the beginning of Fuller Theological Seminary.

"If this school is to be, it should be the best of its kind in the world!" he wrote to Bible scholar Wilbur M. Smith in 1946. "I see this great need, but I am not an educator. I must have the help of men of like vision." As Fuller envisioned the school, the men and women it would prepare for ministry, mission, and evangelism would stand as a bastion of evangelical fundamentalism against the twentieth-century trends of modernism and secularism.

With cofounder Harold Ockenga, theologian and pastor of Park Street Church in Boston, Fuller enlisted outstanding evangelical scholars such as Carl Henry, Everett F. Harrison, Harold Lindsell, and Wilbur M. Smith as the founding faculty. In 1947 thirty-nine men entered the school as its first student body. Among them was Bill Bright, who later founded Campus Crusade for Christ. Classes were held at Pasadena's Lake Avenue Congregational Church until the new buildings were completed on the property Fuller purchased down the street.

From its tiny start, Fuller Theological Seminary has grown to become the largest seminary in North America, with an enrollment of thirty-five hundred. To this day its focus is that of its founder, training men and women to step out boldly in ministry, mission, and evangelism.

Fuller's seminary dream did not interrupt his radio ministry. He expanded coverage through the 1940s, and his message now reached across the United States, Canada, Europe, Africa, Asia, South America, and the Pacific. In the fifties and sixties, as the new technology of television eclipsed radio in popularity, Fuller continued his weekly broadcasts, proving that radio was and still is an efficient, powerful tool for reaching people with the gospel of Jesus Christ. When he died in 1968, five hundred stations around the world were still broadcasting his program.

LEGACY

These days Christians embrace technology in ministry without hesitation. Televisions and fax machines, digital video and multimedia, E-mail messages and Web pages—these tools are used by ministries throughout the world to spread the same message Jesus delivered with lungs and larynx, mouth to ear, from Teacher to note-taking disciples. Until the invention of the printing press, gospel preaching stayed in this medium. And not until Charles Fuller came along hundreds of years later did it move beyond print. We who send and receive the Good News through electronic media have much to thank him for. And those who count on the fact that they can sit in on the teaching of the country's best preachers just by turning on the radio can appreciate the vision of the man who pioneered it all.

At its heart Fuller's lifelong ministry wasn't really about radio or the seminary. These things were merely the means to the end. His call was to preach the truths revealed to him in the Word of God, which he believed with deep conviction. He spoke with the miner in mind, and the hardworking farmer, the soldier, the laborer out in the orange grove. He pleaded passionately with his listeners to recognize their need for Jesus Christ. The message from God to man was spoken not by angels but by a man "of like passions with us." He faced formidable obstacles—the depression, financial burdens, bitter criticism—yet he persevered in his passionate faith to carry out his life's mission: to deliver God's message of salvation to millions. Some of his listeners sat in church pews, others in his seminary's classrooms. Most sat near a radio, connected to him by an invisible wave of radiation.

Preaching the Good News is not something I can boast about. I am compelled by God to do it. How terrible for me if I didn't do it! 1 Corinthians 9:16

1918 –

BILLY GRAHAM

SHARING THE GOSPEL

My one purpose in life is to
help people find a personal
relationship with God,
which, I believe, comes
through knowing Christ.

From the Billy Graham Evangelistic Association Web site, November 1999

In 1934 a group of Christian businessmen from Charlotte, North Carolina, held an all-day prayer meeting in a farmer's pasture. In one of their prayers they asked God to raise up from Charlotte a man who would preach the gospel to the ends of the earth.

The pasture belonged to William Graham Sr., the father of a fifteen-year-old boy named Billy. Within months that boy committed his life to Christ, the first step in a journey that would lead him to fulfill a prayer offered in a pasture.

In Short

Evangelist Billy Graham has preached the gospel to more people on this planet than anyone else in history. His simple, contagious faith, shared through hundreds of evangelistic campaigns, has led millions worldwide to commit their lives to Christ. As the most respected evangelical in the church and as a friend to its most influential leaders, Graham has had an impact on the course of Christianity for half a century.

Faith

William Franklin Graham Jr. was born near Charlotte, North Carolina, on November 7, 1918, four days before the signing of the armistice that ended World War I. His parents, William and Morrow Coffey Graham, strict Scottish Presbyterians, raised Billy and his three younger siblings in the church. When Billy was five years old, his father took him to Charlotte to hear a professional baseball player-turned-preacher named Billy Sunday.

As a teenager the sometimes rebellious Billy hunted, fished, and played baseball. He also attended church, but he was not eager to take it seriously. That changed when he went to hear another traveling evangelist, Mordecai Hamm. At the end of one of the preacher's sermons, Billy was convinced that he needed Jesus. After four verses of the hymn "Just As I Am," he walked to the front of the assembly. At age fifteen he had become a believer, and although he didn't know it then, he would eventually lead millions to do the same thing.

Following his graduation from high school, Billy attended Florida Bible Institute for three years and received a bachelor's degree in theology. While in Florida, he was baptized and became a member of a Southern Baptist church and then began preaching on street corners, in rescue missions, and at small churches. He continued his education at Wheaton College, where he also took on his first and only pastorate, at United Gospel Tabernacle, a Baptist church. During this time he met Ruth Bell, the daughter of a Southern Presbyterian missionary, who had spent her childhood in China and Korea. The two were married on August 13, 1943, soon after Billy's graduation from Wheaton.

FRUIT

While pastor at the Tabernacle, Billy took over as host of a local Sunday night radio program called *Songs in the Night.* The host he replaced, Torrey Johnson, shared Billy's passion for reaching young people with the gospel. Together they conducted large youth rallies that drew thousands of unchurched teenagers to hear Graham preach. When this evangelistic ministry was organized into Youth for Christ International, Johnson, who became president, hired Graham as its first full-time employee. Graham spent the next four years traveling across America and Europe, speaking and organizing local chapters.

Eventually Graham began holding evangelistic rallies of his own. He got a big start in 1949 when he set up a tent at the corner of Washington and Hill streets in Los Angeles, drawing 350,000 people over the twenty-five-day campaign. Before the crusade began, Graham paid a visit to Henrietta Mears, who encouraged the young evangelist through prayer and counsel to carry out the monumental task God had set before him.

The crusade received positive coverage in the newspapers, including those owned by William Randolph Hearst, who was so impressed with Graham's impact that he instructed his editors to push the story. Because of the press, Graham's reputation preceded him in subsequent campaigns throughout the country. His weekly radio program, *The Hour of Decision,* and the television show of the same name, which ran from 1951 to 1954, also helped extend his influence. In 1955 he helped to found *Christianity Today* magazine. The first issue featured articles from Graham as well as his friend Carl Henry, the man who would become editor of what immediately grew into the country's most-read evangelical magazine.

Graham's growing reputation left him open to criticism that he was a real-life Elmer Gantry, enriching himself through evangelism. To counter such speculation and to ensure that the ministry ran efficiently, Graham and others incorporated the Billy Graham Evangelistic Association (BGEA) in 1950. The BGEA embraced strict business practices, provided accountability for Graham and his growing staff, and became a model of integrity to many other ministries who have adopted its methods.

Graham's evangelistic campaigns visited every major U.S. city. He also conducted campaigns overseas, including the remarkable 1954 London crusade, where Anglican pastor John Stott assisted. Many international campaigns followed. And in 1982, at the invitation of the officially atheistic Soviet government and the prompting of Billy's old friend Cameron Townsend, Graham made his first visit to the Soviet Union.

After 1957 he generally held three to five crusades a year, while a number of associate evangelists led crusades in smaller cities and churches. To help ensure that new converts received encouragement and guidance following the crusades, in 1960 the BGEA began publishing *Decision* magazine, whose circulation reached two million by 1988. They also launched a film company, World Wide Pictures, to produce evangelistic films in many languages.

Graham's many books are among the most successful in the

history of Christian publishing. *Angels: God's Secret Agents* sold one million copies within three months of its release in 1975. Among his other books are titles such as *The Jesus Generation, How to Be Born Again,* and his autobiography, *Just As I Am.* Ruth, too, has been a well-received writer, best known for her inspirational books of poetry. The list of films, articles, seminars, and associated organizations that have stemmed from Billy, Ruth, and their organization is staggering.

Early on, Graham realized that the large-scale gatherings were only a part of the overall crusade in every city. To ensure that both the events themselves and the faith they sparked were successful, he goes to a city only when invited by a large number of its pastors. Then his team spends months in each city to unite local churches and ministries, plan the promotion, recruit volunteers, and, most important, to make sure that converts will be plugged in to local churches immediately after the campaign so that they can receive the early guidance that will help their faith to take root and grow. It is these efforts, which are a part of every crusade to this day, that have made Graham and his ministry a model for effective evangelism.

Billy's enthusiasm for evangelism compelled him not only to reach the lost but to disciple others to follow in his steps. In 1962 he began conducting conferences for seminary students to train them in the cause of evangelism. In 1974 his alma mater, Wheaton College, opened the Billy Graham Center, which contains a library, a museum, archives, and an evangelism institute. A similar project in North Carolina, the Billy Graham Training Center, opened in 1987 to equip laypeople to serve more effectively in their churches.

In 1992 the BGEA announced that Graham had Parkinson's disease and would be easing back on his extremely busy schedule. He has continued his crusades but has spoken much less frequently than in the past. In 1996 William Franklin Graham III, Billy's oldest son, was named vice chairman of the BGEA board. Franklin now runs Samaritan's Purse, the mission organization founded by the late Bob Pierce, an old friend from Billy's first days with Youth for Christ. When the time comes for Billy to retire from service, Franklin will be his successor. In the meantime, Billy and Ruth, who have five children, nineteen grandchildren, and eight great-grandchildren, spend most of their time at their home in the mountains of North Carolina.

LEGACY

Since his evangelism career began over fifty years ago, Billy Graham has preached the gospel to more people in live audiences than anyone else in history—over 210 million. The gospel has reached hundreds of millions more through print, television, and film. Graham has been on the Gallup list of "Ten Most Admired Men in the World" an unparalleled thirty-seven times. *Good Housekeeping* has named him among the ten "Most Admired Men" fourteen times and on three occasions has placed him at the top of that list. His picture has graced the covers of all three major U.S. newsweeklies, and in 1996 he received a Congressional Gold Medal.

Perhaps as significant as his half century of evangelism is the effect he has had on the lives of other influential Christian leaders of the twentieth century. Billy has counted among his friends many of the people who have a chapter in this book. And he has met with nearly everyone in this book whose life span crossed into the 1950s. Presidents have sought his counsel; world political leaders have considered it among the greatest of honors to sit with him in prayer. And to this day, whenever he stands at the podium in a jam-packed stadium and says, "Come now," thousands follow him into faith.

For additional information about the Billy Graham Evangelistic Association, see appendix A.

Each of you must turn from your sins and turn to God, and be baptized in the name of Jesus Christ for the forgiveness of your sins. Then you will receive the gift of the Holy Spirit. Acts 2:38

BOOKS BY BILLY GRAHAM

Angels: God's Secret Agents (1975)
Answers to Life's Problems (1994)
Collected Works of Billy Graham (1993)
Death & the Life After (1994)
Hope for the Troubled Heart (1991) (out of print)
How to Be Born Again (1989)
Just As I Am (1997)
Storm Warning (1995)
The Faithful Christian (1994)
Till Armageddon (1993)
To God Be the Glory (with Corrie ten Boom) (1985)
Unto the Hills (1993)

I have often said that the first thing I am going
to do when I get to Heaven is to ask,
"Why me, Lord? Why did you choose a
farmboy from North Carolina to preach to
so many people, to have such a wonderful
team of associates, and to have a part in what
you were doing in the latter half of the twentieth century?" I have thought about that
question a great deal, but I know also that
only God knows the answer.

from his autobiography, *Just As I Am*

1913–

CARL F. H. HENRY

THE GOOD NEWS IS TRULY GREAT NEWS

The coming decade of decision
will be marked either by
evangelical penetration of
the world, or by the world's
penetration of the
evangelical movement and an
inner circle's reactionary
withdrawal into some modern
Dead Sea Caves.

Confessions of a Theologian: Carl F. H. Henry, An Autobiography

In 1933 Franklin Delano Roosevelt became president, an ape named King Kong invaded movie theaters, and Hitler's National Socialists seized control of Germany. But for Carl Henry 1933 was most memorable for another event: It was the year he committed his life to Christ.

A decade later FDR was still president, *King Kong* was gathering dust in a Hollywood film vault, and Hitler's Nazi Party would soon lose its war. But now Carl Henry, armed with a pastorate, a doctorate, and formidable writing skills, was ready to show twentieth-century Christians how to defend and proclaim the fundamentals of the faith.

In Short

From the moment he first found faith, Carl Henry knew it was worth shouting about. At a time when influential theologians and church leaders were selling the latest secularized theologies through well-crafted teachings and publications, many conservative believers offered timid, ineffective rebuttals—or none at all. Henry determined to present the case for fundamental biblical truth with a boldness and excellence that eclipsed the competition. Through the mind of a theologian, the oratory of a great evangelist, and the incisive writing of a veteran newspaper reporter, Carl F. H. Henry has shown us that our faith is worthy of the best we can do to live it, defend it, and pass it along.

Faith

Karl Heinrich, a baker, and his wife, Johanna, were German immigrants who met and married in New York. They named their first child, born January 22, 1913, Carl Ferdinand Howard. World War I began the following year, and when Germany attacked its European neighbors, Germans in America found themselves targets of violent hostility from their own neighbors. Seeking to avoid becoming victims of the awful prejudices, many German immigrants, including Carl's father, anglicized their names. The Heinrich family, now named Henry, also stopped speaking German, even in private.

Carl Henry's father was Lutheran and his mother Roman Catholic, but neither attended church, led family prayers, or taught their children about Jesus. Carl's mother worked hard, feeding, washing, and mending clothes for eight children. His father toiled six days a week at the ovens of a midtown Manhattan bakery. He often came home late and sometimes drunk. Carl had once seen his mother beat her drunken husband with a broomstick. Some years later he heard his father threaten to shoot her. Terrified, Carl crawled from his bed and peered out the bedroom door. Then, in a flash of courage, he walked up to his father, wrestled the gun from his hand, ran back to his bedroom, and threw the weapon out of the window and into the snow.

In 1920 the Henry family moved to a big country house on Long Island, where the children helped raise animals and grow vegetables. Carl's father found another moneymaking hobby— distilling moonshine whiskey—and the Henry home became a retreat for locals looking for relief from Prohibition. Carl often returned from school to find the dining room filled with customers playing poker and sipping shots of undiluted whiskey. Carl Henry had his father's name, but he didn't want to share his reputation, so he began using the middle initials *F. H.* to make the distinction clear.

Carl entered high school in 1925 with an impressive academic record. But no one in his family had ever gone to college, so Carl applied himself to practical studies such as business, typing, shorthand, and commercial law. By his junior year, able to type eighty-five words a minute, he landed a part-time job covering high school sports and other events for a local weekly newspaper. His journalism career had begun.

When the stock market crashed, setting off the Great Depression, Carl was fortunate to find a full-time job with the paper he was already writing for part-time. But the job wasn't reporting; it was selling subscriptions door-to-door, a tough task when no one seemed to have money for luxuries such as newspapers. After a few days of failure, Henry stopped offering subscriptions and instead introduced himself as a reporter. Now instead of slammed doors he was greeted with open doors. People wanted to talk to a reporter. Henry would write up stories he heard and return a few days later to see how the folks liked seeing their names in print. Then he'd sell them a subscription.

While at the paper Carl was befriended by Mildred Christy, a white-haired, middle-aged coworker he would eventually call Mother Christy. This widow had begun praying not only that Carl would become a Christian but that he would eventually enter the ministry. When Carl visited Mother Christy's home, she would tell the gospel story, quote from Scripture, and encourage him to make a commitment. But he would change the subject.

Meanwhile, Carl's journalism skills were being honed through ever-increasing responsibility. By late 1931 he was relief editor at the Islip Press and was providing Long Island coverage for New York papers such as the *Herald Tribune,* the *Evening Post,* and the *Daily News.* Then in 1932 another local paper, the *Smithtown Star,* asked Carl to take the editorship, making him, at nineteen, the youngest editor of a weekly in the state of New York. The following year Carl began to read the Bible. One night he took a drive to give serious thought to what he had read. Returning home, he got caught in a thunderstorm, and as he waited out the squall, he was shaken by a blinding flash of lightning and a mighty roll of thunder. To Carl it seemed like a giant arrow aimed right at him.

A few days later Carl met with a Christian friend. For three hours Carl posed difficult questions, and his friend answered them with intelligence and grace. Finally Carl said, "I'm ready." The two knelt inside the car, and Carl prayed for salvation.

FRUIT

Henry's new faith took immediate hold. After first telling Mother Christy what had happened, he invited sixty people to his house to hear his testimony. Among the family members, friends, and coworkers was his garage mechanic, who made a commitment to Christ that night. Henry's mother did the same a few months later.

Within a year Carl was accepted at Wheaton College, but paying for his education was another matter. He saved carefully before leaving for school, only to be hit with two giant expenses. First, his parents split up, and Henry helped his mother by paying the foreclosure bill on the family home. Then, weeks before he was to depart for Wheaton, he was stricken with acute appendicitis. After being examined, he made a deal with the surgeon: If he didn't feel better by the next morning, he would come in for surgery. He went to Mother Christy's house, where she had assembled a group to pray. When he returned to the doctor the next morning, the pain was gone, and the surgeon released him.

At Wheaton Henry landed a job as a typing instructor after producing stunning letters of recommendation from his former editors in New York. It was in the typing classroom that he met his future wife, Helga Bender, a fellow Wheaton student and daughter of Baptist missionaries in Africa. Five years later they were married.

Henry found work with the *Chicago Tribune* and several local dailies and also did local coverage of the presidential election for the Associated Press. With his part-time reporting and instructing Henry was able to pay tuition and graduated in 1938. Now he was at a crossroads: Continue his journalism career or study for the ministry? He chose the latter, fulfilling the second half of Mother Christy's prayer.

The fall of that year Henry entered both Northern Baptist Theological Seminary and Wheaton's graduate program. In May 1941 he received his bachelor of divinity degree from Northern and three weeks later his master of arts in theology from Wheaton, having supplemented his income by teaching English and American literature, religious journalism, and later, systematic theology. In January 1943, after finishing his student pastorate, Henry was ordained to the ministry at Humboldt Park Baptist Church.

Meanwhile, he also earned a doctorate in theology from Northern and took a position there as professor of systematic theology and philosophy of religion. The journalist from Long Island had four degrees, and now he sought a fifth. While spending his summers teaching at Gordon Divinity School in Boston, Henry studied at Boston University and received a doctorate in philosophy.

Throughout the 1940s Henry poured himself into teaching, speaking, writing, and of course, feeding his own insatiable appetite for learning. But when Boston pastor Harold Ockenga and radio evangelist Charles Fuller invited Henry to help form a new seminary in California, he accepted. Fuller Theological Seminary opened its doors in the fall of 1947, with Henry serving as dean. Among the first class of students was Bill Bright, who later founded Campus Crusade for Christ.

In the early 1950s Billy Graham and other key ministry leaders began discussing the idea of publishing a new Christian magazine that would serve as the evangelicals' answer to the more liberal *Christian Century*. Naturally Carl Henry's name came up in these discussions. His extensive journalism experience, administrative skills, and solid theological foundation seemed fashioned for this very purpose. The first issue of *Christianity Today* came out on October 15, 1956. The magazine was a great success, surpassing *Christian Century* in subscriptions as it entered its second year. Henry contributed many articles and served as its editor for twelve years before departing in 1968.

Upon leaving the magazine, Carl and Helga moved to Cambridge, England. For the first time in many years Henry was free from multiple demanding pursuits. Although he did give a series of lectures while in Cambridge, he did not teach but instead used his time in England to write. He returned to the United States in September 1969 to teach at Eastern Theological Seminary in Philadelphia. Henry also taught as visiting professor of theology at Trinity Evangelical Divinity School in Deerfield, Illinois.

Since the 1970s Henry has served as guest lecturer and professor at several schools and as a speaker on Christian ethics, social issues, evangelism, and world missions. Through his association with organizations such as World Vision and Prison Fellowship, he has addressed audiences throughout the world as an outspoken advocate for biblical truth and Christian social activism. And always a journalist, he serves as a contributing editor to *World* magazine.

LEGACY

Carl Henry grew up outside the church. But when as a young journalist he finally believed the Good News, it struck him as truly *good news,* a story so hot that it *had* to be featured on his life's front page, with a big bold headline so no one could miss it. In nearly forty books, hundreds of articles, and a thousand lectures, Henry has kept this news item out in front for all of us to read.

But one doesn't have to read his writings or hear his lectures to get his take on the gospel story. Henry's vast legacy has ensured that the news continues. His work in a little start-up venture called *Christianity Today* helped to make it the most-read Protestant magazine of the century. He put his mark on a brand-new Fuller Theological Seminary, and at many other seminaries Professor Henry has shaped the lives of a legion of new pastors, missionaries, educators, and other ministry leaders, showing them how to study, apply, and broadcast the Good News because it truly is the best news of all. Not bad for a Long Island newsman.

We have seen with our own eyes and now testify that the Father sent his Son to be the Savior of the world. 1 John 4:14

BOOKS BY DR. CARL F. H. HENRY

Aspects of Christian Social Ethics (out of print)
Confessions of a Theologian (out of print)
Conversations with Carl Henry: Christianity for Today (Symposium series, vol. 18) (1986)
The Biblical Expositor: The Living Theme of the Great Book with General and Introductory Essays and Exposition for Each Book of the Bible (1994)
The Identity of Jesus of Nazareth (1992)
Toward a Recovery of Christian Belief: The Rutherford Lectures (1990)
Twilight of a Great Civilization: The Drift toward Neo-Paganism (1988)

1951–

BILL HYBELS

SEEKING THE SEEKERS

I want spiritual seekers to find a safe place to get answers that will satisfy their hearts and minds. The doors of our ministries are wide open to people who want to scrutinize the faith and see if it makes sense. So often I see that as their questions are answered and their concerns are addressed, they end up becoming followers of Jesus.

Willow Creek newsletter, March 1999

Youth minister Bill Hybels stood before a packed room of six hundred teenagers. They had gathered for an evening of fellowship filled with music, drama, and multimedia, followed by Bill's short presentation of the gospel. When he finished, he invited the students to stand up and receive Christ. So many kids stood up that he thought they had misunderstood him. He made them sit back down as he explained it again. Again they stood up—nearly three hundred students. They stayed for two hours, waiting in line to be counseled and to pray with someone about their decision.

Bill was the last one to leave that night. As he walked out of the church, his knees buckled, and he fell to the ground sobbing. He was overwhelmed by God's actions that night, humbled and grateful that he had been chosen to play a part in them. Then he made a vow: As long as he was in ministry, he would provide a safe place for unbelievers to come, a place where they would be welcomed and encouraged to discover Christ.

IN SHORT

Pastor Bill Hybels revolutionized the way many Christians do church. As a young man he saw the church as a gathering place for the "already convinced," where those who had not yet found faith too often felt uncomfortable and unwelcome. Hybels set out to change this lopsided arrangement. The result is a church in the Chicago suburbs where seekers are sought and saints are fed. Today hundreds of other churches throughout America are following Hybels's lead.

FAITH

William James Hybels was born December 12, 1951, in Kalamazoo, Michigan. His parents, Harold and Gertrude Hybels, ran a potato and onion farm. By age five, young Bill was helping out on the farm, sorting produce, cleaning refrigerator bins, and loading trucks that delivered the produce to restaurants and grocery stores.

His father was successful in the business, a smart, hard worker who passed on these traits to his son. While Bill's friends headed to the beach, Bill headed out to the dusty fields to work alongside crews of migrant workers. From his father and the work they shared, Bill learned discipline and perseverance. He also learned to enjoy the rewards of work done well. His father sent him on ski trips to Aspen and journeys abroad, wiring him money whenever he ran out. Life back home was not dull either. He shared his father's love for cars, boats, and airplanes, and soloed the family plane at age sixteen.

That same year he embarked on another adventure. He was raised in a Christian home and sometime in his childhood had memorized a Bible verse: "He saved us, not because of the good things we did, but because of his mercy" (Titus 3:5). But at a youth camp that year, the meaning of the verse finally hit him, and when it did, it stopped him in his tracks. Salvation wasn't the result of his hard work; it was Jesus who did all the work. Bill decided that it was the greatest thing in the world. He committed his life to Christ.

Between high school, farm work, and world travel, Bill met and started dating a young woman named Lynne Barry. They dated through high school and made plans to marry in college. But Lynne broke off their engagement; Bill took off to South America to heal his broken heart.

Meanwhile, Hybels had been planning to take over the management of the family business. After two years of college he returned home to do just that. But it was becoming clear to him that God was calling him to something else. After a final summer working for his father, he turned in his credit cards and the keys to the cars, the boat, and the plane and began ministering to kids. He led Bible studies and served as a counselor at a Christian camp. As he immersed himself in the environment that had brought him to

Christ, he began to form ideas to help bring teenagers to their Savior.

That summer Hybels ran into Dave Holmbo, an old friend who had been with him at the camp where he met Christ. As the two rekindled their friendship, they discovered a common vision for reaching teenagers with the gospel. Hybels shared his own disappointing experiences of attempting to bring his friends to church, only to have them walk away feeling uncomfortable and unwelcome. The two young men began to form a plan: to create attractive youth events where Christian students could safely and confidently bring their non-Christian friends to hear about Jesus.

On the advice of kids they consulted, Holmbo and Hybels decided that these outreach events should include drama, lots of music, multimedia presentations, and short messages on topics of interest to teenagers. Holmbo was the assistant music director at South Park Church in suburban Chicago, so it was there in 1973 that they launched their program. On their first night, they drew 125 teenagers. Within six months, three hundred kids were showing up. Hybels was offered a staff position at the church. They called their youth ministry Son City.

But in all the excitement, Hybels had not forgotten his high school sweetheart. Though separated for eighteen months, they had never lost touch with each other. Lynne was now out of college, and both she and Bill had grown in their commitment to Christ. She shared Bill's vision for ministry, and the two decided to complete the wedding plans they had made in high school. They were married on May 18, 1974. The wedding was a Son City event: Teenagers served as ushers, the ministry's band members played during the ceremony, and more kids sang at the reception. Nearly one hundred students made the four-hour drive to Kalamazoo to attend.

FRUIT

Six months after the wedding, the groom was back in school. He attended Trinity College in Deerfield, outside Chicago. A professor there opened Bill's eyes to the culture of the early church, where its members had true communion with each other and a strong desire to reach out to unbelievers. That was what he sought with his own youth ministry—and what he began to dream about for a church ministering to *all* ages.

By the summer of 1975 Bill had resigned from his position at South Park Church. He and Lynne, with their friends Dave and Sue Holmbo, set out to start the church of their dreams. But they needed money to do it. Hybels, the twenty-three-year-old son of a produce grower, did what he knew best: He drove down to the farmer's market, bought twelve hundred baskets of tomatoes, and sent the students out to sell them door-to-door. They earned enough money to buy some equipment and start a fund for the rent.

The building they rented, Willow Creek Theater, had seating for 970. Son City West was born. Bill and his founding leaders canvassed the neighborhood to find out what people thought about church—and if they didn't attend, why they didn't. These were some of the responses they received: Church is irrelevant, lifeless, boring, predictable, judgmental, harsh, always asking for money. The survey results were an indictment against churches and a clear guide to Hybels of what their new church would *not* be.

The leadership team decided that their Sunday morning services would be for outreach, aimed to show people that Christ was relevant to their lives. Midweek Bible studies would be aimed at believers who sought to grow in their faith. Their first Sunday service was held October 12, 1975, attended by 125 people. It featured music and drama, a multimedia presentation shown on the theater's giant screen, and a short message.

As the weeks went by, the unique Sunday services drew more and more "seekers," and Bible studies were added to accommodate the growing ranks of believers. In two years, they were filling two services and had developed a discipleship program to fill the need for mature leaders to serve in the burgeoning ministry. By 1979 they had drawn over three thousand people to their Easter service. Several weeks later they began construction on the future home of Willow Creek Community Church, on a 145-acre plot in nearby South Barrington.

The explosive growth of the church was accompanied by many difficulties. In a twelve-month period Bill lost his father, Lynne suffered the first of two miscarriages, and half of the ministry staff left the church due to misunderstandings and a badly handled discipline issue. Hybels was broken by his leadership failings. He met with the board to confess his leadership mistakes and preoccupation with his own teaching at the expense of other important ministry concerns.

As the church entered the 1980s, they felt as if they were starting over, with a better church structure, marriage counseling, more mature leadership, a new building, and elders who directed the church toward a more peaceful, healthier era. They moved into the new facility in 1981.

The church has grown ever since. Willow Creek Community Church now sees nearly seventeen thousand people attend its services each weekend, ministering with a staff of four hundred and volunteers numbering in the thousands. The church still adheres to the strategy with which Hybels began: weekend services to attract the seekers; midweek services and meetings for worship, Communion, and in-depth biblical teaching.

The ministry of Willow Creek has spread far beyond the Chicago suburbs. Throughout the 1980s and 1990s Hybels has invited pastors to visit his church, meet with the staff, and take part in workshops and conferences that convey the strategies that have led to Willow Creek's success. Hundreds of churches worldwide have embraced the Willow Creek model, and many have seen the kind of growth that earns them the description of "megachurch."

In the fall of 1992 the Willow Creek Association (WCA) was formed as a ministry separate from the church to respond to the needs of seeker-oriented ministries worldwide. The WCA assumed responsibility for Willow Creek's church leadership conferences and publications, lifting a tremendous burden from Willow Creek staff members. In less than two years, fifteen full-time employees were working with nearly a thousand churches worldwide. The WCA has crossed denominational, racial, and cultural barriers and encouraged ministries seeking to turn unbelievers into devoted followers of Jesus Christ.

LEGACY

Many young leaders enter church ministry filled with vision and energy, only to be stifled by entrenched traditions and superiors unwilling to change. Some of these leaders give up and leave the ministry. Others give in and lose their zeal. But a few hang tough and carry out the mission God has given them. Bill Hybels is an example of one of those rare young leaders. From his first Son City youth event to the weekly services at Willow Creek, he has not lost the vision: to provide a safe environment for unchurched people to discover the dangerous, transforming message of Jesus.

That transforming message is at work in Hybels, too. Although he was blessed with early success, he did not consider his initial methods as the "absolute success formula" for reaching everyone. As society changes, so must the church's methods of reaching that society. While many of Hybel's original strategies still work today, others do not, and he and his ministry constantly adapt their methods to stay relevant and accessible to new generations with differing needs. Indeed, it is the same strategy employed by the apostle Paul—varying the seasoning of the message to attract people with different tastes to the unchanging truth of Christ.

For additional information about Willow Creek Community Church, see appendix A.

My message and my preaching were very plain. I did not use wise and persuasive speeches, but the Holy Spirit was powerful among you. I did this so that you might trust the power of God rather than human wisdom. 1 Corinthians 2:4-5

BOOKS BY BILL HYBELS

Authenticity: Being Honest with God and Others (1996)
Becoming a Contagious Christian (1996)
Building a Contagious Church (2000)

Colossians: Discovering the New You (1999)

Descending into Greatness (with Rob Wilkins) (1994)

Essential Christianity: Practical Steps for Spiritual Growth (1998)

Exodus: Journey toward God (1999)

Fit to Be Tied: Making Marriage Last a Lifetime (1997)

Honest to God? Becoming an Authentic Christian (1992)

How to Hear God (1999)

Inside the Mind of Unchurched Harry & Mary: How to Reach Friends and Family Who Avoid God and the Church (1993)

James: Live Wisely (1999)

Making Life Work: Putting God's Wisdom into Action (1998)

Network: The Right People . . . in the Right Places . . . for the Right Reason (1996)

Philippians: Run the Race (1999)

Rediscovering Church: The Story and Vision of Willow Creek Community Church (1997)

Romans: Find Freedom (1999)

The God You're Looking For (1998)

Too Busy Not to Pray: Slowing Down to Be with God (1998)

Who You Are When No One's Looking (1989)

1876–1951

H. A. IRONSIDE

SALVATION IN CHRIST ALONE

Christ and ... is a perverted
gospel, which is not the
Gospel. Christ without the
"and" is the sinner's hope
and the saint's
confidence. ... For
salvation itself, Jesus
is not only necessary,
but He is enough.

H. A. Ironside: Ordained of the Lord

For three years Harry Ironside moved up the ranks of The
Salvation Army from cadet to captain, but he was constantly
tormented with the thought that he had "backslidden" and
might lose his salvation. He worked harder and harder, depriving
himself of even the simplest pleasures, confident that he was
making his salvation more secure. Under the strain of this unbear-
able burden of perfection—a weight he had been trying to carry
for five long years—Harry collapsed in exhaustion. He resigned
from The Salvation Army and checked into a rest home. He was
just nineteen years old.

In Short

Harry Ironside learned early the importance of being "saved." But
it took a physical and emotional breakdown to convince him that
it is Jesus who does the saving, not ourselves. When he discovered
this essential truth, his real ministry began: fifty years of powerful
preaching, teaching, and writing.

It has been estimated that from 1916 to 1929 alone, Ironside
preached the gospel and taught the Scriptures sixty-five hundred
times, to a total audience of more than a million people, often
without the aid of a microphone. His powerful street-bred preaching had the energy of a Billy Sunday, the integrity of a Billy
Graham, and the scriptural insight of a master Bible scholar.

Faith

The first son of John and Sophia Ironside was born at home on the
morning of October 14, 1876, in Toronto. Moments later he was set

aside as lifeless. The physician turned to give full attention to the mother, who lay weak and dangerously ill. Forty minutes later, to the doctor's astonishment, the nurse assisting him detected a pulse in the infant. The physician instructed her to immediately place the child in a hot bath. In a moment the newborn Harry let out a lusty cry.

Two years later Harry's father, just twenty-seven, died from typhoid fever. His well-marked Bible, later given to Harry, proved to be a precious legacy. From it, Harry recited his first verse of Scripture, at the age of four: "For the Son of man is come to seek and to save that which was lost" (Luke 19:10, KJV). That Harry was lost and that Christ Jesus came from heaven to save him were the first truths impressed on his young heart. According to *H. A. Ironside: Ordained of the Lord,* Harry's widowed mother knelt with him as a child and prayed a prophetic prayer: "O Father, keep my boy from ever desiring anything greater than to live for Thee. Save him early, and make him a devoted street preacher, as his father was. Make him willing to suffer for Jesus' sake, to gladly endure persecution and rejection by the world that cast out Thy Son; and keep him from what would dishonor Thee."

Throughout Harry's childhood, godly men came to his home, asking him repeatedly, "Harry, lad, are you born again yet?" Harry didn't know what to say. When he was ten years old, his mother moved the family to Los Angeles. Harry and his brother, John, would walk with their mother to Sunday school, passing saloons, gambling houses, and drunken men along the way. Never having seen such behavior, eleven-year-old Harry decided he must start a Sunday school for the neighborhood boys and girls. He had read the Bible ten times through, so he became the teacher. Average attendance was sixty strong.

Harry was twelve when renowned preacher Dwight L. Moody held a great campaign in Los Angeles. Harry went to the first night's meeting, and as it was standing room only, Harry climbed up to a girder and listened to the evangelist from there. He remembered going home that night and praying, "Lord, help me someday to preach to crowds like these and to lead souls to Christ." Two years later one of the godly men who had often visited the Ironsides in Toronto arrived at their home. Harry knew his question before it was uttered: "Well, Harry, lad, I'm glad to see you. And are you born again yet?" Harry hung his head. When the kindly gentleman learned of Harry's preaching, he encouraged him not to preach until he knew he was "saved."

Harry gave up his Sunday school, but instead of making a commitment to Christ, he decided it was time to enjoy himself. Six months later, in February 1890, Harry was at a party trying to have fun. But Scripture verses kept popping into his head, so he went home, crept up to his room, and committed his life to Christ.

FRUIT

Immediately Harry wanted to tell others about Jesus Christ and his gift of grace. Straight to a Salvation Army street meeting he went and spoke on the street corner for the first time of the grace of God so newly revealed to him. He soon became known as "the boy preacher." His pride swelled, and a month later, in a dispute with his brother, John, Harry lost his temper and struck him to the ground. As John taunted him about what a nice Christian he had become, Harry ran to his room in anguish. He sought God's and John's forgiveness and decided that he never wanted to have another evil thought.

"Holiness" meetings drew Harry to the Salvation Army hall. There he learned that when sinners were converted, God forgave all the sins they had committed up to the time they repented, but after that, Christians were on lifelong "probation" and could forfeit their salvation if they fell into sin and did not repent. To maintain a "saved" condition, people needed to reach a place where they were no longer sinful. Harry heard heartfelt stories—one from a lady who told how for forty years God had kept her from sin in thought, word, and deed. Earnestly Harry prayed for and pursued sinlessness.

But the holiness he sought eluded him. He was not alone in his frustration. He began to hear of others who struggled painfully to attain this high standard of Christian living only to fall away discouraged and battle weary. The strain was too much, and Harry gave up the fight and his ministry with it. While Harry spent time in the rest home, he met fourteen other officers whose health had been broken like his. He became cold and cynical and put away his

Bible. God seemed to have failed him, he concluded, and so he sought solace in poetry, history, and science. But God had not forgotten young Harry.

A woman dying of consumption was brought to the home, and Harry's heart went out to her. To him, she was a martyr, laying down her life for a needy world. Truly, he thought, she was holy. To his surprise, she came to him, begging him to read to her because of his holiness. A pamphlet his mother had given him years before caught his attention. Moved by a sudden impulse, he read page after page, hoping to soothe and quiet this dying woman.

Redemption in Christ through his death, the pamphlet stated, was the only means of attaining eternal security. As Harry read, he realized that he had been depending on his own efforts. Could it be that he had trusted Christ to save him but thought that it was his own faithfulness that kept his soul in right standing with God? Harry began to search the Scriptures earnestly. He saw that he had been looking for holiness from within instead of from Christ. Harry realized that the same grace that had saved him, and that grace alone, could carry him.

Harry left the rest home and moved to San Francisco, where he met members of the Plymouth Brethren Church. They encouraged him to remain there and teach the Bible, and soon Harry was in demand as a speaker. He met a former Salvation Army captain, Helen Schofield, and within weeks knew he wanted to marry her. Despite the fact that Harry had no stable income, Helen accepted his proposal at once, and they were married on January 5, 1898. Following Harry's mother's death, the young couple took in Harry's half sister, Lillian. Their own sons, Edmund and John, were born in 1899 and 1905.

While Helen knew that their income might be uncertain for a time, she couldn't have known that the uncertainty would last for more than twenty years. Harry refused to pass a collection plate at any evangelistic service in which he spoke, always trusting that the Lord would provide. And God did provide but often in unconventional ways. Harry would reach out to shake someone's hand and find a coin in his own hand when he was done. Mail would arrive with cash stuffed inside. In his travels Harry would sometimes sleep in trees when he had no money for a room. And occasionally he and his family would get on a train, travel as far as their money would take them, and then get off and look for a place to preach.

Harry remained devoted to his wife, but his zeal for preaching often took him away from home for months at a time. As their young family grew, Helen stopped traveling with her husband. While she was proud of Harry's accomplishments, life was not easy for her. In addition to managing on a shoestring budget, Helen became virtually a single mother with the responsibility of raising the children on her own. Meanwhile, Harry roamed the country, speaking in churches and revival tents, conferences, Bible schools, and seminaries.

In 1930 after Harry spoke at a conference at Chicago's Moody Church, the church invited him to become their pastor. On March 16 of that year he accepted the position on the condition that he could still travel and preach. Over the next eighteen years he did just that, roaming the country on his frequent speaking engagements at churches and Bible conferences.

Helen died on May 1, 1948, and on May 30 Harry submitted his resignation to Moody Church. By this time cataracts had left him almost completely blind, yet he continued to teach, including a series of verse-by-verse studies through the book of Revelation. Before each message someone would read the chapter. Then Harry expounded on that chapter, proceeding from one verse to the next, introducing each verse in its proper sequence and explaining its meaning until he had gone through the entire chapter. Never did he ask to have his memory refreshed by the rereading of a particular passage.

On October 9, 1949, Harry married a Christian widow, Ann Hightower, who assisted him by taking dictation for his last books. Ann was soon widowed again: Harry died of a heart attack on January 15, 1951. He was on a trip to New Zealand, the final journey of a man who had spent his life as a traveling preacher.

LEGACY

Many of Ironside's messages became the core of his writings. His thirty-four expository volumes include eleven Old Testament books, a single volume covering the minor prophets, and twenty-two volumes covering the entire New Testament. The list of other H. A. Ironside books runs to twenty-three titles. In addition he wrote thirty-four booklets and pamphlets and fourteen tracts. Few other Christian writers have been as prolific.

But whatever topic he addressed, Ironside maintained from first to last the same underlying theme: Jesus Christ came to save us from our sins. And our hope for purpose in this life and a guarantee regarding the next one lies in Christ alone. Nothing more and nothing less.

God saved you by his special favor when you believed. And you can't take credit for this; it is a gift from God. Salvation is not a reward for the good things we have done, so none of us can boast about it. Ephesians 2:8-9

BOOKS BY HARRY IRONSIDE

1 & 2 Thessalonians (1997)
Acts (1943)
Colossians (1997)
Crowning Day (1997)
Death and Afterward (1989)
Ezekiel (The Ironside Commentaries) (n.d.)
Galatians & Ephesians (1981)
H. A. Ironside: Ordained of the Lord (1990)
Letters to a Roman Catholic Priest (1989)
Matthew (The Ironside Commentaries) (1993)
Minor Prophets (The Ironside Commentaries) (n.d.)
Philippians (The Ironside Commentaries) (1996)
Proverbs (1996)
Psalms: Book One (The Ironside Commentaries) (1999)
Revelation (The Ironside Commentaries) (1996)
Romans (1928)
The Epistles of John and Jude (1931)
The Levitical Offerings (1986)

1920–

John Paul II

DEFENDING GOD'S CHILDREN AGAINST
THEMSELVES

It is the task of the Church,
of the Holy See, of all
pastors, to fight on the side
of man, often against
man himself.

From a sermon given in 1976 while Karol Wojtyla was still a
cardinal and the archbishop of Krakow

In new robes that distinguished his new responsibilities, Karol Wojtyla, now Pope John Paul II, looked out over the crowd that had filled the square of St. Peter's Basilica for his inauguration. He spoke first in Polish, greeting his countrymen and inviting them to prayer. Then he spoke in Italian. Finally he greeted the world in French, English, German, Spanish, and Portuguese, each language bringing forth applause from a different part of the square. He continued his greetings in Slovak, Russian, Ukrainian, and Lithuanian, giving many their first hint of the truly global vision of this charismatic young pope.

At the conclusion of the mass, John Paul stepped in front of the altar to bless the crowd. Then he surprised everyone. Breaking protocol, he stepped down from the platform and into the square. He spoke first to a group of people in wheelchairs. Then he approached the Polish section, alarming his bodyguards, who feared he'd be trampled in the surging crowd. Instead he was greeted by children. They gave him flowers; he stroked their heads and kissed them. Truly, this was the people's pope.

In Short

Polish Catholic priest Karol Wojtyla survived both Nazi occupation and communist domination to become the most popular and respected pope of the twentieth century. In his writings, messages, and public masses, Pope John Paul II calls Christians worldwide to stand firmly on the church's biblical foundation even as they reach out to love others in the name of Christ.

FAITH

Karol Josef Wojtyla was born May 18, 1920, in Krakow, Poland. He was named for his father, a master tailor. Karol's mother, Emilia Kaczorowska, was the daughter of a packsaddle maker. The Wojtyla family suffered many tragedies. Karol's older sister died before he was born; his mother died when he was nine; and his older brother died three years later. The family's Catholic faith sustained them, and Karol did well in school, showing a passion for poetry, religion, and the theater.

By the start of Wojtyla's second year in Jagiellonian University, Hitler's troops had rolled across Poland, but during their occupation the Germans allowed the university to stay open. Wojtyla pursued studies in literature and philosophy and became involved in experimental theater. It had been his father's dream to see Karol become a priest, but he died in 1941 before his dream came true. A year and a half later Wojtyla entered Krakow's underground seminary.

He also registered for theology courses at the university and became active in an underground student movement that opposed the German occupation and rescued Jews from the Nazi atrocities. Wojtyla saw himself as a philosopher and a moralist but above all, as a Christian and a witness to his faith in Christ. In 1946 Wojtyla was ordained as a priest and immediately left Poland to begin his studies in Rome. Two years later, after receiving a doctorate in sacred theology, he returned to Poland to work as an assistant pastor at a church near Gdów.

In 1948 Wojtyla moved back to Krakow to serve as an assistant pastor at St. Florian's and as a chaplain to students at his old school, Jagiellonian University, which was near the church. His ministry to the university students flourished. He was personable and informal, creating a great spirit of community within the group. He held masses and prayer meetings and took his students hiking, skiing, and canoeing. On bicycling trips one of the students would often have to ride just in front of Wojtyla to keep him on track. Otherwise he might slip into meditation and veer into the trees. During his ministry at St. Florian's he completed a second doctorate, this one in philosophy, at the University of Krakow.

In 1956 he became a professor of ethics at the Catholic University of Lublin. Two years later, at just thirty-eight years of age, Wojtyla was appointed auxiliary bishop of Krakow, and in six more years, after the death of his superior, he became archbishop of Krakow. Just months after assuming this position, he traveled to Rome to take part in the Second Vatican Council. This revolutionary series of meetings transformed the Roman Catholic Church by reaffirming its biblical roots and challenging its members to reach out to the world with both spiritual hope and tangible help.

Archbishop Wojtyla became Cardinal Wojtyla in 1967 upon appointment by Pope Paul VI. His ministry, once limited to Poland, now took him throughout the world and frequently to Rome on official church business. Such business included his place in the conclave that elected Pope John Paul I in August 1978 following the death of Paul VI. After the inauguration Wojtyla left Rome on a trip to Germany. During his time there he received news that the new pope had died, whereupon he returned to Rome.

Following the new pope's funeral, Wojtyla joined the conclave again. It took the members two days and eight ballots to elect the new pope. On October 16, 1978, at 5:15 P.M. white smoke rose from the chimney over the Sistine Chapel. Karol Cardinal Wojtyla had been elected the 264th successor of the apostle Peter to lead the Catholic Church. He took the papal name of his predecessor, becoming John Paul II. At age fifty-eight he became the youngest pope in over a century and the first non-Italian pontiff in nearly half a millennium.

While the Catholic world rejoiced and all Poland cheered, the head of the Soviet Union's KGB prepared for trouble. After years of German occupation followed by Soviet domination, Poland had regained a national voice and an international star. As a priest, professor, archbishop, and cardinal, Wojtyla was a staunch defender of faith and church, but he did not provoke the government. Yet in the Soviet communist system, where faith itself was considered an enemy of the state, Poland's Catholic Church existed in an uneasy and at times tense truce with the communist regime. A Polish pope would only increase this tension.

Indeed, John Paul brought attention to Poland and its church merely by traveling to his home country. Through the words and pictures from journalists who reported his visits, the whole world saw life behind the Iron Curtain, and the Polish people got a glimpse of the freedoms on the other side. Within two years of John Paul's election, millions of Polish workers, encouraged and aided by the church, took part in an illegal strike and gained the right to form independent unions. By the next year nearly ten million workers had joined the Solidarity union. The long march to independence had begun, and it would not end until 1990, when church and labor leaders led the country into free elections.

FRUIT

But John Paul did not become pope to Poland only. Worldwide, Catholics and government leaders knew that he was a force to be reckoned with. From the start he has traveled the globe—to over 160 countries so far—addressing presidents, prime ministers, dictators, kings, and queens, calling them to serve with justice and mercy. And he has been no less shy in addressing the people they govern. His public messages and masses attract audiences in the millions; no other person on the planet has addressed more of its citizens.

To Catholics and non-Catholics, Christians and non-Christians, young and old, his message is the same: to live as Jesus showed us, in obedience to the Father, serving one another in love and peace, justice and mercy, in respect of the precious life God has given us. His actions speak as loudly as his teachings. This approachable, beloved priest did not retreat behind his papal robes. Despite countless death threats and a nearly successful assassination attempt, he has refused to hide from his people. Even as the frailties of old age bring him great discomfort, frequent exhaustion, and dangerous illnesses, he continues to travel the world, greeting his brothers and sisters in Christ with smiles and blessings and open arms.

LEGACY

Displaying tremendous charisma and warmth, John Paul II has truly been a pope of the people. But while he has shown unceasing compassion, he has also stood firm on the moral and social issues facing Catholics around the world, despite whatever unpopularity that brings. He has not hesitated to state strongly the church's stand on matters of marriage and family, the unborn, materialism, secularism, and the sanctity of life. In an age where tolerance has come to be defined as the acceptance of all beliefs and lifestyles as equal, his critics find this combination of compassion and firmness on the issues incongruous. But to John Paul, this combination—compassion and obedience, liberal love and conservative doctrine—is the only expression of faith consistent with Christ and the church he gave to his disciples.

In that sense John Paul II is like many evangelical Protestants. He is unwilling to toss out the truly biblical traditions established by the early church merely because many consider them to be out of sync with current culture. And he's just as unwilling to allow the church to fade into irrelevance through neglect of the physical and social needs of people alive right now. His mission as head pastor of the Catholic Church is the same mission for all Christians: to help God's children find, worship, and reflect the true Head of the church, Jesus Christ.

For additional information about John Paul II and the Roman Catholic Church, see appendix A.

With the help of the Holy Spirit who lives within us, carefully guard what has been entrusted to you. 2 Timothy 1:14

BOOKS BY JOHN PAUL II

A Moment's Peace: Words of Encouragement (1995)
A Pilgrim Pope: Messages for the World (1999)
An Invitation to Joy (1999)
Breakfast with the Pope: Daily Readings (1995)
Catechism of the Catholic Church (1994)
Celebrate 2000: A Three Year Reader: Reflections on Jesus, the Holy Spirit, and the Father (1998)

Celebrate 2000: Reflections on the Holy Spirit (1997)
Celebrate the Third Millennium: Facing the Future with Hope (1999)
Crossing the Threshold of Hope (1995)
Fear Not: Thoughts on Living in Today's World (1999)
In My Own Words: Pope John Paul II (1998)
John Paul II and Interreligious Dialogue (Faith Meets Faith) (1999)
Splendor of the Truth (1993)
Springtime of Evangelization (1999)
The Place Within: The Poetry of Pope John Paul II (1994)
The Way of Christ; The Way of Love; The Way of Prayer (1995)
The Way to Christ: Spiritual Exercises (1994)

1909–

TORREY JOHNSON

REACHING YOUTH FOR CHRIST

I do not challenge you to
something easy. I do not
challenge you to something
that has comforts and
luxury. I challenge you to
something that involves all
that you have, but Jesus
gave his all for you, when He
died on Calvary's Cross.

Reaching Youth for Christ

In 1942 Pastor Torrey Johnson began to pray for opportunities to reach young people in the greater Chicago area. He joined with like-minded pastors, evangelists, and student leaders to create large-scale events that would attract students by the thousands to hear the gospel. The plan took on a grand form in the summer of 1944. Every Saturday night from May 27 to October 14 Torrey, along with friend Billy Graham and others, held rallies that drew over two thousand young people.

When they began having to turn students away for lack of room, they decided to move the rallies to the giant Moody Memorial Church. But the church could not accommodate them until October 28, forcing them to improvise for October 21, the one Saturday for which they had no hall. Torrey moved the rally to the giant Chicago Stadium for one night. Fifteen minutes before the rally started, the stadium's twenty thousand seats were already filled. The program featured messages from athletes and youth evangelists and a twenty-five-hundred-voice choir. Hundreds of young people met the Savior that night. Thus began the ministry of Chicagoland Youth for Christ.

In Short

Pastor Torrey Johnson grew up in a city with hundreds of churches—and tens of thousands of young people who had never found their way into a single one of them. His spirited youth rallies drew students by the thousands to meet other Christian young people and to hear the gospel message. This local ministry to unchurched students became an international organization called Youth for Christ, offering millions of young people world-wide a chance to meet and grow in Jesus Christ.

FAITH

Torrey Maynard Johnson was born March 15, 1909, in Chicago, Illinois. His parents, Jacob Martin Johnson and Thora Mathilda Evensen, were Norwegian immigrants who had met and married in Chicago. Devout Christians, they named their new son after the great evangelist R. A. Torrey with a prayer that the boy would grow up to be such a man. Torrey's father was a sailor before his marriage and then took a succession of jobs, from streetcar conductor to painter to salesman to real estate agent, to keep his young family fed. While he worked long hours, Thora educated the six children and raised them in their faith. The Johnsons attended Salem Evangelical Free Church, so between Sunday school, his parents' Bible lessons and prayers, and a constant parade of pastors and Bible school students visiting the Johnson home, Torrey was immersed in the ways of the faith daily.

Although Torrey was confirmed at age thirteen, he knew he wasn't a Christian: Christianity was in his head but not in his heart. Throughout high school he excelled in swimming, warmed the bench in football, and hung out with the popular students. While he continued to have perfect attendance at church, he later admitted, "I loved sin. I loved the ways of the world, with its worldly pleasures. My companions were the same way, so it would not have been easy to become a Christian."

The summer after he graduated from high school Torrey worked as a building contractor while his parents made plans for him to enter nearby Wheaton College. He didn't want to go to Wheaton, a Christian school, but obeyed his parents' wishes.

During summer vacation Torrey joined his family at their cottage on Wisconsin's Lake Geneva. One night he and his brother went to a concert, where Torrey ran into Evelyn Nilson, a girl who had attended his high school. They went for a walk together that night and continued to see each other frequently for the rest of the summer.

There was just one problem: Evelyn was a Christian, but Torrey was not. Evelyn liked spending time with him—especially when it involved going to church. And while Torrey was interested in the first part, he was not interested in the second. Evelyn held her ground and would not let their relationship move beyond friendship until he shared her commitment to Christ.

Before Torrey left for Wheaton, he made two decisions. First, he would not let the Christian setting there spoil his fun. Second, he would turn down his father's offer of financial help and pay his own way through school. So he moved to Wheaton and got a job peddling ice, a physically demanding occupation that also helped him stay in shape for football. When the owner of the business offered to sell out, Torrey bought the business and used it to cover his school expenses.

Meanwhile, he was having the fun he dreamed of, disregarding the school's rules about gambling, dancing, and going to movies. But one night after the Christmas break, when most of his classmates had not yet returned to school, he got lonely and decided to go to church. He sat in the balcony for the service, all alone except for one other student, Evan Welsh, a football teammate. At the end of the message the preacher gave an invitation. Evan came over to Torrey, saw tears in his eyes, and said, "Come on, Torrey. Tonight's the night for you to give your heart to Christ."

Evan grabbed Torrey's arm, Torrey resisted, and the two football players got into a tug-of-war. Finally Torrey stopped struggling, and the two went forward together. He didn't know it at the time, but Evan and a few other students had been praying for him through the fall term. That night God answered Torrey's classmates' prayers as well as those of Evelyn and his parents.

FRUIT

Now committed to the Lord, Johnson next determined to choose a career. First he decided to become a doctor and in 1927 enrolled at Northwestern University and began working toward a medical degree. He also attended his parents' Salem Evangelical Free Church and was soon leading a Bible study group. Before his second year at Northwestern began, he and Evelyn were engaged, and by December of that year he had changed his mind about becoming a doctor and had reenrolled at Wheaton. He graduated two years later and on October 30, 1930, married Evelyn.

As he finished his work at Wheaton, Torrey decided that he was to be a preacher. His father, delighted that his son might now carry on in the footsteps of his namesake, backed his decision completely. But his mother reminded him that he was not a good speaker. He told her that he believed God would loosen his tongue. Mother and son knelt together, and she prayed in Norwegian and then in English that God would make Torrey a simple preacher so that people like her, without formal education, could understand and receive the Word. Torrey never forgot that prayer. He knew that if he were to preach, he would have to keep the gospel simple.

He took his first pastorate at a Baptist church in Chicago and also joined in evangelistic missions with two men, Bob Cook and Ray Schulenburg. These ministry opportunities took him away from the church frequently, and one day the deacons called him in and asked if he was going to be a pastor or an evangelist. Torrey chose the latter. After just a year at the church he joined Schulenburg to spend the next two years on the road with the traveling evangelist. Then he entered Northern Baptist Seminary and at the same time served as pastor of Midwest Bible Church.

In 1936 Torrey received his doctorate in divinity from the seminary and stayed to teach New Testament Greek and world history. He had continued serving at the steadily growing Bible church, and they were anticipating bringing him on full-time. Now he was faced with another decision: Would his career be that of a pastor or a professor? This time he chose the former.

Five years later Torrey began broadcasting a Sunday afternoon radio program called *Chapel Hour,* and soon on Sunday nights a second program, *Songs in the Night.* But as had happened in the past, Torrey's various ministry pursuits competed with each other, so he eventually relinquished the radio work to another young Chicago minister named Billy Graham. But he continued to carry on other outside evangelistic missions in the Chicago area.

In 1944 the ministry of Chicagoland Youth for Christ (YFC) began with weekly youth rallies and hit citywide fame with the giant event at Chicago Stadium. As Youth for Christ continued holding its rallies, now at Moody Church, Johnson and his old friend Bob Cook released a book, *Reaching Youth for Christ*. Meanwhile, Torrey, Graham, and other youth evangelists from around the country—including Bob Pierce, who later founded World Vision—decided to join forces and form a national ministry with the vision of spreading the work overseas. Youth for Christ International was born in January 1945. The church Billy Graham was serving gave him a year's leave to become YFC's first field man. Johnson became the chairman for the new organization.

Johnson considered resigning from his church position to devote his full attention to YFC, but the growing church chose instead to keep their pastor and hire associates to help him keep up with both his ministries. Youth for Christ flourished under its founder's early leadership, with local ministries opening across the country. More than fifty years later Youth for Christ USA now has more than two hundred local chapters, eight hundred full-time workers, and eleven thousand volunteers working in communities throughout the country. Their ministries include campus Bible studies, camps, missions, outreach events, student evangelism training, crisis-pregnancy centers, AIDS prevention, and work with youth gangs and juvenile offenders. Their international ministries operate in 127 countries.

Torrey's leadership of Youth for Christ continued until 1948. In 1953 Johnson resigned his pastorate at Midwest Bible Church to travel as an evangelist worldwide, which he continued to do until 1967, when he retired from his "on the road" ministry to become pastor of Bibletown Community Church in Boca Raton, Florida, where he served until he retired in 1982.

After this "retirement" Johnson developed and became president of an assisted-care facility in Lancaster, Pennsylvania, and later developed a similar facility in Carol Stream, Illinois, near Wheaton, where he and his wife make their home. He still speaks occasionally and serves on the board of Youth for Christ International.

LEGACY

As a young man Torrey Johnson went from being an entrepreneur to a medical student to a ministry candidate before he became a minister of the gospel. And even then he could not figure out what *kind* of minister he was to be. He turned from the pastorate to evangelism to teaching to the pastorate again. What must surely have been confusing at the time is now clear to us as we look back on his life: This is not the story of a man trying to find the particular ministry that fit him best. It's the story of God preparing Torrey Johnson for a ministry bigger than any one kind. The founding of Youth for Christ required an entrepreneur, a pastor, an evangelist, and a teacher who knew how to reach young people. God had developed Torrey for just such a moment.

Johnson's legacy is the organization he founded, which grew from a local outreach to Chicago's youth to an outreach across the country and to the far corners of the world. Millions of students have met Jesus through the ministry of Youth for Christ. Thousands of these students and their dedicated leaders have gone on to become pastors and evangelists, missionaries and leaders, multiplying the initial impact of Johnson's work to a figure beyond measure. The life of Torrey Johnson is a clear testimony to the fact that God has plans far greater than we can imagine.

For additional information about Youth for Christ, see appendix A.

The believers who had fled Jerusalem went everywhere preaching the Good News about Jesus.

Acts 8:4

BOOKS BY TORREY JOHNSON

Reaching Youth for Christ (1994)

1929–1968

MARTIN LUTHER KING JR.

SEEING THE GLORY OF THE LORD
REVEALED . . . TOGETHER

I have a dream that my four
little children will one day
live in a nation where they
will not be judged by the
color of their skin but
by the content of their
character. I have a
dream today!

From the address given at the March on Washington for Jobs and Freedom, August 28, 1963

It was double D day in the spring of 1963. More than twenty-five hundred excited youngsters had turned out at the Sixteenth Street Baptist Church, fifteen hundred more than the day before. Dr. King led the children, along with adults, on a march into downtown Birmingham. A formation of police and firemen blocked the route. The firemen stood ready, high-powered fire hoses pointed at the marchers. Police dogs growled and strained at their leashes. When the marchers refused to turn back, the firemen opened their hoses, sending columns of water crashing into the children and adults, knocking them down, ripping their clothes, smashing them against the sides of buildings, driving them crying and bloodied into the park. Apparently the term *nonviolent* applied only to the protestors. The other side honored no such restriction.

In Short

Minister, civil rights leader, and Nobel Peace laureate Martin Luther King Jr. became the voice of African Americans and other peoples in their struggle for release from oppression. Many Americans responded to the movement in apathetic silence, while others on both sides of the struggle lashed out in violence. King chose another road: faithful defiance in the face of evil, a gentle call for peace and mercy that drowns out the roar of hatred. His remarkable life, cut short by an assassin's bullet, shows us that obedience is costly but bears immeasurable fruit.

Faith

Martin Luther King Jr. was born in Atlanta on January 15, 1929, the son of the Reverend and Mrs. Martin Luther King. Both his

grandfather, Rev. A. D. Williams, and his father were pastors of
Ebenezer Baptist Church, and both were civil rights leaders.

For the first twelve years of King's life his family, along with
grandparents, aunts, and uncles, lived in a two-story Victorian
house in "Sweet Auburn," the center of black Atlanta. Immersed
in a full family and church life, King grew up in an environment of
Christian love, honesty, diligence, respect for elders, courtesy, and
tolerance. He learned that education led to competence and
culture and that church was the path to morality and immortality.

On a spring Sunday in 1934 King joined his family at a spirited
revival in the packed sanctuary of their church. When the evangelist asked audience members to come forward to receive salvation,
King's sister took off for the pulpit, the first person to respond to
the invitation. King, just five at the time, shot out after her, not to
obtain salvation but to make sure that his sister didn't "get ahead
of him." Faith came gradually for King as he absorbed the teachings of his church and family and made them his own.

As a young teenager he became torn between respect for his
father and his need for independence. He was suspicious of
Sunday-school Christianity and the unbridled emotionalism, the
stomping, clapping, and shouting, that went on in his father's
church services. He doubted that Christianity could ever be
"emotionally satisfying" or "intellectually respectable." Although
he resented much in the church, King admired social gospel
proponents like his father who saw the church as an instrument
for improving the lives of black Americans.

In 1944 King began his freshman year at Morehouse College. In
chapel services the school's president, Benjamin Mays, mesmer-
ized his young disciples by preaching stewardship, responsibility,
and engagement. King was enormously impressed. He saw in
Mays the minister he wanted to be, a rational man whose sermons
were both spiritually and intellectually stimulating and a moral
man who was socially involved.

FRUIT

In 1947 King began assisting his father at Ebenezer Baptist and a
year later was ordained as a Baptist minister. He graduated from

Morehouse College and received a scholarship to study at Crozer Theological Seminary in Chester, Pennsylvania. It was his first experience living away from home *and* living in the North, where race did not determine where a person went or what he did at every moment.

While studying at Crozer, King attended a lecture on the life and work of Mahatma Gandhi that inspired him to delve deeper into Gandhi's teachings on nonviolence. When King graduated from Crozer in 1951 with a bachelor of divinity degree, he was class valedictorian and winner of the Pearl Plafker Award for most outstanding student. He moved on and began doctoral studies in theology at Boston University. While in Boston he met Coretta Scott. They were married on June 18, 1953, at her family's home in Marion, Alabama.

A year later, in May of 1954, the Supreme Court ruled in the landmark *Brown v. Board of Education* case that racial segregation in public schools was unconstitutional. That was a defining moment for King. He rejected offers for academic positions and decided to complete his Ph.D. requirements while working in the South. He accepted a position as pastor of the Dexter Avenue Baptist Church in Montgomery, Alabama. While there he completed his dissertation and in 1955 received his doctorate in systematic theology from Boston University.

King's first big civil rights battle began over public transportation. On December 1, 1955, Rosa Parks, a seamstress in Montgomery, was arrested for refusing to give up her bus seat to a white person. Black residents launched a bus boycott and elected King as president of the newly formed Montgomery Improvement Association. It turned out to be dangerous a appointment.

Within weeks King was arrested on the charge of speeding (he was going thirty mph in a twenty-five-mph zone) and taken to jail. Four days later his house was bombed. Just three weeks after the bombing, eighty-nine people, including King and many other ministers, were indicted for conspiring to prevent the Montgomery Bus Company from operating its business. Despite these attempts to suppress the movement, the U.S. Supreme Court declared Alabama's segregation laws unconstitutional, and Montgomery buses were desegregated in December 1956. On December 21, blacks and whites in Montgomery rode on unsegregated buses for the first time, and King was among them.

The boycott brought national attention to the civil rights movement and thrust King into the middle of it all. In the summer of 1957 over one hundred black leaders joined him in Montgomery to form the Southern Christian Leadership Conference, an organization that strove for desegregation of transportation, public facilities, and housing and fought for equality in voting rights, employment, and education. King served as their president. The following year he met with President Eisenhower and saw the publication of his first book, *Stride toward Freedom: The Montgomery Story*. Three days after its New York release, while King was autographing books in a Harlem department store, an assailant stabbed him in the chest.

At the end of 1959 King resigned from his Montgomery church and returned to Atlanta to assist his father as copastor of Ebenezer Baptist. He divided his busy schedule between time with his family, preaching, his regular ministry responsibilities, and increasingly his civil rights activities.

In the early sixties the movement spread across the country, with King often leading, and sometimes chasing, the protests. Student-led efforts became more common, and many actions turned violent. King pleaded with leaders and protesters to spurn violence, but law enforcement officials often responded to the demonstrations with violence, and when protesters returned it, a peaceful march could quickly escalate into a bloodbath. Even worse, some militant leaders of the movement were actually *encouraging* violence, prodding their followers to strike first. King denounced these leaders and their tactics forcefully and often.

King's peaceful defiance put him at the front of many confrontations with authorities, who could count on arresting him without a struggle. They took advantage of that, and King landed in jail often. At times it seemed that if the members of Ebenezer Baptist wished to meet with their pastor, they had to visit him in jail. Over the course of his life he was arrested thirty times.

On August 28, 1963, King delivered his most famous speech, "I

Have a Dream," at the Lincoln Memorial in Washington, D.C. It was not his first speech before this historic backdrop, but it was the first covered in its entirety by the national networks. The nation heard and saw him plead for justice and freedom. A quarter million people, filling the Mall from the Lincoln Memorial to the Washington Monument, stood to hear his immortal words. Looking back on that day, Coretta Scott King said, "At that moment, it seemed as if the Kingdom of God appeared. But it only lasted for a moment."

That moment ended when, just days later, a bomb blast in a Birmingham church killed four girls. Within weeks the FBI tapped King's phones. His speeches, marches, books, and sermons received increasing attention throughout the country. In December 1964 he traveled to Oslo, Norway, to accept the Nobel Peace Prize, and the following year he spoke out against the Vietnam War, endearing himself to antiwar activists and adding new members to the ranks of his detractors.

Gathering enemies in both the private and public sectors, King's life increasingly became an object of attention. The FBI obtained secret audio recordings of a party King held in his suite at Washington's Willard Hotel. The tapes allegedly contained evidence that King had been having sex with someone other than his wife.

King continued his fight against racism while broadening his efforts to include antipoverty campaigns. Marches grew larger, and many were scarred by the violence King abhorred. If ten thousand joined in the march and just one resorted to violence, it was the violence that grabbed headlines and made the evening news.

In early 1968 the sanitation workers of Memphis went on strike. On March 28 a march King led through the city erupted in violence. One person died, and more than fifty were injured. When King left the city, he was distraught. Returning to Memphis on April 3, he vowed to try again with a nonviolent march. That evening he told the crowd gathered at the Masonic Temple, "I may not get there with you, but I want you to know tonight that we as a people will get to the promised land."

The following day, April 4, 1968, King was shot in the neck while standing on the balcony of the Lorraine Hotel and died at St.

Joseph's Hospital. He was just thirty-nine. When the news of King's assassination hit the streets of America, rioting broke out in several cities. The unrest in Washington, D.C., was the worst in its history. Like so many times before, King's courageous example of nonviolence was shamed by bloodshed.

But just as surely, King's cause prevailed. Four days after her husband's death, Coretta Scott King assumed her late husband's place in leading a massive silent march through the streets of Memphis. Seven days later Congress passed the 1968 Civil Rights Act, prohibiting racial discrimination in the sale or rental of housing. And fifteen years later, years filled with many setbacks but ever greater advances, President Ronald Reagan signed a bill that set aside one day in January as a national holiday to celebrate the courageous, peaceful fight of an Atlanta preacher.

LEGACY

Martin Luther King Jr. dreamed of a day when his nation would live up to its creed—where all people, of all colors, of all cultures, and of all economic backgrounds would stand equally. He dreamed of a nation that would sit together at one table. He dreamed of freedom and justice for all. He dreamed of men and women who would "act justly and . . . love mercy and . . . walk humbly with [their] God" (Micah 6:8, NIV). He believed in the redemptive power of love as an instrument of nonviolent social reform. He believed that the more excellent way was one of love over hatred, despair, and violence. He dreamed that we would one day see the glory of the Lord revealed and that all mankind would see it—together.

For additional information about Martin Luther King Jr., see appendix A.

The glory of the Lord will be revealed, and all people will see it together. The Lord has spoken!
Isaiah 40:5

BOOKS BY MARTIN LUTHER KING JR.

A Knock at Midnight: Inspiration from the Great Sermons of Reverend Martin Luther King Jr. (Peter Holloran, editor) (1998)
I Have a Dream (1997)
Strength to Love (1996)
Stride toward Freedom: The Montgomery Story (out of print)
The Measure of a Man (1988)
Trumpet of Conscience (out of print)
Why We Can't Wait (1991)

1898–1963

C. S. LEWIS

SEEKING GOD WITH INTELLECT
AND IMAGINATION

Look for yourself, and you
will find in the long run
only hatred, loneliness,
despair, rage, ruin, and
decay. But look for Christ
and you will find Him,
and with Him everything
else thrown in.

Mere Christianity

On November 22, 1963, the world saw the passing of three influential men: John F. Kennedy, who showed us the power of the human spirit to shape our earthly course; novelist Aldous Huxley, who painted frightening pictures of that same humanity run amok; and C. S. Lewis, who took us on a journey from the longings of humanity to their fulfillment in the God-man Jesus Christ.

IN SHORT

Irish-born writer and English professor C. S. Lewis is the best-known Christian author of the twentieth century. His timeless children's stories, fantasies, and apologetics continue to delight and challenge Christians and non-Christians of all ages. His writings as well as his own life's story show us that we are to grasp God with both intellect and imagination, both mind and heart.

FAITH

Clive Staples Lewis was born in Belfast, Ireland (now Northern Ireland), on November 29, 1898. His brilliant, bookish parents, Albert and Flora Lewis, kept an extensive library at home, and it was here that the young boy, whom his family and friends called Jack, explored other worlds through the words of writers such as Arthur Conan Doyle, Henry Wadsworth Longfellow, and Mark Twain.

Jack's own world was shaken at age ten when his mother died of cancer. On her deathbed she presented him with a Bible, hoping that it would provide solace for him in the trying days ahead. In it she had inscribed: "From Mommy, with Fondest Love, August 1908." Recalling her death later, Lewis wrote: "All settled happiness, all that was tranquil and reliable, disappeared from my life." Jack decided that no God could be so cruel as to take his mother away, and by his early teen years he had become a confirmed atheist.

Lewis's father, a well-heeled lawyer and member of the genteel class, shipped sixteen-year-old Jack off to England to be tutored by an old family friend and former headmaster, William Kirkpatrick. In Lewis's three years with the man he called "The Great Knock," he devoured his tutor's academic fare: Greek, Latin, and Italian literature, critical thinking, skepticism, and atheism. The protégé became master of all these things. It was during this time that Lewis also discovered George Macdonald's *Phantastes*. This fantasy story was his first exposure to good Christian literature, and it struck him like a "new world." But it would be years before he entered that world himself.

In 1917 nineteen-year-old Lewis left "The Great Knock" for the halls of Oxford University. A tour of combat duty in France during World War I interrupted his studies for a time, but otherwise he seldom ventured from this intellectual haven. When his friend Paddy Moore was killed in the war, Lewis virtually adopted Mrs. Moore as his mother, moving in with her in 1921 and living with her until 1950, when she moved to a nursing home the year before her death. Indeed, Oxford became Lewis's lifelong home; even when in later years he taught at Cambridge, he kept his place in Oxford and commuted home on weekends.

At Oxford Lewis poured himself into his studies, read voraciously, and developed friendships with brilliant thinkers. Most influential among them was Owen Barfield. In his own intellectual inquiry Barfield had become a theist, and in frequent debates with his friend, he opened Lewis's mind to consider the idea of God. He also dispatched Lewis's "chronological snobbery," the idea that whatever is "out of date is on that account discredited." With that fallacy out of the way, Lewis was free to seriously consider writers of the Middle Ages and the Renaissance and eventually the writings of George Macdonald and G. K. Chesterton, whose religious views were definitely founded on old ideas. In a debate that ran for years, the relentless Barfield eventually convinced his opponent of the existence of "The Absolute."

Lewis's father's death in 1929 forced Lewis, now a professor at Oxford, to turn again to questions about God and eternity. A year and a half later, Warnie, his older brother and best friend, confessed his Christian faith. By August 1931 the two brothers were attending church together, an activity they had not shared since their boyhood. A month later Lewis got into a discussion with Hugo Dyson and J. R. R. Tolkien, two friends and fellow academics. The topic was metaphor and myth and whether the biblical accounts of Christ were either of these things. Of these three men, only two were Christians, but a few days later Lewis, the odd man out, wrote: "I have just passed on from believing in God to definitely believing in Christ."

FRUIT

Looking back on his return to the faith he had abandoned as a teenager, Lewis claimed that it had begun with George Macdonald's *Phantastes* many years earlier and that through it all Macdonald had been with him. Now Lewis was ready to learn from him much that he had not been ready to learn from him before. And in the spirit of his fellow traveler, Lewis began to write of his faith with brilliance and imagination.

Over the next three decades Lewis created a substantial body of Christian work. He became a highly acclaimed writer of apologetics, science fiction, children's literature, and fantasies—or as Lewis liked to call them, "fairy tales for adults." While fully capable of discussing Christianity at the highest of intellectual levels, he chose to impart the principles of the faith in books written to the common man. Yet he would not sacrifice sound reasoning for the sake of easy reading. He treated his readers as intelligent skeptics who were unworthy of anything but the best, most reasoned case he could make.

In his most famous apologetics book, *Mere Christianity*, as well as in fantasies such as *The Screwtape Letters* and *The Great Divorce,*

Lewis's case for Christianity is compelling and clear. In works such as his children's series, The Chronicles of Narnia, and the science fiction series, The Space Trilogy, Lewis expressed faith through brilliantly crafted fantasy and allegory. In virtually everything he wrote he seemed to have the non-Christian reader in mind. Others used their writings to address the needs of Christians; Lewis was an evangelist. He was after those who, as he had for many years, rejected Christianity as unreasonable. He would show them the contrary: Faith in Christ was reasonable, and even better than that, it provided the reason for living.

One person he convinced was Joy Davidman Gresham, a writer in New York. She was Jewish by birth, communist by choice, and extremely intelligent. In her own journey to Christ she had read some of Lewis's books, and in the late 1940s she began corresponding with him about questions of faith. The two met in 1952 while Joy was seeking a British publisher for a book she had just written. They continued their correspondence afterward, and when Joy's husband left her for another woman, she and her two young sons moved from New York to London.

What began as a professional friendship became a romance. It was a difficult match. Joy's family in America resented her conversion; her sons resented the move to England, and her ex-husband resented paying child support. Most of Lewis's friends did not like her and avoided the couple's company. Nonetheless, the couple overcame these difficulties, and in 1956, a year after Lewis left his position at Oxford to teach at Cambridge, Joy and Jack were married.

Now a new set of difficulties beset them. Joy was diagnosed with cancer. Their life together became a test of love and faith in the midst of difficulty as they dealt with her treatments, tried to raise two active boys, and were ostracized by Lewis's friends. The deeper things of love and faith prevailed, and for a few short years Joy greatly inspired her husband's writing before the cancer took her life in 1960.

Joy's death struck Lewis deeply, but he continued to write books, including a small volume that told the state of his heart,

A Grief Observed. And when he died on November 22, 1963, he still had two more books awaiting publication at the printer.

LEGACY

On secular university campuses today it is rare to find an outspoken Christian professor. The few who dare to proclaim their faith do so amidst the silent scorn or spoken ridicule of their "enlightened" peers. It is easy to imagine that this prejudice is a recent phenomenon, that in Lewis's day Christian academics received more respect. But such was not the case. While the reading public celebrated Lewis's works, many of his colleagues shunned him. They criticized his beliefs and resented him for calling himself a professor even as he stooped so low as to write silly stories for children and religious fanatics. While Lewis felt their rejection, he did not allow it to deter him from his chosen path.

We can be delighted that he didn't. His volume of Christian work is the most widely read in the twentieth century, providing children and adults, believers and skeptics a view of a faith shaped with both superior intellect and vivid imagination. While most of his peers filled dusty library bookshelves with the dull discoveries of their intellectual pursuits, C. S. Lewis fills our minds with a God as real as he is fantastic.

You must love the Lord your God with all your heart, all your soul, and all your mind.

Matthew 22:37

BOOKS BY C. S. LEWIS

Aslan's Triumph (1998)
C. S. Lewis on Faith (1998)
C. S. Lewis on Grief (1998)
Christian Mythmakers (1998)
Mere Christianity (1999)
Readings for Meditation and Reflection (1998)
Screwtape Letters (1996)

Space Trilogy (1996)
The Abolition of Man (1996)
The Case for Christianity (1996)
The Complete Chronicles of Narnia (1998)
The Great Divorce (1996)
The Problem of Pain (1996)
The Wood between the Worlds (1999)
Till We Have Faces (1998)

1881–1937

J. GRESHAM MACHEN

STANDING FOR BIBLICAL TRUTH

What I need first of all is not exhortation, but a gospel, not directions for saving myself but knowledge of how God has saved me. Have you any good news? That is the question that I ask of you. I know your exhortations will not help me. But if anything has been done to save me, will you not tell me the facts?

Christian Faith in the Modern World

In 1814, as the British army approached the United States Capitol, a senate clerk scrambled to save the new country's precious documents from destruction. He took them to a hiding place in the countryside, thus keeping them out of British hands and the flames that soon ravaged the besieged Capitol. The clerk's name was Lewis Henry Machen.

A century later his grandson, John Gresham Machen, fought to preserve something he considered even more precious: the orthodox teachings of the Reformed faith.

IN SHORT

Professor J. Gresham Machen's textbooks on New Testament Greek are standard fare for seminary students nationwide. But he is best known for his tenacious stand against the modernism that swept through the church in the first part of the twentieth century. Machen refused to compromise on what he saw as the fundamentals of the Christian faith, and his fight for orthodoxy birthed a seminary and established a new denomination: the Orthodox Presbyterian Church.

FAITH

John Gresham Machen (pronounced MAY-chen) was born in Baltimore, Maryland, on July 28, 1881, the second son of Arthur Webster and Minnie Gresham Machen. The Machen family had a long Southern aristocratic history with strong church ties. Gresham's great-grandfather had settled in colonial Virginia, and his grandfather had served as a clerk to the secretary of the senate and as an elder in Washington's Fourth Presbyterian Church. His mother, a graduate of Wesleyan College, had published a book in 1903 entitled *The Bible in Browning*.

Machen was raised in a home that set great value on good education, logical thinking, and precise reasoning. After attending a private school specializing in the classics, Machen entered Johns Hopkins University and graduated with highest honors in 1901. At the urging of his pastor he went on to Princeton Seminary, where he majored in philosophy, receiving bachelor of divinity and master of arts degrees by 1905. Following Princeton, Machen spent a year studying the New Testament in Germany. Among his German instructors was Wilhelm Hermann, a professor of systematic theology at the University of Marburg.

In Germany, far from family and familiar culture, Machen came to a crossroads in his faith. One road was more familiar to him, the faith he had embraced as a child and studied at Princeton, founded on the teachings of an inerrant Bible. The other road, modernism, was intellectually progressive and popularly appealing, a belief that the teachings of the Bible were subject to new interpretations adapted to modern culture. Machen's rigorously logical mind would not allow him to take a middle road. To him, orthodoxy and modernism were mutually exclusive. If one was paved upon truth, the other had to be counterfeit. Which road would he take?

For Machen, the question was as much about personal identity as intellectual certainty. After much study and soul-searching, he chose the road of orthodoxy, the road that he believed had been paved by the first church and reopened by another German theologian, Martin Luther, in 1517. But he did not forget all he had studied of modernism, and later he would use this knowledge against it.

In 1906 Machen was called to Princeton to teach courses on the New Testament. He lamented the lack of passion for Christ among scholars and sought through his teaching to reveal and pass on the zeal he had. To loosen up his overly serious students he filled the first classroom session in each semester with jokes and stunts. For the rest of the semester his students could count on him for comic and at times eccentric behavior.

He had a habit of reading the morning mail while catching their errors as they declined Greek nouns. In the midst of his lectures he might bump his head against the wall, balance something on his head, or write entire conjugations on the blackboard—backwards. After class his students could challenge him to a game of tennis. His unorthodox way of teaching orthodox faith endeared him to students and reminded them that joy was indeed part of God's plan.

Machen taught at Princeton for twenty-two years. During this time he turned his New Testament curricula into textbooks and published articles that caught the attention of other theologians. In 1914 he was ordained in the Presbyterian Church. He also began to speak out against modernism, which had crossed the Atlantic and was creeping into Princeton Seminary and the Presbyterian denomination it belonged to. Machen was becoming known as a staunch defender of Reformed orthodoxy.

His most important book in the debate was *Christianity and Liberalism,* published in 1923. Machen's attack on modernism was not just a stand for the "fundamentals"—inerrancy of Scripture, Christ's virgin birth, vicarious atonement, etc.—but a challenge to the whole of Reformed Christianity. Although seen as an ally of fundamentalists, he preferred to call himself a Calvinist, maintaining that Christians needed more: a historical perspective, an appreciation of scholarship, historical confessions rather than skeletal creeds, and the precise formulation of Christian doctrine.

The battle between modernist and orthodox camps grew through the 1920s. In 1924 the Presbyterian Church adopted a more liberal stance, and in the summer of 1929 Princeton's board reorganized to reflect this. Machen resigned in protest. Within weeks of the start of the new fall term a like-minded group of students and faculty members met to form a new school. Westminster Seminary opened in September, with Machen delivering the inaugural address to its first class of fifty students.

Although now out of the denomination's flagship seminary, Machen was not out of the church—yet. It took a battle over missions to do that. In 1933, concerned that the denomination was sending out increasingly liberal missionaries, Machen and others formed the Independent Board of Foreign Missions. He was elected president. The following year the church's legislative body, the general assembly, declared Machen's mission board unconstitutional. He was tried by a judicial commission for violation of his ordination vows, found guilty, and suspended from ministry.

A year after his conviction Machen and others who objected to the denomination's liberal direction broke free and formed a new Presbyterian denomination, which became known as the Orthodox Presbyterian Church. At the opening general assembly of the new church, Machen, its first elected moderator, declared the joy he found in what many considered a tragic schism: "On Thursday, June 11, 1936 the hopes of many years were realized. . . . What a joyous moment it was! How the long years of struggle seemed to sink into nothingness compared with the peace and joy that filled our hearts! . . . With that lively hope does our gaze turn now to the future! At last true evangelicalism can go forward without the shackle of compromising associations!"

The future of the new denomination was bright indeed, but Machen's own future was short. His many years on the front lines of this battle had seen victory in the formation of Westminster Seminary and the new denomination. Now he was joyous but tired. Over the Christmas holiday of that same year Machen took a train from Philadelphia to the subzero plains of North Dakota to preach at the request of a pastor friend. Just before New Year's Eve he checked into a Bismarck hospital, scarcely able to breathe. It was pneumonia, and far more serious than he imagined. He died on New Year's Day 1937 at the age of fifty-five.

His pastor friend came to pray with him in the hospital on that last day. Machen told him of a vision he had had of heaven: "It was glorious, it was glorious," he repeated. A little while later he added, "Isn't the Reformed faith grand?"

FRUIT

J. Gresham Machen was a man of seeming contradictions. He could trace his family line to colonial America and find in it great men and women who passed faith and patriotism on to their children. He never married, never had children, never passed on these traits to a new generation of Machens. Yet his progeny were his students, his seminary, and his denomination, and they carry the torch still.

He could hold his own in just about any intellectual circle. Many in these circles concluded that doctrine must be influenced by time and culture and that those who thought otherwise did so in ignorance. But Machen's belief in the unchanging tenets of faith came not from nostalgia or from careless thinking but through precise reasoning that rivaled that of his liberal peers. And while he expressed his passionate beliefs through humor and camaraderie with his students, he could just as easily cut off an opponent—even a friend—with a fiery retort that left no room for rebuttal.

Machen poured himself into the doctrinal issues of his day, but he was just as outspoken on public policy, from family friend President Wilson's idealist war aims to Roosevelt's social security program to the "alarming bureaucratization of the United States." And all the while he found time to write extensively and insightfully, remain involved in the lives of his students, and serve as an early mentor to men who would have far-reaching effects on twentieth-century Christianity, including journalist Carl Henry, Harold Ockenga (cofounder of Fuller Seminary), and Bible scholar Wilbur Smith.

LEGACY

Four centuries before Machen made his compelling case for doctrinal truth, another professor posted ninety-five theses on a chapel door. Like Martin Luther, Machen immersed himself in a heated debate over doctrine instead of succumbing to the pressures of a powerful church. Both theologians were "excommunicated" from their churches. Each played an essential role in clarifying what the church is about and how we are to practice the faith on which the church is founded. To this day these questions are fiercely debated. For those who question the relevance of the ancient Scriptures to life in today's world, the life and work of J. Gresham Machen make a formidable argument for the timelessness of truth.

For additional information about J. Gresham Machen and his work, see appendix A.

All Scripture is inspired by God and is useful to teach us what is true and to make us realize what is wrong in our lives. It straightens us out and teaches us to do what is right. It is God's way of preparing us in every way, fully equipped for every good thing God wants us to do.

2 Timothy 3:16-17

BOOKS BY J. GRESHAM MACHEN

Christianity and Liberalism (1923)
God Transcendent (1996)
Learn or Review New Testament Greek (1998)
New Testament Greek for Beginners (1999)
The Christian View of Man (1984)
What Is Faith? (1996)

PETER MARSHALL

THE HARMONY OF ABILITY
WITH HUMILITY

I feel ... I am not yet ready for the
responsibilities and the dignities which
would be mine as minister of the
New York Avenue Church. I am too young,
too immature, too lacking in
scholarship, experience, wisdom, and
ability for such a high position. Time
alone will reveal whether or not I shall
ever possess these qualities of mind and
heart that your pulpit demands.

From a letter to New York Avenue Presbyterian Church in Washington, D.C., in 1936,
declining their pulpit, from which he would later preach to presidents and senators

One starless night, walking back from a nearby village, young Peter struck out across the lonely Scottish moors. The only sounds were of wind through the moorland, the wild birds clamoring as his footsteps disturbed them, and the bleating of sheep. Suddenly he heard an urgent call:

"Peter!"

He stopped and called back, "Yes, who is it? What do you want?" For a second he listened, but there was no response. Thinking he must have been mistaken, he walked a few paces. Then he heard it even more urgently:

"Peter!"

He stopped and peered into the darkness, then stumbled and fell to his knees. Putting out a hand to catch himself, he found nothing. He was on the very brink of an abandoned limestone quarry. One more step would have sent him to certain death. He had no doubt whose voice it was. God had saved him—saved Peter Marshall for something great ahead.

IN SHORT

Scottish-born Presbyterian minister and chaplain of the U.S. Senate, Peter Marshall had the voice for magnificent preaching, the charisma to draw immense crowds, and a humility that made everyone from high school students to senators want to know the God he served. The fruit of his ministry continues to ripen long after his premature death.

FAITH

Peter Marshall was born in 1902 in Coatbridge, Scotland. His father, an insurance man and church member, died when Peter was four.

His mother was a woman whose strong faith empowered her to survive the hardship and raise Peter with a similar trust in God.

In his early twenties Marshall worked as an engineer and helped out with his Congregational kirk's youth. He volunteered to teach Sunday school, lead the youth choir, and serve as a scoutmaster. But volunteer work was not enough for him, and he determined to give his life to full-time service. Soon after his decision, he nearly walked into the quarry, and he knew that in saving him, God was confirming his call.

Sensing that God wanted him to go to America, he booked passage. In 1927 the twenty-five-year-old Marshall arrived at New York's Ellis Island with conviction in his heart—and enough money in his pocket to last him two weeks. He found a job in New Jersey and after working and saving for a year, headed south to Birmingham, Alabama, to look up an old friend he knew from his school days in Scotland. In Birmingham he attended a Presbyterian church, where the pastor took Marshall under his wing. The members of his Sunday school class raised money to send him to Columbia Seminary in Atlanta.

Although he did not have a proper college degree when he entered, the school made a rare exception and allowed Marshall to complete the courses for a divinity degree. He graduated magna cum laude in 1931 and was ordained into the Presbyterian Church that same year. Nonetheless, he felt an educational inferiority because of his lack of a formal education, a feeling that would stay with him throughout his life.

Fruit

As a young minister fresh out of seminary, Marshall was offered two positions, one at a small church in Covington, Georgia, the other at Westminster Presbyterian Church in Atlanta. He chose the former and, after gaining confidence in his ministry duties, took the position at Westminster when it was offered to him again a few years later.

Marshall was well suited for the pastorate and well liked by his congregations. He had a Scottish brogue and precise diction, and spoke with an engaging dramatic voice. His tall frame and broad shoulders dominated the pulpit. His charisma drew crowds to the church; his immigrant voice for the common man kept them coming back. Marshall's commanding presence harmonized with a penetrating humility that made his messages of Christian faith real and believable. His Sunday services were filled to overflowing, and at times people stood in line in the rain just to get into the church.

As the preacher drew crowds, the crowds drew publishers. He received many offers to publish his sermons. But he never felt his sermons were good enough, rejecting offer after offer with a written reply: "Perhaps later . . ." Meanwhile, the young minister met Catherine Wood, a student at Agnes Scott College. They were married on November 4, 1936.

On their honeymoon the newlyweds visited New York Avenue Presbyterian Church in Washington, D.C. The church had been seeking Marshall as their pastor. He declined. His letter turning down the invitation revealed much about his own heart: "I am too young, too immature, too lacking in scholarship, experience, wisdom, and ability for such a high position. Time alone will reveal whether or not I shall ever possess these qualities of mind and heart that your pulpit demands."

Time did tell. The church persisted, and Marshall finally felt God's hand leading him to accept. In the fall of 1937, at age thirty-five, he moved to Washington. His messages were as popular there as they were in Atlanta. When the sanctuary filled up, the church installed loudspeakers in the chapel, which served as an overflow room. Still, on many Sundays over five hundred people were turned away. Marshall's services acted like a leveling ground, attracting people of all classes, incomes, and occupations, from judges to postal workers, senators to file clerks, executives to their hired help.

His audiences appreciated his nonecclesiastical demeanor, especially when his son, wee Peter, was born, and he began using stories of his son's antics as illustrations. Teenagers loved his youthful sincerity. Twelve young people comprised the youth group when Peter arrived. He immediately began teaching a Sunday school class for senior high and college students. Before long, the youth group had grown to two hundred.

In 1938, within a year of his arrival in Washington, Marshall received two great boosts to his ministry. On January 26 he was granted U.S. citizenship. This removed a hurdle to ministry in the nation's capital. Then on May 30 he was granted a doctorate from Presbyterian College in Clinton, South Carolina. Although it was merely honorary, it was an affirmation of his immense, albeit largely informal, education and eased a bit of his mostly self-imposed stigma for not having received other degrees. He would now be referred to as Dr. Marshall.

A decade after receiving his citizenship, Marshall received his greatest honor. His ministry to senators, long conducted as pastor of a church many Senate members attended, became an official government appointment in 1947 when he was confirmed as chaplain of the U. S. Senate. His prayers were now delivered on the senate floor and carried across the country through the press. In his trademark style he prayed not in ecclesiastical language but in words the common man could understand.

His ministry in the Capitol opened doors of faith for many senators. One remarked, "I never know whether Dr. Marshall is praying for me or at me." Another said, "We felt the impact of Dr. Marshall's prayers, so we wanted to know him better." Many took that opportunity and became Christians when they did.

While Marshall was always personable and eager to share his faith, the rugged Scotsman in him had difficulty expressing his deep feelings—even to his wife. Catherine, whose own ministry was profoundly influential, confessed in her book *A Man Called Peter* that he had but one place he could always open up, and that was in prayer. He called God his "Chief," and it was to the Chief that he poured out his soul.

Perhaps it was his intense passion for the Chief's work in both congregation and Congress that accelerated a serious heart condition. Marshall suffered his first heart attack before being voted in as Senate chaplain. He knew that his condition was not good but resisted all attempts by others to slow him down. He did not fear death; he wanted to live life to the fullest for the Chief, to whom he entrusted his health. His second attack came in 1949, just weeks after President Truman's inauguration.

Peter Marshall did not recover. He died on the morning of

January 26, 1949, at age forty-six. Hours earlier, when he was informed by his physician that he must go immediately to the hospital, his humor still showed through: "I take a dim view of that. What a revoltin' development this is!"

LEGACY

As a young minister, Peter Marshall saw more people walk through his church doors than most pastors see in a lifetime. His great communication abilities could quite easily have led to a rewarding writing and speaking career and to a long series of ever more prestigious churches. But humbled by the greatness of his Chief and the shortcomings he saw in himself, he turned down nearly every offer he received. He chose instead to follow God's leading and that leading only.

These two qualities—humility and great ability—often become each other's enemy: Talent often brings pride, while deep humility often requires that we set aside our natural strengths to allow God to work through our weakness. Yet in Marshall, these two qualities resulted in a formidable combination. It was his humility that gave substance to his naturally powerful voice.

Unfortunately, this same humility keeps most of us from reading his words. The man whose messages could have filled volumes never published a book. But we can know him through the great work of Catherine Marshall. In her biography of Peter, she lets us listen in on the great communicator in his pulpit and the humble servant baring his soul to the Chief.

Seek first his kingdom and his righteousness, and all these things will be given to you as well.
Matthew 6:33, NIV

BOOKS BY PETER MARSHALL

First Easter (Peter and Catherine Marshall) (1995)
The Prayers of Peter Marshall (Catherine Marshall) (1989)

1890–1944

AIMEE SEMPLE McPHERSON

ANGEL IN THE SERVICE OF THE KING

Put first things first.
To take Him as your
physician, accept Him
as your Savior first.
The fountain lies open,
the precious blood is
still efficacious to
cleanse from sin.

Sister Aimee: The Life of Aimee Semple McPherson

F ollowing a revival meeting the young widowed evangelist took up a collection. It came to $65. She headed to the next town, where she heard a man had a tent for sale. He told her he would sell it to her for $150. When she informed him that $65 was all she had, he agreed to give it to her if she would take it without inspecting it. She had no choice.

When Aimee opened the tent, she found the canvas full of rips and holes and eaten with mildew. She and the other women went to work patching the holes and sewing the tears, and they managed to get it up that evening for Sunday's meeting. Halfway into her sermon the canvas shrieked and tore over her head. The crowd lost interest in the sermon, their attention drawn to the canvas roof about to collapse on them.

In Short
Canadian-born American evangelist Aimee Semple McPherson started her ministry on a street corner, toured the country with a tent, and settled in Los Angeles to build a church that would multiply itself across the world. In the first half of the twentieth century she was the country's most celebrated Pentecostal, one of its most adored and ridiculed personalities, and the founder of the Foursquare denomination.

Faith
Aimee Kennedy was born October 9, 1890, in Salford, Ontario. Her father, James Morgan Kennedy, had entered into a scandalous marriage with his young housekeeper, Mildred "Minnie" Pearce,

who was thirty-five years his junior. Minnie had been brought in to care for the ailing Mrs. Kennedy, and after the first Mrs. Kennedy died, Minnie became the second Mrs. Kennedy and eventually Aimee's mother.

Minnie's uncle and guardian was a Salvation Army officer, so she raised her only child as a Salvationist. As a young girl Aimee lived on a farm, where she had few friends but the animals. She attended school only because she had to and showed her disdain by being disrespectful to authority, audacious, and rebellious. But she excelled at speaking, winning her first award at age eleven.

For a time in her teen years Aimee became an atheist. But Christianity was all she knew—it was the basis for everything in her home, her life, and her community, so her atheism did not last long. Her conversion took place when she was seventeen. A Pentecostal evangelist, Robert Semple, came to town and preached on repentance from the book of Acts. Aimee later wrote: "My very soul had been stripped before God—there was a God, and I was not ready to meet him." Aimee fell in love with God that night. Six months later, on August 12, 1908, she married the evangelist who had introduced her to God.

Shortly after, Aimee badly sprained her ankle and sensed that God was telling her to go to the elders of a church. They prayed over it, and she was instantly healed. Thus began her belief in the ministry of healing, a ministry that would last over three decades.

Robert Semple was Aimee's mentor in ministry. She watched him preach and played piano and prayed for new believers at his services. In 1910 they traveled to China on a missions trip. Along the way they stopped in England, and Aimee received a surprise invitation to preach at a Pentecostal gathering. Aimee preached her first full sermon before an enthusiastic crowd of fifteen thousand in London's Royal Albert Hall.

After their stop in London, the Semples completed the journey to China. Aimee disliked China immensely and was eager to return home. But the couple was struck by dysentery, and though Aimee recovered, Robert did not. He died in Hong Kong five days after their second wedding anniversary. A month later the young widow gave birth to a daughter, Roberta Star.

Mother and daughter returned from China by way of New York City, where Aimee met a young accountant named Harold McPherson. He fell in love and proposed to her. They were married February 12, 1912. The bride kept both of her husbands' names and became known as Aimee Semple McPherson. A son, Rolf, was born a year later.

Aimee began preaching regularly and teaching Bible studies. Her mother, Minnie, joined them to help out with the children. But as Aimee's ministry success increased, her interest in Harold diminished. Three years into their marriage she packed up the kids and her mother and left him.

FRUIT

In 1915 Aimee led her first public revival at Mount Forest, Ontario. A woman preacher was a novelty, and families came from all over to see her. Some thought she was a witch, but most were simply attracted to her beauty. Young people were especially drawn to her. She frightened and stimulated and evoked strong emotions. During her Mount Forest revival, hundreds were converted, and dozens received healing.

She didn't seek a healing ministry, but as news spread that healings occurred in her meetings, thousands came to her. Not everyone was healed, and for some the healing was only temporary, but many claimed complete healing from diseases and disabilities.

In 1916 Aimee took her ministry on the road and bought a tent to hold the large crowds. Thus began a seven-year traveling campaign that ended in Los Angeles. Along the way she traveled the East Coast from New England to Florida twice and coast to coast six times—no simple feat in the days before interstate highways and uninterrupted pavement. Aimee, her mother, and her two children traveled in a 1912 Packard that she called the Gospel Car. Along one side, in six-inch-high painted letters was the message "Jesus Is Coming Soon"; the message on the other side read "Where Will You Spend Eternity?"

Traveling from town to town and sleeping on the roadside, Aimee often preached up to ten times a day. She spoke from the backseat of her car with a megaphone at her mouth, a miniature organ in her lap. She led gospel hymns, preached, and invited listeners to come to Jesus. Men and women knelt by the running boards and gave their lives to Christ.

Like most Pentecostal preachers, Aimee's message drew great numbers of immigrants, the poor, and the working class. Her audiences were often racially diverse and were composed of unbelievers as well as Christians of all traditions. Nearly everywhere she went she was met with hecklers, and at least once the crowd turned into an angry mob, which she managed to silence through prayer.

Press reports of Aimee's amazing ministry spread throughout the country. By the time she arrived in Los Angeles, she was famous: She was mobbed by reporters, scandalized in print, and gossiped about from church pulpits. If her healing spectacles weren't enough to pack the house, her theatrics filled all the empty seats. In the last years of her tent ministry Aimee felt led to establish a "permanent tent" in Los Angeles. Construction began in 1921. Angelus Temple was dedicated on New Year's Day 1923. The domed building had excellent acoustics, fifty-three hundred seats, and two balconies—a colossal structure designed for resounding worship.

In her new ministry home, Aimee's legendary theatrics took on even greater proportions. She borrowed livestock and zoo animals to use on stage, donned costumes, and relied on props and scenery to support her sermons. Calling upon her Salvation Army heritage, she wrote gospel lyrics to popular songs and employed a thirty-six-piece brass band. She recruited a hundred-voice choir as well as several trios, quartets, and other choral groups, filling the hall with music in every service.

The Temple became a tourist attraction. It also served as the church home to a diverse group of local citizens, including Klansmen and Gypsies, police chiefs and hoodlums, politicians and hundreds of Hollywood celebrities. Now a celebrity herself, Aimee brought in famous speakers and preachers and sought creative advice from Charlie Chaplin. As the press continued to call her a charlatan, she now found herself being defended by respected journalists, including H. L. Mencken, who was no big fan of religion himself.

Aimee called the message of her ministry the "Foursquare Gospel," a term inspired by her reading of the prophet Ezekiel's vision (1:10) of creatures with four faces: man, lion, ox, and eagle. To her, the man was Jesus the Savior; the Lion of Judah, the giver of the Holy Spirit; the ox, the Healer who bears our burdens; and the eagle, the eternal Christ who will come again.

Aimee was not the first person to use the *foursquare* term or to make these connections from the prophecy. The Elim Foursquare Gospel Alliance, founded in Ireland in 1915, was built on the four cornerstones of regeneration, baptism in the Spirit, divine healing, and the Second Coming, and these principles influenced the founders of the Assemblies of God denomination soon after.

The growing ministry at Angelus Temple took on the "foursquare" principles too and eventually became a Pentecostal denomination known as the International Church of the Foursquare Gospel. It would count as its founding date the dedication of the Temple in 1923.

Her church reached out to laborers, widows, and orphans, its commissary distributing necessities to those in need throughout the community. Through her sermons, which were carried on her radio station, KFSG, she mobilized her audience to raise support for the unemployed and relief for the victims of earthquakes and other disasters. She used her radio platform to demand pay raises for firefighters and police officers who assisted the victims of these disasters. In the late 1920s she visited England, toured the Holy Land, and, to no one's surprise, suffered a nervous breakdown. She stayed out of the pulpit for nearly a year. A few months after her recovery, on September 13, 1931, Aimee married David Hutton. Her third marriage would last just three years.

When Aimee traveled, her celebrity status earned her personal interviews with world leaders; and when she returned, her popularity at home gave credibility to her political appeals on their behalf. As World War II approached, she returned to the U.S. to lead American clergy in denouncing the works of Hitler and Mussolini, and when America entered the war, she took to the streets to sell war bonds.

She never saw the end of the war. On September 27, 1944, at the age of fifty-three, Aimee died of an accidental overdose. At the time of her death the Foursquare denomination she founded was comprised of 410 churches in North America, two hundred mission stations, and twenty-nine thousand members. By the end of the twentieth century, the International Church of the Foursquare Gospel had become one of the fastest growing denominations in the world, with 2.8 million members and nearly twenty-five thousand churches ministering in ninety-nine countries.

LEGACY

Aimee Semple McPherson lived a dramatic, tragic, victorious life. She became a folk hero to the city of Los Angeles, adored and scorned by press and citizens alike. From 1926 to 1937 her name appeared in the news columns of the *Los Angeles Times* at least three times a week. She faced forty-five lawsuits, went through two divorces, and suffered painful disputes with ministry workers and family members.

McPherson is testimony to the fact that God uses imperfect people to carry out his perfect work. Despite Aimee's many foibles, sins, and scandals, God used her to change the lives of millions. She shared the gospel with unbelievers, brought relief to the suffering, and founded a church that has reached across the globe.

For additional information about Aimee Semple McPherson, see appendix A.

"My gracious favor is all you need. My power works best in your weakness." So now I am glad to boast about my weaknesses, so that the power of Christ may work through me. Since I know it is all for Christ's good, I am quite content with my weaknesses and with insults, hardships, persecutions, and calamities. For when I am weak, then I am strong. 2 Corinthians 12:9-10

BOOKS BY AIMEE SEMPLE MCPHERSON

In the Service of the King (1927) (out of print)

HENRIETTA MEARS

TEACHING THAT ROCKS THE WORLD

There is no magic
in small plans. When
I consider my ministry,
I think of the world.
Anything less than
that would not be
worthy of Christ nor
of His will for my life.

Henrietta Mears and How She Did It!

Three hundred college students sat on cushions on the floor at the First Presbyterian Church in Hollywood, California. Chinese lanterns hung from the ceiling, and girls dressed in kimonos served tea and Chinese cookies. Laughter filled the hall as the teacher entered, wearing an elegant kimono and perching precariously in a rickshaw.

Henrietta climbed down from the rickshaw, laid aside her fan, and in her deep, resonant voice, began to deliver a challenging message. Her students were profoundly moved as they heard of the great need in Asia. Just a few months later the College Department at First Presbyterian sent two doctors and two nurses to help missionaries in Formosa.

IN SHORT

If the success of a teacher is measured in the lives of her students, then Henrietta Mears deserves the title Teacher of the Century. This remarkable Sunday school teacher inspired some of the century's most influential Christians, revolutionized the field of Christian education, and returned nobility to the name "Teacher."

FAITH

Henrietta, the youngest of seven children, was born to Ashley and Margaret Mears in 1890 in Fargo, North Dakota. Her father was a businessman, her mother a homemaker, and her maternal grandfather a respected pastor in Chicago. As the baby in the family, Henrietta got special attention from her mom, who would read and pray with her in the mornings after the older kids had left for school. By age seven, little Henrietta was ready to confess her faith. She stood before the congregation to answer the questions for membership, becoming the youngest member of their church.

As Henrietta grew into a young woman, her eyesight began to deteriorate. Eyeglasses helped, but the doctors believed her vision would continue to decline, leaving her blind by age thirty. The diagnosis lit a fire in her faith. Believing that God had a purpose for her life, Henrietta determined to study everything she could before her eyesight failed. Against medical counsel, she enrolled at the University of Minnesota to study chemistry; despite her failing vision, she graduated with honors. Her life's work was now formed: She would become a teacher and influence thousands of other teachers along the way.

FRUIT

For several years after college, Henrietta taught high school chemistry in Minnesota public schools. But her real passion for teaching was expressed in her spare time. She took on a Sunday school class of high school girls at her Minneapolis church. By the end of the year, she had 250 students. After ten years, three thousand young women had passed through her Sunday school classes. Through prayer, she became firmly convinced of the purpose to which God had called her when he led her into teaching: It was not just teaching, but teaching that developed leaders who could penetrate the world with the gospel of Jesus Christ.

In confirmation of that call, Henrietta received an invitation to leave public school education and enter the ministry full-time. The offer came from Dr. Stewart MacClennan of First Presbyterian Church in Hollywood, California. MacClennan had heard of her remarkable "spare time" ministry and believed she was just what the church needed for their director of Christian education. She took the call and moved to California.

Her first task was to evaluate the church's existing Sunday school material. She was appalled. One lesson she reviewed proposed that the apostle Paul survived the shipwreck at Malta (Acts 27–28) because he had "eaten carrots and was strong." Henrietta boxed up the material and returned it to the publisher, explaining that she could not use any lesson that denied the miraculous in Scripture. She searched for other materials for her classes but found nothing that passed her muster. So she set out to write her own.

Her philosophy of Christian education was simple: It had to be biblically based and taught by teachers who were faithful to the Bible's teachings. True to that philosophy, she and her teaching team wrote lessons that were bold, challenging, captivating—and effective. In just three years Sunday school attendance grew from four hundred to four thousand.

Word of her curriculum spread from church to church, and requests for the material came pouring in from around the nation. Pastors and teachers were crying out for effective, biblical teaching materials. In response to that cry, Henrietta and a group of businessmen founded Gospel Light Press, one of the first publishers in the Christian education field. This company grew to become Gospel Light Publications and Regal Books, publishing curricula, books, and Bible study materials for Christians worldwide. Among its best works is *What the Bible Is All About,* a collection of Henrietta's teaching notes edited into an engaging, practical journey through the entire Bible.

Reading Henrietta's work, it's clear that the author is not a person who merely knew the Bible and wrote what she knew. Her passion for God's Word leaps off the page in wonder and excitement, like that of a child who has discovered something spectacular and cannot wait to share it. That's what set her apart. To the thousands and thousands of students who passed through her Sunday school classroom, she was a passionate teacher, thrilled as much by the students who grasped God's Word as by the Bible itself.

Her best efforts went to her college classes. She knew that these young people were next year's leaders, missionaries, pastors, and teachers. To attract the kind of students most likely to fill such positions, she worked hard to cultivate an atmosphere of prestige. One of those she drew into the group was a promising young man by the name of Bill Bright. At a Wednesday night Bible study, Bright heard Henrietta teach from Acts 9—the story of Paul's conversion on the road to Damascus and his world-changing response to God's call. After the lesson, Henrietta asked her students to go home and ask God what mission he had planned for them. Bright returned to his apartment, knelt, and prayed. In his new faith, Bright began a ministry that became Campus Crusade for Christ.

Henrietta was to play another important part in the shaping of Bright's life. At a college retreat, Bright introduced her to his fiancée, Vonette Zachary, a young woman who had just graduated from the university and was not a believer. Henrietta pulled her aside for a conversation. She explained the reality of knowing God in very logical, scientific terms. Vonette placed her faith in Christ.

Retreats played an important role in Henrietta's ministry. But in southern California in the 1930s, decent, affordable retreat facilities were hard to find. So Henrietta decided to create one. She discovered a private resort in the San Bernardino mountains valued at $350,000. Through prayer and miraculous intervention, Henrietta laid claim to Forest Home in 1938, for $30,000. Each year since, several thousand young people throughout California and beyond have experienced God at this wonderful place, through teaching and worship in the refreshing spirit of its visionary founder.

It was to this new retreat center in 1949 that another young Bill came to meet with Henrietta before preaching at his first big crusade. Billy Graham was feeling the pressure of the monumental task before him. Henrietta prayed and counseled with him, encouraging him to renew his trust in the Lord, to believe what the Bible promised. The Los Angeles crusade was a success, and many more followed.

Such was the effect this tiny Sunday school teacher with the thick glasses had on thousands of young leaders and future leaders. Her students and protégés became missionaries and evangelists, founded great churches and ministries, and multiplied her own ministry a thousandfold. Henrietta reclaimed the vocation of Christian education from what was once largely boring, impractical, and unbiblical into a passionate, active, life-changing exploration of God and who he wants us to become. Chances are, if you've been touched by effective teaching in the church, you're a part of Henrietta's legacy too.

LEGACY

Henrietta didn't know the meaning of a small plan. To her, every action, every relationship was an opportunity to carry out God's greater plan. She couldn't know exactly how her students would change our world. But she could believe in a God who knew such things, so she did her part with passion and wonder and hope and trusted God to polish those she shaped.

For additional information about Gospel Literature International, see appendix A.

Let us hold unswervingly to the hope we profess, for he who promised is faithful. Hebrews 10:23, NIV

BOOKS BY HENRIETTA MEARS

What the Bible Is All About (1997)
What the Bible Is All About 101: Old Testament: Genesis—Esther Group Study Guide (1996)
What the Bible Is All About 102: Old Testament: Job—Malachi Group Study Guide (1996)
What the Bible Is All About 201: New Testament: Matthew—Philippians Group Study Guide (1996)
What the Bible Is All About 202: New Testament: Colossians—Revelation Group Study Guide (1997)

THOMAS MERTON

LIVING IN THE MYSTERY

Jesus made no compromise with a merely
worldly society. Confronted with kingship,
His answer was not even a word—it was
rejection and solitude. But he emerged from
his solitude to teach of a "society" that
was to be one flesh and one bloodstream
with himself, a mystical union of all men
in His Body, where solitude and the common
life are realized perfectly both together
at the same time.

The Sign of Jonas

S eeking refuge from a world that had pulled him into its most tempting corruptions, Thomas Merton entered a monastery to pursue the Incorruptible. Seven years later he emerged from his refuge for the first time for a six-hour sojourn into the outside world. When it was over, he was a changed man. "The world was not so wicked after all. Perhaps the things I resented about the world when I left it were defects of my own that I had projected upon it," he contemplated.

Perhaps there could be coexistence. He had seen the image called Man, and saw through that image the presence and grace of the Creator of all images. As the gates closed behind him once more, instead of fear, he carried compassion. And in his compassion, he began to write to those in the world, to help them discover the one whose sojourn in this world gave us a vision of the next.

IN SHORT

For over two decades Catholic monk Thomas Merton wrote about the God he pursued from inside the monastery gates. His widely read books on prayer, contemplative living, social action, and many other topics are embraced by Catholics and Protestants alike. He has inspired millions to pursue the incorruptible God from the confines of our corruptible world.

FAITH

Thomas Merton was born January 31, 1915, in Prades, France. His father, Owen Merton, was a landscape painter from New Zealand. His American mother, Ruth Jenkins, had studied interior design.

The cosmopolitan couple moved to New York when Thomas was a year old. When his mother died five years later, he lived with his grandparents much of the time as his father spent long periods away from home to pursue his painting career. Eventually his father landed back in France, and ten-year-old Thomas went to live there too—but in a boarding school.

Three years later father and son moved again, this time to England. Thomas was placed in another boarding school. He joined in the pastimes of his fellow students: drinking, smoking, and pursuing girls. These things became habits he would indulge for many years. In the summer of his sixteenth year, he found out that his father had an inoperable brain tumor. Owen Merton died a few months later. His father's death was tragic, but after spending most of his life away from him, Thomas carried on at boarding school as before.

A year after his father died, between the end of his studies at the boarding school and the start of his first term at Cambridge University, Thomas was given a jolt that turned his attentions to God. In his room one night, he was suddenly overwhelmed by a sense that his father was in the room with him. As Merton described it, "The sense of his presence was as vivid and as real and as startling as if he had touched my arm or spoken to me." The sensation was momentary, but in its wake it exposed the state of his soul. "And now, I think for the first time in my whole life I really began to pray . . . praying out of the very roots of my life and of my being, and praying to the God I had never known, to reach down towards me out of His darkness. . . ."

The next day Thomas did something else for the first time—he went to church, knelt down, and prayed. He went away feeling "reborn" and full of joy. Soon afterward he took a trip to visit his grandparents in the United States. He went to church there and read the Bible and tried to pray. But his boarding-school lifestyle had not left him, and he was soon up to his old habits again.

At Cambridge, Merton lived large. He skipped classes, drank heartily, ran up bills he could not afford, got into fights, and was arrested for partaking in a dangerous car stunt. But two things checked his excesses. The suicide of an acquaintance exposed the despair he himself felt inside. And the girl he had slept with got pregnant and gave birth to a son. Merton was pursued by a lawyer, but his guardian kept the case out of court by making a financial settlement. Merton took off to America and had no further contact with either the girl or their son. Years later both were killed in the German air raids on London.

Safe in the U.S. but racked with guilt, Merton entered New York's Columbia University. He took courses in Spanish, German, and French Renaissance literature, pledged a fraternity, ran cross-country, drew cartoons, and wrote for the school magazines and newspapers. He smoked and drank heavily while becoming intensely active in every pursuit he could find. After receiving a bachelor's degree, he stayed at Columbia and got a master's degree in English, thinking he would like to be a university professor. But even as he pursued women and lived hard, Merton began again to consider his soul, knowing that who he was and what he wanted to become were still very far apart. Finally, he went to Mass one Sunday—the first Sunday he had been sober since returning to New York. He was now ready to pursue God.

On November 16, 1938, Merton took his first Communion after being baptized into the Catholic Church. The weeks he had spent getting ready to be received into the church were some of the happiest he had ever had. But still the old habits died hard. He attended Mass often through the week, went to confession, and took Communion—and went to wild parties, got terrible hangovers, and had affairs with women. Meanwhile, he worked on a Ph.D., wrote poetry and novels, and provided book reviews for the *New York Times* and the *Herald Tribune*.

One weekend on a trip with some friends, Merton was suddenly taken by the idea of becoming a priest. He told his friends, who were baffled. But on the way home, he stopped into a church, praying, "Yes, I want to be a priest, with all my heart I want it. If it is Your will, make me a priest—make me a priest."

Finally, he had found the motivation to change his ways. He quit smoking, gave up heavy drinking, attended Mass daily, and applied with the Franciscan order to begin his training. He felt he must tell them about his old life, so he confessed the drinking, the parties, the affairs, and his son. The Franciscans advised him to withdraw his application.

Merton was heartbroken. It was no longer a question of whether he wanted to lead an obedient life. It had moved from a desire to a necessity. "There could be no more question of living just like everybody else in the world. There could be no more compromises with the life that tried, at every turn, to feed me poison. I had to turn my back on these things." For the first time, he saw faith not as a means to a vocation but as the hope of life itself. "All I knew was that I wanted grace, and that I needed prayer, and that I was helpless without God."

Fruit

At this critical point in his faith journey, Merton got involved in a ministry to children in Harlem. At the same time, he was considering entering a monastery. He had to make a choice. Would he stay in the city and serve, or would he forsake the world, and even this good ministry, to seek God from the depths of his being? In his journal he wrote: "I return to the idea again and again: 'Give up everything, give up everything!'" On December 10, 1941, at the age of twenty-six, he entered the Gethsemani, a Trappist monastery in Kentucky. He was ordained in 1949 and made a novice Master six years later.

His first book written from the monastery, *The Seven Storey Mountain,* was an autobiography. Published in 1946, it became a best-seller and a classic and established its author as a prominent religious figure and Catholic writer. In 1948 he visited the world outside the monastery and returned to the monastery with a new purpose to his life. His insight on prayer and the contemplative life was meant to be shared with the world, and he wrote prolifically on these subjects for the next two decades.

In the 1960s Merton turned to more controversial issues such as race relations, violence, nuclear war, and economic injustice. He wrote a series of antiwar articles for *Catholic Worker,* urging people to understand the psychological forces operative in themselves and in society. In 1964 he was admonished by his superiors not to write further about nuclear war. He chided popes, bishops, and theologians for not condemning it. Merton saw prayer and social action as interdependent and could not embrace one without the other.

Merton's writing of this period caused much controversy, but it was his secret passions that nearly brought him to disaster. While hospitalized for a back problem, he met a student nurse who had read one of his books. The two began a friendship that became romantic, and they carried on a secret relationship. Merton declared his love and wondered how he could live without her. When his superior discovered what was going on, he ordered Merton not to contact the young woman again. The relationship ended.

Thomas Merton was killed in an accident while attending a meeting of religious leaders in Bangkok. He died on December 10, 1968, twenty-seven years to the day from his entrance into the monastery.

LEGACY
Thomas Merton lived a wild, worldly life before entering the ministry. He had seen the world, indulged in its pleasures, and had come up wanting. What he wanted most was a completeness, a filling of something that humanity couldn't supply. When he found this missing piece in God, he abandoned all else to pursue him.

Some question the wisdom of such a radical act. How can a person who removes himself from society serve as a light to its members? Merton shows us how. His writing, forged in monastic isolation, gives us a unique view of our world as seen from another one. He was regarded by many as a spiritual master, a brilliant religious writer, a man who embodied the quest for God and human solidarity in the modern world. Over sixty volumes of his writings are in print in English, with foreign translations in publication the world over. He was a leader in monastic renewal, making Western Catholic monasticism accessible to the world through his writings. Much of the current interest in contemplative living among Protestants can be traced to him.

Through Thomas Merton, Christians of all traditions have been exposed to the mystery of the complexity of life, in all its earthiness, reaching for that which is divine.

[The grace of God] teaches us to say "No" to ungod-
liness and worldly passions, and to live self-
controlled, upright and godly lives in this present age. Titus 2:12, NIV

BOOKS BY THOMAS MERTON

Ascent to Truth (1989)
*At Home in the World: The Letters of Thomas Merton and Rosemary
    Radford Ruether* (edited by Mary Tardiff) (1995)
Bread in the Wilderness (1986)
Contemplation in a World of Action (Gethsemani Studies in Psychological
    and Religious Anthropology with Robert Coles) (1999)
Contemplative Prayer (1971)
Courage for Truth (1994)
Dancing in the Water of Life: Seeking Peace in the Hermitage (with
    Robert Daggy) (1998)
Elected Silence: The Autobiography of Thomas Merton (1949)
Last of the Fathers (1982)
New Seeds of Contemplation (1972)
No Man Is an Island (1978)
Run to the Mountain: The Story of a Vocation (1997)
The Asian Journal of Thomas Merton (1973)
The Collected Poems of Thomas Merton (1980)
The New Man (1978)
The Other Side of the Mountain: The End of the Journey (Journals of
    Thomas Merton, vol. 7, 1967–1968) (1998)
The Seven Storey Mountain (1990)
The Silent Life (1975)
The Wisdom of the Desert (1970)
Thoughts in Solitude (1976)

1865 – 1955

JOHN MOTT

CALLING YOUNG LEADERS TO SERVE

The only program which can
meet all the alarming facts
of the situation is the
worldwide spread
of Christianity in its
purest form.

The Evangelization of the World in This Generation, expressing
Mott's view of his life calling to evangelism

The famous preacher Dwight L. Moody held his first College Students Summer School in July 1886 in Mt. Hermon, Massachusetts. Halfway through the one-month conference, a group of young men met on their own to talk about missions. Fourteen students signed a solemn pledge to enter the mission field. They continued to meet, talk, and pray about missions, and soon there were twenty-one signatures. Then fifty. By the end of the conference the list contained one hundred names of the students who would become known as the Mt. Hermon Hundred.

John Mott was number twenty-three. He had no idea that his pledge to enter the mission field would lead tens of thousands of students after him to do the same.

IN SHORT
Missionary, Christian ambassador, and Nobel Peace laureate John Mott did more to mobilize young men and women to ministry than any other leader in the first half of the twentieth century. At a time when denomination, race, and nationality isolated Christians from each other and prevented large-scale missions efforts, Mott recruited legions of Christian students of all traditions, colors, and nations to overcome the things that divided and to work together in the one thing that united: the cause of Christ.

FAITH
John Raleigh Mott was born in Sullivan County, New York, on May 25, 1865, just weeks after Abraham Lincoln's assassination.

Four months after his birth his parents moved the family west to a farm in Postville, Iowa. John's father, John Stitt Mott, bought a partnership in a retail lumberyard in Postville and eventually bought out his partners' interests and later his competitors'. He also added a line of hardware to sell to the area's farms, and when the town was incorporated, he became its first mayor. The junior John's mother, Elmira, completed Postville's "First Family" as a vigorous, attractive, intelligent woman with an insatiable appetite for learning. Together the Motts raised their children to cherish their Christian faith and their community.

As a boy John understood that the family business would be his when he was ready for it. He learned bookkeeping and kept a meticulous inventory of the business's wares. While working in the lumberyard, he also learned how to serve an international assortment of customers as immigrant farmers from England, Germany, and Scandinavia settled in the area. Even in America's heartland John was being exposed to a much wider world.

In 1879 an evangelist from the Young Men's Christian Association came to Postville. John, now thirteen, attended a revival and made a commitment to Christ. Later another visiting minister took an interest in John and sparked his interest in going to college. So at age sixteen he left the family business and entered Upper Iowa University, a Methodist school. He became a dedicated student, grew in his faith, excelled at speech and debate, and had several articles published in the school newspaper. As he discovered his talent for persuasive communication, he also developed a desire to attend a better school.

In September 1885 John arrived at New York's Cornell University. Immediately he became involved in the University Christian Association, and in December he was elected vice president. At the end of his first year at Cornell the campus ministry selected John to attend Moody's College Students Summer School, where he signed the mission pledge that would direct the rest of his life.

FRUIT
After graduating from Cornell, Mott received several ministry offers. The one he accepted was with the college ministry of the

Young Men's Christian Association. His position put him in contact with student ministries on many college campuses throughout North America. This led him to help form an umbrella organization, the Student Volunteer Movement for Foreign Missions, which incorporated the campus ministries of several organizations. Mott was elected chairman of what became known as SVM upon its formation in December 1888, a position he would hold until 1920.

Early in his ministry Mott met Leila Ada White, the sister of an associate. He fell in love at first sight. They were married on Thanksgiving Day in 1891. She accepted his total preoccupation with his work, beginning with organizing student campus ministries while on their honeymoon. In the ministry she became his editor and confidante and objective honest critic. She also helped to slow him down when he was overdoing it. They had four children, who often accompanied their father on his national and international trips.

In 1895 John and Leila sailed to England to begin a twenty-month tour of student ministries in other countries. Before the tour, Mott saw the formation of the Federation of Student Christian Organizations, the world's first global association of student ministries. Mott became the general secretary.

Working through his national ministry, SVM, in association with overseas ministries connected with the Federation, Mott helped to coordinate the sending of many students into the mission field. By 1906, the twentieth anniversary of his Mt. Hermon Hundred pledge, nearly three thousand student volunteers had been sent overseas. They constituted two-thirds of the missionaries sent from the United States. Each year Mott traveled the country, speaking at colleges and conferences, inspiring students to answer God's call to missions.

President Woodrow Wilson, a childhood friend from Iowa, noted Mott's superior motivational and organizational skills as well as his diplomatic acumen. Wilson invited Mott to become ambassador to China, but Mott respectfully declined, convinced that to accept would be a betrayal of the call he had received from God.

But when America entered World War I, Mott served his country in another way. Rallying his national and international ministries, he sent volunteers to Europe under the auspices of the YMCA to minister to battle-weary soldiers and to bring relief to prisoners of war on both sides. Former president Taft called attention to the effort, declaring it one of the greatest works of peace in the history of war and crediting Mott's organizational genius and inspiring leadership for its success.

Mott's work with the YMCA continued after the war. In 1926 he became president of the World's Alliance of Young Men's Christian Associations, spearheading its efforts to inspire young people to work for peace between nations. And after World War II, he traveled throughout Europe, conducting the work of rehabilitation among its victims and reforging the links between national ministry and humanitarian organizations that had been established after the first war. In recognition of these efforts, Mott received the Nobel Peace Prize in 1946.

Among Mott's greatest accomplishments were his efforts to bring Christians together. Many denominations and organizations insisted on working alone in the mission field, often creating discord and competition and leaving their student missionaries isolated and unsupported by their Christian brothers and sisters. Mott saw missions not as a call to churches but as a command to the church worldwide. He organized and assisted in the leadership of many important international conferences, led the work of the International Missionary Council, and served as a tireless diplomat to bring Christian ministries together for their common purpose.

Just as he sought to remove human barriers to evangelism in other parts of the world, Mott worked to see such walls torn down in the United States. In the segregated South, where churches were among the most segregated of all institutions, he worked with a movement that brought black and white Christians together in integrated associations. He did the same in his own organizations, seeing to it that skin color would not keep Christians from carrying out Christ's work.

This larger God-ordained mission was the focus of everything he did. The organizations he served in—the Student Volunteer Movement, the YMCA, the Student Federation, the International Missionary Council—flourished under his leadership for a generation. In his hands they were instruments for creating a spirit of Christian love from which peace could flow.

John Mott died at his home in Orlando, Florida, at the age of eighty-nine, bringing to an end a long and fruitful life of inspiring tens of thousands of young people to Christian service, to the mission field, and to the cause of peace. But his legacy lives on through the lives of the students he inspired, students who became ministers and missionaries and leaders, who in turn inspired another generation of students to break through the human barriers that keep Christians from each other and from the people they are called to serve.

Legacy

John Mott was an ambassador for Christ among the nations. Few men have traveled in so many countries or spoken to so many people. And it is likely that none has inspired as many young men and women to enter the mission field. Indeed, Mott's influence on just one such student, Cameron Townsend, led this young man to found a Bible translation ministry that spans the globe. Mott's role in the lives of countless other future leaders is immeasurable.

The students who flocked to Mott's organizations, joined him in worldwide missions conferences, and followed his leading overseas were Protestant, Roman Catholic, and Orthodox, coming from every Christian tradition on earth. Mott sought to shape them into Christian leaders whose love transcended the frontiers that separated people. All races had a valuable contribution to make to the spiritual community, he believed. And all races and nations needed Christ to reveal himself in all his power and glory. "God is our Father," Mott said. "But if God is our Father, then we are all brothers, and no frontiers or racial divisions can separate us from each other."

For additional information about the YMCA, see appendix A.

All this newness of life is from God, who brought us back to himself through what Christ did. And God has given us the task of reconciling people to him. For God was in Christ, reconciling the world to himself, no longer counting people's sins against them. This is the wonderful message he has given us to tell others. We are Christ's ambassadors, and God is using us to speak to you. We urge you, as though Christ himself were here pleading with you, "Be reconciled to God!"

2 Corinthians 5:18-20

BOOKS BY JOHN R. MOTT

The Evangelization of the World in This Generation (1972)
The Moslem World of Today (1986)

1926–

J. I. PACKER

KNOWING GOD

The question is, can we say, simply,
honestly, not because we feel that
as evangelicals we ought to, but
because it is a plain matter of fact,
that we have known God, and that
because we have known God, the
unpleasantness we have had or the
pleasantness we have not had,
through being Christians
does not matter to us?

Knowing God

I n 1933 a bully chased a shy seven-year-old student out of the
school and onto a busy street, where he was struck by a passing
truck and thrown to the ground. He was rushed to the hospital
with a crushed skull. The surgery was successful, but the boy was
left with a small hole in his skull where the fragmented bone had
been removed. Forced to wear a protective metal guard, he was
sidelined from sports and ostracized by his peers. But he looked
forward to one thing: a bicycle for his eleventh birthday.

James Packer's cautious parents bought him a typewriter
instead.

In Short

While other children played, young J. I. Packer wrote stories and
read books to pass the time. These hobbies developed in him a
superior ability to think critically and logically, and when he
became a Christian, he applied his mental skills to his faith. The
result of all that thinking has elevated this theologian, professor,
and writer to a place among the greatest Christian minds of the
twentieth century. For thousands of his students and millions of
his readers, Packer has blown the dust off theology, transforming
its study into a thrilling quest to know God.

Faith

James Innell Packer was born July 22, 1926, in Twyning, Gloucester-
shire, England, to James and Dorothy Packer. His father was a rail-
way clerk, his mother a schoolmistress. As a child J. I. was something
of a loner. His awkward shyness made it difficult for him to relate to

other children. Still, he dreamed of becoming a star cricket player—a dream that was dashed the day of his horrible accident. The aluminum plate he wore to protect the hole in his skull made him a bit of a curiosity—he could hold his friends riveted as he told the gory details—but the novelty wore off long before the plate disappeared, as he was forced to wear it until he entered the university.

As a result of his "curious features," the already shy J. I. distanced himself even further from others, passing the rest of his childhood in a lonely melancholy. But the typewriter he received instead of a bike pushed him into the larger world of his own imagination. The stories he wrote worked the muscles of his innate linear thinking and analytical skills, sharpening his ability and appetite for learning.

In his teenage years Packer applied some of his thinking to the topic of faith. He attended the local Anglican church and was confirmed there at age fourteen. The following year he began having conversations about religion with a frequent chess opponent who happened to be the son of a Unitarian minister. The discussions set Packer's mind to considering the differences between the teachings of these rival religions.

His logical thinking led him to the errors in Unitarian doctrine, but it also led him to ask, What is true Christianity? The search to find the answer started in a just-published book a teacher had assigned to him, *The Screwtape Letters* by C. S. Lewis. He also began a vigorous study of the Scriptures, reading from his grandmother's Bible because he didn't have one of his own. As a result of his inquiry he determined intellectually that the historical Christian faith was real.

Packer entered Oxford's Corpus Christi College in the fall of 1944. A committed Christian friend had encouraged him to seek out members of the campus InterVarsity ministry. Packer followed his advice. A month after his arrival, he was sitting in a church service when a picture formed in his mind. Packer saw himself standing outside, looking into a home where a party was in progress. The meaning was clear: While others were in the faith, he was still on the outside. When he walked out that night, he knew he was a Christian, in both mind and heart.

In his new faith Packer continued to investigate the historical doctrines and current practices of the church. He found various and conflicting views. With the many shades of faith he found, none passed his intellectual examination and met his real spiritual needs.

A known bookworm, Packer was asked to work in the library of the Oxford Inter-Collegiate Christian Union (OICCU) at Saint Aldate's Church, one of the larger churches in the city, known for its significant student ministries. As he began reading the books under his care, he found an edition of Puritan John Owen's *On the Mortification of Sin in Believers.*

The Puritans presented their doctrine in a way that was as theologically solid as it was spiritually alive. Packer determined that this was exactly what he wanted to do himself: With theological substance and spiritual fervor he would combine the Anglican with the evangelical, the old with the new, the truth with the passion to live it.

FRUIT

Packer decided he needed two things to pursue his ministry vision: further theological training and ordination in the Church of England. He did his doctoral work at Oxford on the Puritans and spent some time teaching. His examination of Puritanism prompted him to publish articles on the subject and to organize an annual conference for others who were studying the Puritan ways. The conferences were a success, in part because a prominent minister, David Martyn Lloyd-Jones, enthusiastically endorsed and chaired them.

Shortly before Packer's ordination in 1952 a friend asked Packer to cover for him at a speaking engagement. He did not enjoy public situations, but he agreed to do it. When Packer finished his message that night, everyone left the room, leaving him standing alone at the speaker's table. A young nursing student by the name of Kit Mullett spotted him in his awkwardness and came up to greet him. This act alone caught Packer's attention, but when she told him that he reminded her of her pastor, Martyn Lloyd-Jones, he was smitten.

Packer went home that night, but he didn't get much sleep. He couldn't get his mind off Kit. They were married on July 17, 1954, the week after the groom had turned in his five-hundred-page doctoral dissertation.

Meanwhile, Packer had been serving as a curate in an Anglican church. Among his many duties was teaching the doctrine class to the youth. He left this position in 1955 to become assistant lecturer at Tyndale Hall in Bristol, a theological school with a strong emphasis on biblical study.

Packer's first book, *Fundamentalism and the Word of God,* was published in 1958. In it he demonstrated rationally that authentic evangelicalism carried all the intellectual rigor that the liberals presumed to be their domain.

From the response of his students and readers Packer knew that his work was addressing a great longing for spiritual vitality among Anglicans. In 1961 he left his teaching position at Tyndale Hall to join the staff at Latimer House, a think tank and resource center for evangelicals, where Packer played an instrumental part in its formation and direction. Working with other prominent church leaders, Packer helped lead a major renewal movement in Britain's mainline churches that lasted through most of the 1960s.

But as the evangelical fervor grew, so did the discord. Some leaders, including Packer's old friend and Puritan Conference partner Martyn Lloyd-Jones, believed evangelicals should leave the Anglican and other mainline denominations and join or establish churches that embraced their doctrine.

Packer was an evangelical. He was also an Anglican. He would not desert the Church of England. Nor would he desert his non-Anglican friends. To Packer they were all brothers and sisters in Christ, bound together to bring renewal not just in the churches but in the *church.* This commitment cost him dearly. In 1970, after Packer published a book with two Catholics, Lloyd-Jones formally "disfellowshipped" his old friend from the movement the two had helped to start. This ended the Puritan Conferences as well as Packer's positions on various evangelical boards and committees.

Cut off from the evangelical movement, Packer also faced a crisis within his own denomination. Having left Latimer House in

1970, he returned to Tyndale Hall to serve as principal. This school, as well as other theological schools in Britain, was facing a steady decrease in students, resulting in fewer and fewer candidates for ordination. To deal with the problem the Anglican Church proposed merging Tyndale Hall with another school. When Packer responded to the proposal, he presented evidence to show that the merger was unworkable. In reply, the commission decided to close the school altogether.

Packer tried furiously to save his college. After much debate the Church of England's governing board decided to open a new school, to be called Trinity College, which would embrace and impart an evangelical vision. But when the school came into existence on January 1, 1972, Packer was passed over for the position of principal and was given the title of associate principal instead.

The "lesser" position came with a silver lining: Packer now had more time to travel, speak, and write, and he put this time to immediate use. His book *Knowing God* was published in 1973. When the book came out, Packer immediately gained international acclaim. By 1992 *Knowing God* had reached the million mark in copies sold. The success of this book convinced Packer of the importance of relating theology and spirituality. Yet in Britain his "Anglican evangelicalism" still seemed to many to be a contradiction in terms.

But across the Atlantic it was a different story. There, evangelicals found his passionate view on doctrine as refreshing as it was biblical. When the famous "Battle for the Bible" erupted in the U.S., with many Christian leaders fighting over the issue of inerrancy, Packer was invited to participate in the meetings as an objective outsider. Out of this debate came the International Council on Biblical Inerrancy (ICBI), which he helped to found in 1977.

The year before ICBI's founding, Packer was invited to take the theology chair at Regent Theological Seminary in Vancouver, British Columbia. He requested that the position be held open for a few years so that his departure from England would not be viewed as walking out on the Church of England. The school agreed.

Packer moved to Canada and took the position at Regent, as promised, in 1979.

His ministry and the school where he teaches have flourished ever since. In breaks from his own courses Packer continues to write and to lecture at seminaries throughout North America. And as always he finds himself in the middle of controversies and battles between evangelicals and Christians from mainline traditions despite his consistent, vigorous commitment to Reformed theology and his unwillingness to give any ground on critical theological issues.

LEGACY

It's not hard to discover J. I. Packer's purpose in life; it's printed on the cover of 1.5 million books: *Knowing God.* This is what he set out to do before he became a Christian, and his own faith was the first result of that pursuit. The pursuit led him to rediscover the Puritans and their refreshing melding of doctrine and passion. It brought him to ordination in the Anglican Church and to a fight to ensure an evangelical presence in its seminaries.

The pursuit continues. He has written, edited, or contributed to over fifty books, devotionals, commentaries, Bibles, and encyclopedias. And he continues to teach at Regent and to lecture at other schools, reaching thousands of ministry candidates each year.

Despite immense pressure, criticism, and ostracism from his evangelical compatriots, Packer refused to abandon his denomination. He remained an Anglican because he found a biblically solid, intellectually sound foundation beneath his church's dusty traditions and liberal distractions.

Through the example of his life and the deep wisdom in his writing, J. I. Packer has redefined theology as not merely wrestling with biblical texts and their ideas but with the living God. He shows us that the wrestling match starts in both mind *and* heart and continues as it engulfs the church God has given us, drawing the world's spectators into the fray.

So, my dear brothers and sisters, be strong and steady, always enthusiastic about the Lord's work, for you know that nothing you do for the Lord is ever useless. 1 Corinthians 15:58

BOOKS BY J. I. PACKER

A Quest for Godliness: The Puritan Vision of the Christian Life (1994)
Decisions: Finding God's Will (1996)
Evangelism and the Sovereignty of God (1991)
God Has Spoken: Revelation and the Bible (1994)
Growing in Christ (1994)
Illustrated Manners and Customs of the Bible (1997)
In God's Presence: Daily Devotions with J. I. Packer (1998)
Knowing and Doing the Will of God (1995)
Knowing Christianity (1999)
Knowing God (1973)
Life in the Spirit: A 30-Day Personal Bible Study (1996)
Meeting God: 12 Studies for Individuals or Groups (Lifebuilder Bible Studies) (1989)
Never beyond Hope: How God Touches and Uses Imperfect People (2000)
Rediscovering Holiness (1994)
Revelation (Crossway Classic Commentaries) (1999)
The Collected Shorter Writings of J. I. Packer (1999)
Truth and Power: The Place of Scripture in the Christian Life (1999)

1934–

LUIS PALAU

MOVING THE MASSES TOWARD CHRIST

My wish and desire is that
people get right with God,
settle the big question, and
die happy knowing they
will be with Jesus.

Calling America and the Nations to Christ

In the 1960s and 1970s a young Argentine evangelist swept across Latin America with crusades that filled soccer stadiums to overflowing and saw tens of thousands make decisions for Christ. Soon he ventured overseas to Spain and Britain, Germany and the Soviet Union. There was one country, however, where he would not hold a campaign. Despite a burden to answer the many invitations he had received from cities across America, the country in which he was now a citizen, he felt that he could not enter this mission field without the blessing of its elder statesman-evangelist, Billy Graham. He made up his mind to give Graham a call.

But Billy beat him to it. After reading an article in *Christianity Today* about the success of Luis Palau's crusades around the world, he called Luis and told him to "get on with it"—wherever God led him to preach. With his model and mentor's blessing Palau brought his worldwide crusade to America too.

IN SHORT

Teenage Luis Palau first heard Billy Graham on the radio in his native Argentina and prayed that God might make him an evangelist to the masses too. God answered his prayer. Ten years later Palau began an evangelistic campaign for Christ that spilled out of Latin America and poured across the globe. To date, over half a million people have followed him to Christ. And after three decades of mass evangelism his prayers and plans make it clear that he considers himself just halfway into his career.

FAITH

Luis Palau was born on November 27, 1934, in Buenos Aires, Argentina. His father, Luis, was a successful construction businessman with Spanish roots. His mother, Matilde, came from French and Scottish ancestry. The young Luis's multicultural heritage would shape his view of the world and eventually draw him into a career that spanned the globe.

His religious heritage was blended as well. His parents were nominally Catholic, members of the official church in Argentina. They had their son baptized into this church although they themselves were not believers. But while he was still a boy, Luis's parents met Christ through the "tent-making" ministry of a Shell Oil executive, a committed Christian and associate of Luis senior. His parents' new commitment to Christ and compassion for the lost had an effect on the junior Luis. But as a boy he was "hot tempered and quick tongued," so their Christian teaching brought him much guilt but no conversion.

Seeking to provide the best possible education for their son, the Palaus sent Luis to a British boarding school near Buenos Aires. Two years later the young scholar's father died of pneumonia. Luis arrived home from school too late to say good-bye. The next year, in 1945, Luis moved to another boarding school in Argentina: Saint Alban's College, part of the Cambridge University Overseas Program.

In February 1947, in the heart of the Argentine summer, twelve-year-old Luis met Christ. He was at a summer camp sponsored by his school, a camp he didn't want to attend because he knew it was part of a conspiracy by his mother and headmaster to get him converted. Luis had heard the gospel many, many times, but late one night in his tent his counselor woke him so that he might hear it again. They sat on a log in the rain, and when they were done talking, Luis had accepted Christ. Palau remembered what happened next: "Back in my tent, by the light of my flashlight, I wrote in my Bible: 'February 12, 1947, I received Jesus Christ.'"

His first years of faith were rocky ones. After the death of Luis's father the family suffered severe financial problems, which Luis was quick to blame on the "privileged and educated English." He left his English Bible on a train, set aside his faith, and later, when he had returned to that faith, he purchased a Bible in Spanish. But his rigorous British education and the associations he made in school kept him in the English world, and in his later teen years he accepted a trainee position with the Bank of London in Buenos Aires and decided on international banking as his career. Palau excelled in his work and received a series of promotions that eventually led to an executive position at another branch.

Meanwhile, his faith blossomed. In 1952 he first heard Billy Graham on the radio and prayed that God would lead him to become an evangelist like Graham. He immersed himself in biographies of great church leaders and evangelists such as Martin Luther, John Calvin, George Whitefield, John Wesley, Dwight L. Moody, and Billy Sunday and read books by influential Bible teachers Oswald Chambers, J. I. Packer, and many others. He began an extensive personal Bible study, became active in a local church, and was soon speaking at outdoor evangelistic meetings and on the radio. The young man was so consumed with becoming a minister that his coworkers at the bank began calling him Pastor.

There was just one problem: Despite his best evangelistic efforts, no one was following him to Christ. Palau made a decision: He told God that if he did not confirm Luis's calling by the end of the year, Luis would still serve him but would give up the idea of evangelism. God responded. One day at a Bible study Palau attended the leader didn't show up, so Luis stepped in. When it was over, a woman had come to Christ. Her conversion was so dramatic that Luis walked all the way home, crying and confessing that he would answer the call to evangelism.

FRUIT

By 1957, while Palau was still in his early twenties, he and other young believers had organized a tent-evangelism and radio ministry in Argentina. In two more years he left his position at the bank and joined an American-based missions organization working in Latin America. At a conference in Argentina he got an offer from

American pastor Ray Stedman to come to the U.S. to attend seminary. Palau declined, feeling that he could not afford to set aside his ministry for the four years it would take to attain a degree. Later Palau received the same offer again, but this time it was agreed that Palau could attend the much shorter graduate program at Multnomah School of the Bible.

Palau accepted, moved to Portland, Oregon, and graduated from Multnomah School of the Bible (now Multnomah Biblical Seminary) in 1961. He left with more than a degree. While there he met Patricia Marilyn Scofield, a fellow student, and the two were married.

Life for the newlyweds moved quickly. Palau joined the mission group Overseas Crusades, now known as OC International, and completed its seven-month training program in Detroit. By the end of 1962 Luis had become a U.S. citizen and was serving as Spanish interpreter for Billy Graham at a crusade in Fresno, California. In the next year he was ordained at Stedman's Peninsula Bible Church in Palo Alto, California, saw the birth of his twin sons, and took a church-planting assignment in Colombia with OC International.

Through the remainder of the decade Palau's ministry expanded across Latin America. His regular radio broadcasts in Colombia began in 1965 and were soon picked up by stations in other countries. They continue today, daily reaching a Spanish-speaking audience estimated at twenty-two million. In 1968 in Bogotá Palau held his first large-scale evangelistic crusade, drawing twenty thousand. In the late sixties and early seventies he ran crusades in Mexico, Honduras, and Peru, with some crusades seeing over one hundred thousand people in attendance. Soon he was holding Spanish-language crusades in Nicaragua, Bolivia, and Spain.

In 1978 the Luis Palau Evangelistic Association (LPEA) was formed, with headquarters in Portland, Oregon. By the end of the decade Palau's crusades had branched out to the non-Hispanic world too, in Germany and Britain, and in Australia through a partnership with Billy Graham. And after that significant phone call from Billy Graham telling Luis to "get on with it," Palau began to expand his ministry to the United States with Graham's blessing.

Throughout the eighties and nineties he has held dozens of massive crusades on several continents, preaching in English and Spanish and in dozens of other languages through interpreters. The list of countries is great, including most of Eastern Europe and Asia, regions long closed to such large-scale forms of evangelism.

In Latin America, where Palau has concentrated much of his attention, Marxist radicals have often challenged Luis's ministry, calling him a Yankee imperialist, and a widespread negative press has accused him of changing the customs and culture of the people. Palau has been a gracious opponent, praying with those willing to meet with him, inviting student activists to join in his crusades, and allowing even the negative publicity to attract thousands of people who come to hear for themselves what the controversy is all about. To all who dare to listen, Palau offers a faith that transcends class, culture, and politics.

Although more than thirteen million people worldwide have heard the gospel from Palau's own lips and twice that many have heard him through radio, Palau considers these numbers insignificant in comparison with the hundreds of millions who have never heard about Jesus. He looks to the future with great hope and strategic plans to reach those who so far have been left behind. As he writes in his autobiography, *Calling America and the Nations to Christ*, "Some people think I'm joking when I say it, but I plan to preach until I'm ninety-two, as the Lord gives me strength. I may not be as vigorous, but my mind can be as clear. Certainly my knowledge of the Lord and Scripture ought to be better. If the invitations keep coming, I want to preach until the very end."

LEGACY

Some people wonder if the days of effective mass evangelism are nearing an end. If they are, the millions who attend crusades by Graham, Palau, and other renowned evangelists don't know it. While Luis Palau encourages one-on-one evangelism, he believes that mass evangelism plays an essential role in societies: "It's eventually necessary to move the masses, sway public opinion, influence the thought patterns of the media. Simply put, a nation will not be changed by timid methods. It must be confronted, challenged, hit with the truth again and again, forcefully, in the power of God's Holy Spirit."

Palau implemented this strategy behind the Iron Curtain before it fell, and he returned to multiply the fruit after it did. He envisions a day when such evangelism can take place in the Middle East. Some may scoff, but Luis has seen God open closed cultures before, and he plans to be there when it happens again. Once a message is shouted in a stadium, it cannot be silenced in the streets.

In the sunset of Billy Graham's career of evangelism, many see his Hispanic protégé as the next "Billy." To those who speak Spanish, the world's third most common language, Luis Palau already is.

For additional information about the Luis Palau Evangelistic Association, see appendix A.

Go into all the world and preach the Good News to everyone, everywhere. Mark 16:15

BOOKS BY LUIS PALAU

A Biblical Look at the Family (1991)
A Man after God's Heart (1998)
Calling America and the Nations to Christ (1994)
Dream Great Dreams (1984)
Experiencing God's Forgiveness (1984)
Experiencing Personal Renewal (1992)
God Is Relevant: Finding Strength and Peace in Today's World (1997)
Healthy Habits for Spiritual Growth (1994)
How to Lead Your Child to Christ (1991)
Say Yes! How to Renew Your Spiritual Passion (1995)
The Moment to Shout (1999)
The Only Hope for America (1996)
The Peter Promise: Powerful Principles from the Life of Peter (1996)
The Schemer and the Dreamer (1999)
What Is a Real Christian? (1985)
Where Is God When Bad Things Happen? (1999)
Your New Life with Christ (1996)

1 9 3 0 –

JOHN PERKINS

PREACHING THE WHOLE GOSPEL—
RECONCILIATION WITH GOD AND WITH MAN

Does the gospel—that is, the
gospel as we presently preach
it—does it have within itself
the power to deal with racial
attitudes?

Let Justice Roll Down

A horrified sixteen-year-old John Perkins rushed to the doctor's office. His brother Clyde had been shot by a deputy marshal. *Please live,* the words screamed in his head. *Please live!* The year was 1947. Clyde, twelve years older and a decorated World War II veteran, had been like a father to John.

Now Clyde, home from the service, had taken a girl to the movies in town. They were standing in the back alley at the theater's "colored-man's" entrance and had been talking too loudly. A passing deputy yelled at Clyde to shut up, clubbed him, then shot him twice in the stomach. He was unconscious when his little brother pleaded in his ear. Clyde died during the night.

IN SHORT

John Perkins fled Mississippi to escape a fate similar to that of his murdered brother. Yet as God had once done with Moses, he called John home to lead his people to freedom. And as with Moses, God thrust John into a great struggle against racism, oppression, and injustice. Perkins paid a high price for his obedience, trading a comfortable life in California for a world of hurt—jail, beatings, anxiety illnesses, and despair.

Over time John's direct work has brought hope, faith, economic freedom, and social justice to tens of thousands. And his legacy, including the continuation of social programs he started and the ever-expanding

1980
Named the
Distinguished Black
American in the
*International Who's
Who of Intellectuals*

1980
Named
Mississippi's Most
Outstanding
Religious Leader

1983
Named to
President Reagan's
Task Force on
Food Assistance

1999
Received Prison
Fellowship's
eleventh annual
William
Wilberforce
Award

ministries of individuals he has inspired, has reached millions
across the country and throughout the world.

Faith

John Perkins was born in 1930 into a tough family living in a
sharecropper's house in rural Mississippi. During Prohibition the
Perkinses were bootleggers and gamblers and were known for their
fighting. When John was born, his mother, Maggie Perkins, had
pellagra, a painful disease that results from a diet deficient in
protein foods. Because his mother was unable to nurse him, the
baby grew weak, until his grandmother found a sharecropper who
gave them milk from his cow. Seven months after John was born,
his mother died; his father, Jap, left home; and John's grandmother, who had already raised nineteen children of her own,
took in all five Perkins children. Eventually she gave three of them
away, but because John was little, she kept him.

After Clyde was killed, John's relatives thought it best for him to
leave town, and they sent him west. In California he found a job
that paid blacks and whites equal wages, something he had never
seen before. What's more, there was no segregation; everyone
worked together.

In 1949 on a visit to Mississippi, John met Vera Mae Buckley, a
young woman from a good churchgoing family. Vera Mae was the
closest John had come to Christianity. He had never heard the
simple truth of the gospel and knew nothing about Jesus Christ.
For two years they wrote back and forth, but just as they made
plans to get married, John was drafted into the Korean War. The
two were married just before John left for Okinawa. But his military stint nearly destroyed his marriage. In their first four years as
husband and wife the two had been together just twenty-one days,
and John was unfaithful throughout his time in the army.

After his discharge in 1953 John moved back to Monrovia, California, and sent for Vera Mae. John had a good job paying good
money, but his unfaithfulness continued, and Vera Mae, deeply
hurt and pregnant with their first child, moved back to Mississippi. Although on the brink of divorce, they wrote letters, and
John realized he truly loved Vera Mae. Eighteen months later she

moved back to California and introduced John to his son, Spencer, the first of their eight children.

In the spring of 1957 Vera Mae sent Spencer to a children's Bible class at a church down the street. Spencer started coming home asking if he could say Bible verses before dinner, and John observed the changes taking place in his son's life as a result of the church.

Spencer kept asking his dad to go with him to Bible class, and finally John agreed. Immediately the church members enveloped the family, inviting the Perkinses to services and Sunday dinners and taking them under their wing. Through a Bible study on the life of the apostle Paul, John realized that he didn't have what Paul had, and at twenty-seven he turned his life over to Jesus.

FRUIT

John immediately began sharing Christ with others. He gave up gambling; he read everything he could get his hands on, and when he and Vera Mae got involved in Child Evangelism Fellowship, he found something that he never would have expected: white Christians. Among them was Wayne Lee, an old Presbyterian elder who spent two years discipling John.

At one point John accompanied two Christian businessmen on a trip to California to visit prison camps, where a majority of the population was black. As John spent time with the young boys there, he sensed a growing conviction that God wanted him back in Mississippi, to identify with his people, to help them break the cycle of despair by showing them Jesus Christ through real biblical teaching. The family moved on June 9, 1960.

That first summer Vera Mae and John organized vacation Bible schools. They started with ten children and at the end of two weeks had over one hundred. Soon they were teaching in the schools in seven counties, reaching ten thousand children a month. John also began to teach Bible classes at Prentiss Institute, a black junior college, and many people accepted Christ.

By 1964 they were building a Bible institute, had bought a bus, and were forming a congregation, Berean Bible Church. They opened a child-care center in 1964, and the ministry, now named

Voice of Calvary, eventually included three basic thrusts: evangelism, social action, and visible community development.

Involving his white brothers and sisters in the ministry moved more slowly: The Ku Klux Klan threatened white ministers who helped John Perkins. His ministry was blossoming in the time of the civil rights movement, when committed men and women were fighting a tremendous battle for justice and equal rights for black people. While John applauded their commitment, he lamented the fact that few of the movement's leaders were equally committed to Christ. Perkins reasoned that human effort alone could not attain justice. Justice must start with God's strength and with the gospel that called men to Christ for forgiveness. On the other hand, the church, by prayer alone, could not change the current justice system, so Perkins decided to act. The Voice of Calvary ministry began a campaign to educate and register voters.

He and his family received threatening phone calls. Cars began appearing at night, carrying armed white men who sat and watched his house for hours, inching closer and closer. Finally the formation of a volunteer guard group discouraged the silent Klan vigil.

Despite the difficulties, the ministry persevered. In 1967 they developed the Federation of Southern Co-ops, dedicated to the development of local resources and local income. In 1968 the Voice of Calvary officially began the Leadership Development Program, raising up leaders to tutor and conduct Bible classes for younger students. In 1969 they got a farmers' co-op off the ground, buying fertilizer directly from the wholesale distributor and providing co-op members with tremendous savings. In 1969 in the wake of Hurricane Camille and a devastating tornado in Simpson County, Voice of Calvary provided food and clothing to the victims. And through it all Perkins labored to share the gospel.

Just before Christmas 1969 Perkins, Doug Huemkle, a young white volunteer from California, and seventeen others went to a police station to check on a young black man who had been arrested. Immediately they were arrested without cause. Shouting through barred prison windows, Perkins called for a boycott of the town's businesses to pressure the authorities for their release. Vera

Mae and others took action, bypassing nearby stores to shop out of town. The prisoners were released.

Two months later, on February 7, 1970, John and Doug were driving some students who had attended a rally back to their college. The police stopped them, arresting Doug and putting him in the police car alone and then arresting the nineteen students. On the way to the police station Doug was beaten. John and two other ministers immediately went to the police station, where they were arrested the moment they arrived. Once inside the building they were kicked in the head, ribs, and groin and were beaten unconscious, at times with a leather blackjack. Their attackers shaved two of the men's heads and then poured moonshine whiskey over their bleeding scalps. At one point, the officers played Russian roulette with Perkins at the end of the gun and tortured the men with forks. The beating lasted all night.

For two years following that horrendous night, the ministers and students searched for justice, battling the state and law enforcement in court. It took a heavy toll: Six months after his beating John suffered a heart attack. As Perkins lay in the hospital following his heart attack, he promised God he would not repay evil with evil but would return evil with good. He left the hospital with renewed conviction.

In 1973 Perkins joined fifty-two other evangelicals to hammer out a public document known as "A Declaration of Evangelical Social Concern." It called evangelical Christians to move against all forms of social injustice. Perkins spent more time traveling and speaking, often to white suburban evangelicals at their churches, conferences, and schools.

In 1982, drawn by the deep needs in northwest Pasadena, an area full of racial tension, John and Vera Mae moved back to California and developed Harambee Christian Family Center, the John M. Perkins Foundation for Reconciliation and Development, and Door of Hope. In 1989 John convened a meeting in Chicago of Christian leaders from across America, bound by a single commitment to express the love of Christ in America's poor communities at the grassroots level, and the Christian Community Development Association (CCDA) was born. In a few short years CCDA has grown from thirty-seven founding members to over three thousand individuals and nearly four hundred churches and ministries serving in thirty-five states and more than one hundred cities.

The ministry John Perkins built lives on through his children. Several have taken over projects begun by their father. John and Vera Mae recently moved back to Jackson, Mississippi, where today, John is deeply involved in his community, practicing as he preaches his three Rs: *relocation* of people to serve within a community of need; *reconciliation* of people across racial lines and other lines of antagonism; and *redistribution* of skills and resources, which comes as educated, affluent people join together with the poor in their communities.

LEGACY

Throughout his ministry John Perkins has carried out two important missions: evangelism and social reform. Indeed, he cannot conceive of a credible Christian faith that doesn't contain both. To Perkins, true social reform cannot occur without prior reformation of the heart through reconciliation with God. And true reformation forms in us the heart of Jesus, who sees and feels each act of injustice, every instance of human suffering and commands us to work for justice and help those who hurt. Many Christians align themselves with just one of these missions: evangelicals on one side, social activists on the other. John Perkins shows us that true Christianity is found only in the full embrace of both.

For additional information about the Christian Community Development Association, see appendix A.

God has put the body together in such a way that extra honor and care are given to those parts that have less dignity. This makes for harmony among the members, so that all the members care for each other equally. 1 Corinthians 12:24-25

BOOKS BY JOHN PERKINS

Beyond Charity: The Call to Christian Community Development (1993)

He's My Brother: Former Racial Foes Offer Strategy for Reconciliation
    (with Thomas A. Tarrants III and David Wimbish) (1994)

Let Justice Roll Down (autobiography) (out of print)

Restoring At-Risk Communities: Doing It Together and Doing It Right (1996)

Resurrecting Hope (with Jo Kadlecek) (1997)

With Justice for All (1982)

1906–1982

J. B. PHILLIPS

A COMPASSIONATE GUIDE,
A WOUNDED HEALER

If we are to be successful
translators, we cannot afford to
be detached. We must feel to the
full the love and compassion,
the near despair and the
unshakable hope . . . and
the bitter hostility of this
most extraordinary short
period of history.

The Price of Success: An Autobiography

As a minister in the Church of England, Rev. John Bertram Phillips taught from the Authorized Version of the Bible, the three-hundred-year-old translation commissioned by King James I. Its reverent tones, archaic pronouns, and curious sentence constructions suggested the richness of its message and the deep roots of the faith it revealed. But it was incomprehensible to the students in his youth group. What Phillips saw with clarity, they squinted to comprehend.

In desperation, Phillips set out to liberate God's Word from the restrictive language used to convey it. His work illuminated Scripture for his own students and released its power to millions who have read his translations.

IN SHORT

Many know of J. B. Phillips's *The New Testament in Modern English,* but far fewer know that this revolutionary pastor, writer, speaker, and Bible translator suffered from deep inner turmoil, self-doubt, and depression. It was from this wounded heart that Phillips translated the New Testament—words, he believed, written by Christians in difficulty for Christians in difficulty. In his wonderful, life-tested writing, he continues to guide many readers through familiar dark places, straight to the throne of God.

FAITH

J. B. Phillips was born in Barnes, near London, in 1906. His parents were a curious pair. His mother was highly intelligent, rarely affectionate, dependable, a woman of integrity. Not a motherly type but a great friend to her son. J. B.'s father alarmed and disturbed him. He was driven by ambition, often ridden with anxiety, frequently impatient and irritable, a God-fearing, churchgoing perfectionist, whose character left a permanent mark on J. B.'s sensitive nature.

By 1915 J. B.'s mother, who had previously been diagnosed with cancer, was bedridden. Shortly thereafter, just before turning eleven, J. B. was struck with double pneumonia and pleurisy and was not expected to live. But J. B. frustrated the doctor's prediction and was soon on the mend. Treatments for his mother, however, were ineffective, and she died in 1921 after battling her disease for ten painful years. J. B. could not comprehend how God could have let such a terrible thing happen to this wonderful woman, and in anger he gave up religion.

As a teenager J. B. jumped into wireless broadcasting—radio—working hard to afford the hardware that went with the new technology. His first paid writing assignments came through the "wireless" press. He loved the classics, especially Homer and Horace, and he was eventually accepted at Cambridge's Emmanuel College as a student of classics. He entered school as an avowed atheist and never attended chapel, but before long, members of both the Student Christian Movement and the Cambridge Inter-Collegiate Christian Union made a significant impact on him. In the spring of 1925 he gave in to their entreaties and began attending a daily prayer meeting. In July he attended a Christian convention and eventually decided to "throw his lot in" with the Christians. As graduation approached, he decided to join the staff of Sherborne Preparatory School for a year and had a vague idea of later becoming a parson.

FRUIT

Early in his ministry career J. B. had another close call with death. He was rushed to the hospital with severe abdominal cramps and for the second time in his life heard a doctor say, "He probably won't last the night." Once again he proved the doctor wrong. When he recovered, he shrank from reentering the life of a curate, which resulted in his being sent to a psychiatrist. Dr. Leonard

Browne, a Christian, helped J. B. work through the deeper issues that troubled him. Not quite ready to enter the pastorate, J. B. got a temporary position as editorial secretary for the Pathfinder Press. His main work was to produce a quarterly magazine, the *Pathfinder*. This gave him much experience in the art of editing and typesetting, skills that would serve him well in his future.

In 1936 J. B. met and courted Vera Jones. Her utter reliability, integrity, beauty, and charm overwhelmed him, and they were married on April 19, 1939. Less than five months later Hitler attacked Poland, setting off World War II. J. B. became priest-in-charge of Church of the Good Shepherd when the rector left his post to rejoin the army. In October 1941 the church was destroyed in a German air raid, and when several of J. B.'s parishioners lost their homes, he and Vera provided housing and other essentials for the bombing victims.

It was J. B.'s frustrations in teaching the church's youth club that led him to begin translating Scripture verses he knew and loved into a language that made them relevant to the lives of his students. The first set of translations J. B. completed for his Sunday night meetings became the text of his book *Letters to Young Churches*. With written encouragement from C. S. Lewis and a personal visit from Ruth and Billy Graham, J. B. continued his translations and other writings, including *The Gospels in Modern English* and *Your God Is Too Small*, and made broadcasts on the BBC.

J. B. continued his writing, preached at missions and conferences, produced broadcasts on the BBC, and responded to growing stacks of letters from his admirers. He translated several more books of the Bible and wrote radio scripts on the life of Jesus. The inevitable compilation of his translations, *The New Testament in Modern English*, was first published in 1958.

Then suddenly, in 1961, while he was working on a translation in the Old Testament, Phillips stopped writing. His drive, vision, and energy vanished, and he fell into depression. For a brief period in 1962, with the encouragement of a friend and the help of Vera, J. B. rallied to the task of completing the translation, which was published in his book *Four Prophets*. But shortly thereafter, as J. B.

was autographing copies of the book, an utterly irrational panic
seized him. Again he fell into a deep depression and experienced
an emotional breakdown.

When a doctor at the clinic asked him to try expressing his
mental pain through writing, J. B. wrote about what he called the
diminution of the personality: an erosion of the self, alienation,
and self-condemnation. As he wrote, talked, and worked through
his pain, he discovered what it meant to walk by faith. He realized,
as only those who have suffered can, that humans are allowed to
pass through the pain and humiliation of mental anguish so that
they might know God more deeply.

J. B.'s journey through depression transformed his faith and
changed his writing. After completing *Honest to God* and *The Pass-
over Plot*, which disturbed many in the 1960s, he wrote *Ring of
Truth: A Translator's Testimony*. In it he shared his life story and
wrote frankly about his afflictions, giving his many admirers in the
English-speaking world an honest look inside the mind, heart, and
soul of the man who dared to translate the New Testament into a
language we could all understand.

After a prolonged illness J. B. died in his home on July 21, 1982.
While he never lost his faith in God, he never ceased to struggle
against mental anguish. He also never failed to lead others to the
same God who was his source of comfort.

LEGACY

Great works tend to overshadow a person's other noble efforts.
The ministry of J. B. Phillips is no exception. Today we know him
best for his writings, especially his translation of the New Testament. But his church ministry, teaching, speaking, and radio
broadcasts ministered to hundreds of thousands throughout Britain for many years.

The least-known of his ministries was his correspondence with
those who wrote to him. It is no coincidence that he found in
letter writing an effective vehicle for the gospel. After all, his own
Bible translations started in the apostle Paul's poignant letters to
the new churches. Phillips knew the power of a personal message.
Those who corresponded with him knew it too. After reading his

translations, they wrote to him in the belief that a man who could transform two-thousand-year-old words into fresh, very personal messages would care enough to reply.

They were right. This gentleman scholar conscientiously answered thousands of letters with soul-searching questions on life and faith. To the end of his life he continued to reply with words of comfort and counsel, encouraging his readers as well as himself to stand firm in faith in all circumstances.

Knowing that Phillips wrestled with self-doubt and emotional turmoil may make us sad for him, but it also allows us to trust him. He knew the only treatment for the heart's deepest pains. He tested it on himself and then cared enough to share it with us.

This means that if we experience trouble it is for your comfort and spiritual protection; for if we ourselves have been comforted we know how to encourage you. 2 Corinthians 1:6, Phillips

---

BOOKS BY J. B. PHILLIPS

Four Prophets (1963)
Ring of Truth: A Translator's Testimony (1977)
The New Testament in Modern English, revised edition (1996)
The Price of Success: An Autobiography (1985)
Your God Is Too Small (1997)

Bob Pierce

LIVING JUST BEYOND
WHAT'S HUMANLY POSSIBLE

It is only when we reach our
limits that God has most
room to work.

Bob Pierce, as quoted in Franklin Graham's *Rebel with a Cause*

On a trip to China in the late 1940s, Youth for Christ evangelist Bob Pierce visited a mission school for girls on the small island of Kojedo. In his simple, energetic way he shared the gospel story with the young students and encouraged them to go home and tell their parents they were going to live as Christians.

Richard Gehman's book *Let My Heart Be Broken with the Things That Break the Heart of God* relates that the next morning one of the school's missionaries met Bob. She was carrying a little girl in a bloodstained dress. Her back was bleeding. The girl had done as Bob said, and her father caned her for dishonoring his ancestors. The livid missionary placed the frightened, crying child in Bob's arms and said, "You told this poor little girl to do that. Now you take care of her. If you think you can come in here, preach, and not do anything, you are wrong."

Bob was struck to the core. No one had ever held him accountable for the consequences of his message. Now he held those consequences in his arms. He emptied his pocket—five dollars—and gave it the missionary. It was enough to buy cloth for a new dress, a slate for the child's schoolwork, and rice to feed her four hundred classmates. Bob promised to send the same amount each month, and then he wrote the girl's name in his Bible. Near it he wrote, "Let my heart be broken with the things that break the heart of God."

IN SHORT
Chastened yet inspired, the evangelist returned home with a vision to serve the hurting, homeless, hungry, and persecuted, and he

founded a ministry called World Vision, which would become the largest Christian development and relief organization in the world. Years later he formed another world-changing organization, Samaritan's Purse.

The ministry of Bob Pierce stands among the greatest in the twentieth century, even as his personal life falls among those most tragic. While many Christians err on one side, pouring their lives into family and self and thus neglecting the needs of a hurting world, Bob erred on the other: The needs of the world—the world for which Jesus died—pierced his heart and consumed his life, while the needs of his own family went unmet. Yet despite that tragedy, God used this flawed, brilliant man to change our world.

FAITH

Robert Willard Pierce was born on October 8, 1914. He was raised in a Christian home and committed his life to the Lord at age twelve. Bob got an early start in Christian leadership. His family attended a Nazarene church in the Los Angeles community of Watts, and Bob served as the church's youth group president. He led the group on treks to the shopping center, where they sang and gave testimonies—and endured heckling from their non-Christian friends. Bob studied for ministry at Pasadena Nazarene College, married his wife, Lorraine, and the couple had three daughters, Sharon, Marilee, and Robin.

FRUIT

As a young man, Pierce plunged into the Youth for Christ movement. Evangelists held large rallies to bring in young people who had gone unreached by traditional church ministries. Bob was instrumental in organizing outreaches in the Los Angles area. The movement became a formal organization in 1944 when he and eleven other evangelists, including Billy Graham and Torrey Johnson, created the national ministry Youth for Christ. While Graham's and Johnson's rallies helped spread the ministry across the U.S. and into Europe, Pierce set his eyes on Asia.

In the late 1940s he traveled to China to speak to university students. During a three-day break in his schedule he flew to

Kunming, a city in southern China. Soon after Bob touched down on the weed-covered airstrip, a young missionary named Beth Albert met him and took him to the China Inland Mission Home.

Within minutes of their arrival a little Chinese girl, her leg twisted from the effects of malnutrition, crawled into Pierce's lap. "She's mine," Beth said, explaining that she had purchased the girl when her mother had come with three starving children, wanting to sell one of them so she could buy food for the other two. Beth borrowed the money and paid the mother for her little girl.

In addition to caring for a child, the missionary looked after a community of lepers. Soldiers were ordered to shoot any leper found in the city, so a colony had formed eight miles out of town—to which Beth walked every day. She taught them how to make bricks out of mud to build shelters and how to grow their own food. She procured medications and taught others how to administer them. And she received no outside support. Her mission agency had cut off her funding.

Pierce was humbled by Beth's sacrifices, amazed that someone could give up everything to minister to discarded people on the other side of the world. He took photographs of everything he saw to remind himself of this unnoticed ministry and to show others what he had seen. Soon after leaving Kunming, Pierce visited the island of Kojedo, where he took more pictures and spoke the words that got a little girl beaten.

By the end of Pierce's trip he knew he had to support the missionaries he had met. He told God he would spend his life finding people like Beth Albert and coming alongside them so they could carry on their work. The problem was, Bob had no money of his own, so he took what he did have: pictures and memories and a vision for supporting the ministries he had seen. He began to raise money. This was the start of World Vision. Instead of training, sending, and supporting large numbers of its own missionaries, World Vision could direct its resources to existing overseas ministries.

When the new communist government of China forced missionaries to leave, many at gunpoint, World Vision launched a campaign to support those trying to care for the legions of orphans in war-ravaged Korea. In 1953 Pierce launched World Vision's child-sponsorship program, allowing caring Christians to assist individual children through monthly gifts that went toward food, education, health care, and vocational training. From the success of this program in Korea the sponsorship program spread to other Asian countries, then into Latin America and Africa.

A 1962 earthquake in Iran killed 120,000 people and devastated the country, spurring World Vision to create a new mechanism for reaching out to disaster victims. The World Vision Relief and Development Organization was founded to provide emergency relief in response to disaster. Pierce, now head of a giant international ministry, continued his travels worldwide, searching for worthy ministries like that of Beth Albert, encouraging missionaries, and as always, returning home to share their stories.

But as he sought to meet the needs of thousands overseas, he neglected those at home. His marathon travel schedule and overwhelming office responsibilities kept his time and attention on the ministry. Meanwhile, his own family had begun to unravel. But despite mounting troubles in his home, Pierce believed he was doing the right thing. In her book *Days of Glory, Seasons of Night,* Bob's daughter Marilee Pierce Dunker quoted him as once saying, "Doesn't Luke 14:26 say we must hate mother and father, wife and children to be Christ's disciple? . . . Well, that's what I'm doing." When someone asked about his long absences from home, her father would reply, "I've made an agreement with God that I'll take care of His helpless little lambs if He'll take care of mine at home."

Sadly, Pierce's obsession with ministry destroyed the family home. His marriage ended in divorce; his children were bitter. Even more tragically, one of his daughters committed suicide. The greatest needs were those of his own family, but he didn't comprehend them until it was too late. And in the process, he lost World Vision too.

In 1970, still reeling from his family turmoil and his departure from World Vision, Pierce started a new ministry called Samaritan's Purse. He modeled its mission on Jesus' parable of the Good Samaritan: The traveler saw someone in need and without hesitation came to his aid. Pierce wanted his new ministry to do the same, keeping its eyes and heart open to hurting people and simply serving them wherever they were.

Early on, Pierce had shared his vision with Franklin Graham, the son of his old friend Billy. Franklin was impressed with both Pierce and his vision. He saw in Pierce a flawed, complicated, yet ever passionate man with a clear biblical vision to serve the needy. The two traveled together overseas to see some of the projects Samaritan's Purse was supporting and to search for new needs. During the trip Franklin learned that Pierce had leukemia. It was clear that Pierce knew his time was short and that he wanted to pass the baton to Franklin.

In 1978, confined to a wheelchair, Pierce visited Sami, a ministry friend in Beirut. Lebanon was in the midst of a civil war, and the church service the two friends attended together ended with the sound of shelling. Sami took Pierce back to his hotel on the other side of the divided city. The shelling was worse by the time they arrived at the hotel, so Sami, unable to drive safely back to his home, stayed with Pierce in his hotel room.

That night, as shells burst around the city, the two friends prayed. Hour upon hour Pierce poured out his heart, pleading for missionaries, pastors, leaders, and those they led in every part of the world. He had met many people, and he prayed for everyone he could remember.

Bob Pierce died a month later, on September 6, 1978. He summed up his own life well in one of the last things he wrote, quoted here from Franklin Graham's *Rebel with a Cause:* "I want to testify that my whole life is a story of God rewarding faith, and overcoming my flaws, and overcoming my ignorance, and overcoming my resentment to discipline, and in the end overcoming every suffering with His glory and His triumph." People from all over the world came to the funeral. And Franklin Graham, the man Pierce had wanted to succeed him, became the head of Samaritan's Purse.

LEGACY

Bob Pierce's legacy is enormous. Samaritan's Purse, which continues under Franklin Graham's leadership, has an annual budget of eighty-five million dollars. Its ministries include Operation Christmas Child, World Medical Mission, and Franklin Graham Festivals. In addition, Samaritan's Purse has gone at the drop of a hat to provide relief to war-torn areas in Africa and even Albania and Serbia.

What began as a child-assistance initiative called World Vision has matured into a program that helps transform entire communities with water programs, health-care education, agricultural and economic development, and strategic Christian-leadership activities. World Vision now serves over sixty million people in 103 countries.

The remarkable scope of Bob's ministry came about because he was always pushing the limits of faith. He knew as a human he could accomplish good things. But to him, that wasn't nearly enough: As Franklin Graham writes in *Rebel with a Cause,* Pierce said, "Faith isn't required as long as you set your goal only as high as the most intelligent, most informed, and expert human efforts can reach." Bob preferred to work from a wonderful, precarious place he called "God room": "Nothing is a miracle until it reaches the area where the utmost that human effort can do still isn't enough. God has to fill that space—that room—between what's possible and what He wants done that's impossible."

For additional information about World Vision and Samaritan's Purse, see appendix A.

"Now which of these three would you say was a neighbor to the man who was attacked by bandits?" Jesus asked.

The man replied, "The one who showed him mercy."

Then Jesus said, "Yes, now go and do the same."

Luke 10:36-37

1861–1918

WALTER RAUSCHENBUSCH

SOCIAL REDEMPTION

I felt that every Christian
ought to in some way or
other participate in the
dying of the Lord Jesus Christ,
and in that way help
to redeem humanity.

Social Gospel in America

On the first Sunday of May in 1891 a Baptist minister ventured into London's Hyde Park. While well-dressed Londoners took their places in pews of the city's stately churches, a throng of ill-dressed workers descended on the park to hear various speakers expound their socialist views from atop soapboxes and other makeshift platforms. Listening to these secular "preachers," the minister leaned to his American companion and asked, "Where would Christ be if he were in London?"

His friend replied, "Here, talking to the multitudes on the social question."

When Walter Rauschenbusch returned to America, he climbed his own Baptist soapbox to address that social question.

In Short

Baptist minister, scholar, and writer Walter Rauschenbusch introduced America to the "social gospel," Christ's message not just of individual redemption but of social redemption through the kingdom. His writings challenged Christians and non-Christians alike to respond to the social needs gripping the newly industrialized world, and they continue to generate controversy about the role of the church in the institutions of man. Many consider Rauschenbusch the father of the social gospel and the chief instigator of Christian social activism in the twentieth century.

Faith

On October 4, 1861, Caroline Rauschenbusch gave birth to a son. When her husband, August, heard the news, he prayed in his native German, *"Walt, Herr, über diesem Kind"* (Rule, Lord, over this child). They named the boy Walther, a contraction of the first two words of the prayer. Although most would call the boy Walter, he preferred the German form of his name until he was in his early forties.

Walther was born in a German community in Rochester, New York. His parents had emigrated from Germany years earlier to do mission work among other German immigrants. When the work was completed, they settled in Rochester, where August took a teaching position at Rochester Theological Seminary. He was a proud German Baptist and a third-generation pastor, who prayed that his son would carry on both traditions. He sent his family back to Germany when Walther was four, and when they returned to America four years later, Walther was rooted in his German heritage. For the rest of his life, he felt at home in both countries.

After a rigorous, classical education in Rochester and in Germany the young Rauschenbusch was intent on becoming a fourth-generation pastor and entered the University of Rochester and Rochester Theological Seminary at the same time. During his seminary years he became disillusioned with his inherited theology. As society grappled with the booming industrial economy, the expanding urban population, and the poverty and other social ills that festered as a result, Rauschenbusch felt that the church was losing touch. He found comfort in the writings of liberal thinkers and began to question the tenets of orthodox theology. He knew that those who held the old doctrines dear, including his father, would be mortified if he moved in this new direction.

Rauschenbusch completed seminary and was ordained. Now he had a solid education in conservative theology, a growing compassion for the disadvantaged—and many unanswered questions about how the two fit together.

FRUIT

In 1886 Rauschenbusch left Rochester to become pastor of the Second German Baptist Church in New York City, the heart of urban, immigrant America. It was an opportunity to test his convictions: He would live in near poverty, deny himself, and minister like Christ to the poor and abused. Day after day he witnessed the conditions the members of his congregation and their neighbors endured. He was convinced that poverty was not inevitable, that it could be eliminated, and that God summoned Christians to battle against it. He called his congregation's attention to the need to change economic and social patterns. The "salvation of society," he said, has too long been neglected by the church; "the best way to get the self ready for heaven," he added, "is to get the world ready for God."

His life's mission had begun to form. Much of the teaching he had received in seminary focused on only half of the gospel: an individual's redemption from sin in Jesus Christ. What had gotten short shrift was the social component. Christ had demonstrated love for the people around him—the poor, the sick, the oppressed—and called us to do likewise, not just individually, Rauschenbusch believed, but as the church. Addressing pastors in his denomination in 1889, he explained his "social gospel": It was not adequate to wait for changed individuals to eventually correct social wrongs. The church must now mount a direct corporate attack upon "the wrongs of human society and the unjust laws of the community to bring about righteousness."

During his service at Second German Baptist, Rauschenbusch continued to develop this ministry philosophy in his preaching, speaking, and writing. Meanwhile, his hearing, which had begun to give out years earlier, was now interfering with his pastoral duties, so in 1891 he resigned. He got by with lip-reading and, later, with a mechanical hearing aid, but throughout the rest of his life he would fight recurring bouts of loneliness and depression and the temptation to indulge in self-pity.

After leaving Second Baptist, Rauschenbusch traveled to Europe. He spent six weeks in Britain observing the work of the Salvation Army, where much of its London ministry was being run by the General's daughter, Evangeline Booth. He visited food depots, shelters, and other Army ministries, impressed by General Booth's strategies for "soul saving and society saving." In Germany Rauschenbusch spent much time in formulating his social gospel on paper. These writings would be published sixteen years later as

Christianity and the Social Crisis. When he returned to America, his new theology was formed. He proclaimed it at the 1892 Baptist Congress: "The whole aim of Christ is embraced in the words 'the Kingdom of God.' In that ideal is embraced the sanctification of all life, the regeneration of humanity, and the reformation of all social institutions."

His theology of social reform took root in some of the pastors in his audience, and they formed a study group called the Brotherhood of the Kingdom, which met periodically over the next twenty years to pursue Rauschenbusch's ideas and promote the social gospel across the country. Before the century was over, Rauschenbusch married Pauline Ernestine Rother, a German teacher from Milwaukee, and began teaching German at Rochester Seminary. In 1902 he became professor of church history.

In the same year Rauschenbusch began taking serious public action on his ideas about social reform. He fought for lower utility bills for low-income families and accepted invitations to speak on social and political issues. In 1907 he saw the publication of *Christianity and the Social Crisis,* the book he had written sixteen years earlier. It catapulted Rauschenbusch and his social gospel into the public forum. Many church leaders praised it. But the Baptists, the denomination he most wanted to influence, did not receive his message well. In 1912 he followed this groundbreaking work with another radical book, *Prayers of the Social Awakening.*

By 1913 Rauschenbusch's fame had spread so widely that when a national magazine, the *Independent,* asked its readers whom they considered the most useful American, Rauschenbusch's name was listed among those of inventor Thomas Edison; student-missions advocate John Mott; revivalist Billy Sunday; and Charles Sheldon, the author of *In His Steps.*

In 1914, as conservative and liberal church leaders battled theologies and the role of the church in social reformation, America looked ahead to war with Germany. Rauschenbusch found himself caught in the middle of both conflicts. He was a minister of the gospel *and* a social reformer—and an American *and* a German. Longtime friends rejected him for one reason or another, and the situation only worsened when the United States entered the war in 1917. In his increasing isolation, both social and aural, he grew hostile and lonely. By the end of that year, he was facing yet another battle: cancer.

Walter Rauschenbusch died on July 25, 1918. He did not live to see the end of World War I, nor did he live to see the true extent of the church battle his social gospel created.

Legacy

Like most institutions, the church often operates like a ship on the ocean. Walter Rauschenbusch saw this ship listing far to one side, the result of too many passengers clinging to the rail of individual redemption. He responded by standing against the opposite rail of social redemption and calling Christians to move toward him. His purpose was not to bring everyone to *his* side of the deck but to invite them to stand squarely in the middle and to use his weight on the far rail to counterbalance those who clung unmoving to the other. He sought an even keel.

Long after Rauschenbusch left this ship, its passengers are still trying to figure out where to stand. Christians the world over continue to argue about how the church is to proclaim Christ's eternal redemption on the one hand and the kingdom's social redemption on the other. While Rauschenbusch believed that both sides of the gospel were essential, he spent his life proclaiming what he saw as the neglected side: the *social* gospel of the kingdom of God.

Pray like this: Our Father in heaven, may your name be honored. May your Kingdom come soon. May your will be done here on earth, just as it is in heaven. Matthew 6:9-10

BOOKS BY WALTER RAUSCHENBUSCH

A Theology for the Social Gospel (1997)
Christianity and the Social Crisis (1992)
The Origins of Walter Rauschenbusch's Social Ethics (1994)

WALTER RAUSCHENBUSCH

The Righteousness of the Kingdom (Texts and Studies in the Social Gospel, 2)
  (1999)
The Social Principles of Jesus (out of print)

By reason of the pity and sympathy which the

Lord Jesus Christ has implanted in my heart,

I have not been able to look on the things

I see about me unmoved, or without thinking

on the causes of those sad appearances.

Walter Rauschenbusch, speaking to a Baptist audience
in 1889, from *Walter Rauschenbusch: American Reformer*
by Paul M. Minus

1 8 9 3 – 1 9 5 7

DOROTHY L. SAYERS

THE PURSUIT OF A PASSIONATE EXCELLENCE

The only Christian work is
good work, well done.

Dorothy L. Sayers Society Web page

A s a young girl Dorothy lived in the shadow of the walls of
       Britain's Oxford University. She dreamed of life on the
       other side of that wall, the life of a student. The trip across
that wall wasn't so difficult; it was the degree that took some time.
On October 14, 1920, at the age of twenty-seven, Sayers stood
proudly with the first class of women to have earned degrees there.
Five years earlier she had completed her studies in modern
languages at Oxford, taking a coveted first place in her examina-
tions. But she had received no diploma, only a "title to a degree."
Women, when properly chaperoned, had been allowed to attend
lectures for half a century and more recently had been given the
opportunity to take exams.

   Now for the first time the efforts of the these female students
were rewarded with degrees. To Sayers, the ceremony itself was
significant not because Dorothy *the woman* had achieved something great but because it signified that Dorothy *the person* had
done good work, well done.

IN SHORT

In the first half of the century some considered Dorothy Sayers's
lifestyle outrageous; all considered it unusual: Oxford graduate,
controversial Christian apologist, witty antagonist, motorcycle
enthusiast, saxophone player, a person intolerant of fools. This
highly educated, talented British novelist, essayist, medieval
scholar, and anthologist expressed self-doubt and confidence,
loneliness and generosity, sadness and enthusiasm. Sayers became

for many people a symbol of British faith, leading many to view faith in Christ as worthy of consideration.

Dorothy Sayers broke ground not only as a woman in her day and age but as a Christian writing to secular society. Her influence was subtle, but she received profound respect as a writer—a writer who was committed to excellence. She paved the way for Christians to pursue "mainstream" activity, moving beyond the shelter of the church to the world to bring the message of Jesus Christ to the dark corners of society.

FAITH

Dorothy Leigh Sayers was born in Oxford on June 13, 1893, the only child of Rev. Henry Sayers, headmaster of Christchurch Cathedral Choir School. Her father was quiet, gentle, scholarly, and religious but not evangelical. He believed his daughter's faith would come by association, not by indoctrination. The reverend was no great preacher, but he excelled as a teacher and soon recognized his little girl's learning potential. So he educated her as he would have a son in an age when such distinctions made a difference. This meant providing her with a tutor, in Dorothy's case, a French governess.

Studying and playing by herself left Dorothy lonely much of the time, which prompted her to read scores of children's books, novels, and detective stories. As a minister's daughter she participated in the church, singing in the choir and saying her catechism. She was a precocious child with a gift for languages, and she learned Latin and French from her governess by the age of seven. In her teens Dorothy was sent to a boarding school in Salisbury, where she enjoyed her subjects but was lonely and socially miserable. She won a scholarship to Oxford and entered Somerville College in 1912, where she studied modern languages, French literature, and German and did extremely well, finishing with First Class Honors in 1915. She found lifelong friends in some of the intelligent women who also dared to break through the society of men at Oxford, including Muriel St. Clare Byrne and Marjorie Barber.

Like Mary Ann Evans (better known to her readers as George Eliot), Sayers found that women of great intellect but little beauty were held in low esteem. Even as a child she seemed to know she was no beauty. As a young woman she was not unattractive, with an appealing round face and a long neck but with a large bone structure that she did not bother to corset as many women of her day did to gain a tiny waist. After an unfortunate illness in her teens she was left partially bald. If she could not be beautiful, she decided with humor, she would wear a great wig with a black bow, a purple gown and parrot earrings, and would smoke a cigar.

In the 1920s she earned her M.A. and went through a wild period. Disliking the lack of passion often found in academic life, she took an editorial position at Blackwell's, the Oxford publishers, and published two volumes of poetry during that period. In 1922 she served as an advertising copywriter at Benson's, a London advertising agency, where she played with words and created jingles. In 1923 she published her first novel, *Whose Body?* introducing Lord Peter Wimsey, her nobleman-detective hero who ultimately appeared in fourteen volumes of novels and short stories.

Sayers's romantic life was turbulent and often sad. By nature unrefined and a bit of a seductress, she had many beaux, but she did not fall deeply in love until she was twenty-nine. Journalist John Cournos claimed not to believe in marriage and pressured her to live with him instead. She broke it off a year later. While on the rebound she had an affair with a married car salesman and motorcyclist. She became pregnant and delivered the child in secret. Her son, whom she named John Anthony, was raised by a cousin, but Sayers sent him letters, visited him regularly, and sent him to boarding school and later to Oxford.

Two years after John's birth, in 1926, Sayers married Captain Oswald Atherton Fleming. While "Mac," as she called him, gave her son his last name, he did not want John living with them. Dorothy and Mac were comrades at first and enjoyed each other's company, but as her success grew, his diminished. He became unhappy and began to drink and treat her badly. She never left him, instead supporting the household and paying his pub bills until his death shortly before her own.

Sayers's faith began with her father's model of Christian sympathy, generosity, forgiveness, and love. But she would go on to write that she thought Christ to be the "bonny outlaw" who sought people out individually, like the lover in a ballad, and lured them away from the herd. Her love of metaphysical poets and her imitations of them showed her taste for fire and passion in religion. Some blasphemed and persecuted Christ, she said, but it was the Christians who managed to make Christ dull.

FRUIT

It was at Oxford that she studied religion and began to develop her own rational approach to official doctrines, influenced tremendously by G. K. Chesterton. Sayers was an intellectual Christian who loved the subtle play of theology and the logic of the church fathers. In work after work she returned to the value of the Nicene Creed and the battle for orthodoxy. As a person thrilled with ideas and motivated by them, she hated wrong thinking or fuzzy logic. She insisted on the necessity for the correct structure of thought and faith as a framework for emotional commitment. Her own intensity grew and deepened throughout her life. She never shifted from her original foundations, which were firmly fixed.

But as she grew older and faced more complex problems and deeper pain, she centered her life in her faith. One writer noted that while Sayers had an uncanny understanding of humanity's complexities, she was enthralled with the simple story of a birth two thousand years ago.

In the 1930s Sayers lost the two people she counted on most in life—her parents. Without their support and comfort her mood darkened, and the output of her work reached a frenzied pace. In the following decades she continued to write widely, editing anthologies of mystery stories, translating medieval French poetry, lecturing for the BBC, reviewing books for the *Times,* and always continuing the Wimsey saga. She had once considered putting an end to the hero, but her friend Muriel St. Clare Byrne persuaded her to collaborate in putting Lord Peter on stage. The play, *Busman's Honeymoon,* enjoyed a successful debut in 1936.

The stage fascinated Dorothy. She had been asked to write a play for the Canterbury Festival. The result, *The Zeal of Thy House,* was well received, and she followed it with six more plays, the most momentous of which was *The Man Born to Be King*, written for a broadcast on the BBC's children's hour.

When Sayers's success freed her from financial worries, she turned to the scholarly pursuits that had always interested her, writing religious dramas and Christian apologetics and expounding Christian dogma through lectures, essays, radio talks, and books. Sayers enthusiastically volunteered for church work, even while immersed in the intellectual life of wartime and postwar London as a medieval scholar.

Her last great work consumed her intensely for over a decade. Dante's writings had long intrigued her. Now she taught herself Old Italian and made a translation of *The Divine Comedy* unmatched for its popularity and the clarity of its notes. She also found time to finish her translation of the *Song of Roland* from the Old French. Ironically, just as Dante died in the writing of *Paradiso*, Dorothy Sayers died on December 17, 1957, in the midst of translating it.

Dorothy Sayers was an influential writer in both the secular and the religious arenas. She was a contemporary of Aldous Huxley, Virginia Wolfe, and D. H. Lawrence. Among the Christian writers of her time Dorothy Sayers is listed among British authors such as Owen Barfield, G. K. Chesterton, C. S. Lewis, George Macdonald, J. R. R. Tolkien, and Charles Williams (many of whom were part of a group known as The Inklings), well known for their impact on contemporary literature and Christian thought. Together they produced over four hundred books, including novels, drama, poetry, fantasy, books for children, and Christian treatises.

LEGACY

Two themes—passion and excellence—flowed through the life and work of Dorothy Sayers. Thousands of American teachers have delighted in her translation of *The Divine Comedy*. Hundreds of thousands of students in American and British universities have studied Dante through Sayers. Mystery-story addicts know of her through her characters Lord Peter Wimsey and Montague Egg. The English public knows her for her radio broadcasts during World War II, her plays over the BBC, and her numerous letters and articles in various British papers. Christians know her liturgical dramas. Women know her for her life and her book *Are Women Human?*

Sayers had an insatiable appetite to know and to experience. That appetite led her to great pain, great joy, and an unsatisfied intellect. The morality of the scholar was important to her. Scholarship, she had always suspected, was the work she was set on earth to do. And she did it with all her heart. To the end she drove herself hard, living the philosophy she expressed in these words: "The only Christian work is good work, well done."

Never be lazy in your work, but serve the Lord enthusiastically. Romans 12:11

BOOKS BY DOROTHY L. SAYERS

Catholic Tales and Christian Songs (1918)
Clouds of Witness (1995)
Creed or Chaos? (1996)
Crime on the Coast & No Flowers by Request (1984)
Hangman's Holiday (short stories) (1995)
Lord Peter Views the Body (1995)
Lord Peter: The Complete Lord Peter Wimsey Stories (1995)
Opus I (collection of poetry) (1916)
Striding Folly (short stories) (1972)
Strong Poison (1995)
The Comedy of Dante Alighieri the Florentine: Hell (L'Inferno) (1988)
The Documents in the Case (1995)
The Five Red Herrings (1995)
The Man Born to Be King: A Play-Circle on the Life of Our Lord and Savior Jesus Christ (1990)
The Mind of the Maker (1987)
The Nine Tailors (1980)
Unnatural Death (1995)
Whose Body? (1995)
Willie Collins: A Critical and Biographical Study (1977)

1912–1984

FRANCIS SCHAEFFER

THE RENAISSANCE OF CHRISTIAN TRUTH

We not only believe in the existence of
truth, but we believe we have the truth . . .
a truth we can share with the twentieth-
century world. Do you think our
contemporaries will take us seriously if
we do not practice truth? In an age that
does not believe that truth exists, do you
really believe that we will have
credibility if we do not practice truth?

The Great Evangelical Disaster

P riscilla, the oldest of Francis and Edith Schaeffer's three daughters, called to ask if she could bring home a fellow student from the University of Lausanne for the weekend. "She looks as if she has stepped out from a *Vogue* cover, but she has so many questions. She is studying oriental religions—she needs Daddy to talk to."

It was 1955. The Schaeffers lived in a chalet they affectionately called *L'Abri*, "The Shelter," in a village nestled in the Swiss Alps. It was not a good weekend for visitors. The water heater and furnace were broken, and the Schaeffers were without a refrigerator and washing machine. Nonetheless they welcomed the visitor warmly. Conversations that started during the day continued at mealtime. Long walks offered perfect opportunities for more questions and answers. Francis read from the Bible, led family prayer time, and then allowed time for more questions. That was the weekend the ministry of L'Abri was born.

In Short

Millions of Christians who have never heard of Francis Schaeffer have been touched by his influence because he initiated or revitalized many important ideas now embraced by evangelical Christianity. He inspired an army of evangelicals to become serious scholars, encouraged women who chose roles as mothers and homemakers, solidified popular evangelical opposition to abortion, prodded evangelicals out of their cultural ghetto, and gave currency to the idea of intentional Christian community.

FAITH

Francis August Schaeffer was an only child, born in Philadelphia on January 30, 1912. The drunken doctor who managed to aid Francis's mother in birthing the child forgot to register the birth at the proper office. In that year C. S. Lewis was thirteen years old, Salvador Dali was eight, Jean-Paul Sartre was seven, and Picasso had already painted his *Demoiselles d'Avignon*. The work of these men would shape the philosophy of this boy, who grew up to be one of the century's most influential Christian voices.

The boy's parents were not Christians, so as Francis grew older, his father told him that if he wanted to go to church, he could take his pick. Francis chose practically, picking the church that had a Scout troop. While Francis was in high school, one of the church's Sunday school teachers asked him to help a Russian immigrant learn English. The immigrant, who happened to be no less than a White Russian count, wanted to start out by reading Catherine the Great, but Francis figured it would be best to start with something easier. He went to the bookstore to pick up a beginner's English reading book. By mistake the bookstore sent Francis home with the wrong book—Greek philosophy.

The book sparked an interest in Francis that changed his world. His mind devoured philosophy; he read everything he could get his hands on. As his knowledge increased, so did his ability to comprehend the questions the philosophers were asking, questions that, he soon discovered, led to more questions but to no real answers. The preaching in church didn't help. Just more questions without answers. And if he had no real answers to his own questions about God, how could he call himself a Christian? He couldn't. He became an agnostic.

But his questions about God didn't stop. To find answers he decided it was time to actually read the whole Bible. Six months later he was convinced that God was real and that the Bible was God's revealed Word to mankind. In 1930 eighteen-year-old Francis prayed to receive Christ as his Savior. At a church debate two years later Francis met Edith Seville, and they were married in 1935.

FRUIT

Intending to enter the ministry, Schaeffer enrolled at Hampden-Sydney College, then went on to Gresham Machen's new Westminster Seminary in Philadelphia. Shortly after Machen died, Schaeffer left Westminster, and he and Edith founded Faith Theological Seminary. In the 1930s, while Schaeffer's faith was being formed, America was struggling through the depression, and the church was arguing between fundamentalist and modernist theologies, the one side holding to the Bible's absolute reliability, the other not. Schaeffer came out on the side of the fundamentalists, and in his final years of study and after he graduated, he and Edith took every opportunity to speak out in defense of the conservative doctrine.

As a pastor of several churches throughout Pennsylvania and Missouri, Schaeffer was grieved at the compromise he saw in mainline Protestant denominations. In the late 1940s he toured Europe on behalf of the American Council of Christian Churches and, to his astonishment, saw even greater needs there. He and Edith decided to move to Switzerland to work with youth. In 1948 the Schaeffers founded the Children for Christ ministry in Lausanne. With three daughters and a son, Schaeffer was familiar with the challenges of teaching young people. In the meantime he continued studying, touring, and lecturing.

In 1955, after that first weekend of searching for the truth with Priscilla's college friend, the Schaeffers formally opened L'Abri. It was to be a home for solid Bible teaching where anyone could come and participate in a thought-provoking search for truth. Students began to come every weekend. L'Abri became a haven of spiritual rest and discovery for truth seekers worldwide.

Schaeffer developed a pattern of meals, walks, and a Sunday service, all designed to stimulate conversations about philosophical and religious ideas. While a passionate defender of biblical inerrancy, a doctrine under increasing attack in evangelical circles, he seldom quoted from the Bible. He was more apt to talk about philosophy or art. L'Abri saw a steady stream of visitors through the remainder of the 1950s, but in the mid-sixties, as questioning authority and "the establishment" became a cultural phenomenon, the Schaeffers' Swiss ministry drew young people by the thousands. Constant prayer kept L'Abri going, with God bringing along just the right people and finances to keep the doors open.

When fifty-three-year-old Schaeffer returned to America in 1965 for a visit with evangelical leaders, few knew what to make of him. A curious composition of old and new ideas, he dressed in Alpine hiking knickers and knee socks and spoke with the wisdom of a classical philosopher about issues taken fresh from the headlines. But gradually his work gained recognition. Schaeffer continued to expand his ministry, speaking and writing to Christian audiences. In 1968 his first two books were published: *Escape from Reason* and *The God Who Is There*. In those books Schaeffer showed how other philosophies failed to adequately address real-world problems and how Christianity was a reasonable faith with real solutions to the dilemmas facing our culture.

The U.S. Supreme Court's 1973 *Roe v. Wade* decision, which legalized abortion on demand, drew Schaeffer's attention back to America. In the book *How Should We Then Live?* he addressed the foundational problems that led to this devaluing of human life. Such a breakdown of values, he argued, would eventually lead to further violations of human life, such as euthanasia. With his son, Franky, and former Surgeon General C. Everett Koop, Schaeffer published *Whatever Happened to the Human Race?* which tackled these social issues specifically.

Nonbelievers frequently criticized Schaeffer, but, surprisingly, so did believers, who objected to his bold stand for the explicit, consistent application of the Bible. He stood without personal compromise to demonstrate that Christianity should not be compromised either. Most of all, he showed the evangelical community that faith was nothing to be ashamed of: Christianity could hold its own in the face of secular philosophy.

When Schaeffer was diagnosed with cancer in 1981 and given just six months to live, he continued to teach. His illness, with its long and sometimes debilitating treatments, gave him fresh opportunities to address nationwide medical concerns. When Schaeffer died in his home on May 15, 1984, President Ronald Reagan offered a fitting eulogy: "It can rarely be said of an individual that his life touched many others and affected them for the better; it will be said of Dr. Francis Schaeffer that his life touched millions of souls and brought them to the truth of their Creator."

Schaeffer was a prophet in his time. Students, professionals, and academics from around the world came to learn from him. He left an imprint on the careers of a diverse group of influential Christians, including Jerry Falwell, Pat Robertson, Jack Kemp, Chuck Colson, Randall Terry, C. Everett Koop, Cal Thomas, and Tim and Beverly LaHaye; musicians Larry Norman and Mark Heard; and scholars such as Harold O. J. Brown, Os Guinness, Thomas Morris, Clark Pinnock, and Ronald Wells.

The ministry that started in that humble Swiss chalet grew into L'Abri Fellowship, an international study center with branches in England, the Netherlands, Sweden, and the U.S. Schaeffer's books still spark discussion among a worldwide readership, and his films and taped lectures are shown in churches just now discovering that this man who left us years ago knew more about the challenges we'd be facing than just about anyone alive today.

LEGACY

Francis Schaeffer succeeded in communicating the truth of moral, biblical Christianity through a formidable combination of vibrant faith, intellectual integrity, and demonstrative love. In Schaeffer, reality did not hamper truth; it revealed it. He understood the relationship between what a person believed and how that belief affected the choices he made; the pairing of truth with action, philosophy with practice—and the result of wrong ideas carried to their fatal conclusions. Schaeffer spent a lifetime seeking truth and showing us what that truth looks like in a real-world faith.

You must worship Christ as Lord of your life. And if you are asked about your Christian hope, always be ready to explain it. 1 Peter 3:15

BOOKS BY FRANCIS SCHAEFFER

25 Bible Studies: Two Contents, Two Realities (1996)
A Christian Manifesto (1981)
Art and the Bible (1973)
Escape from Reason (1968)
Francis A. Schaeffer Trilogy (1990)
Genesis in Space and Time (1972)
He Is There and He Is Not Silent (1972)
How Should We Then Live? (1983)
Letters of Francis A. Schaeffer (edited, with introductions by Lane Dennis) (1986)
Pollution and the Death of Man (with a new concluding chapter by
    Udo Middelmann) (1992)
The Church at the End of the Twentieth Century (1994)
The Complete Works of Francis A Schaeffer (5 vols.) (1985)
The Finished Work of Christ: The Truth of Romans 1–8 (1998)
The God Who Is There (1998)
The Great Evangelical Disaster (1984)
The Mark of a Christian (1984)
True Spirituality (1979)
Whatever Happened to the Human Race? (with C. Everett Koop)(1983)

1921 –

JOHN STOTT

BASIC CHRISTIANITY

The task of evangelism
cannot be delegated to the
few. Worship and witness
go hand in hand. We are
all called to worship, and
we are all called to witness
in some way.

John Stott: The Making of a Leader

On the last night of a one-week student mission at Cambridge University, the chapel was filled to overflowing with chairs set in the aisles, visitors spilling into the choir stalls, people standing in every available space, and students being turned away. To students whose underdeveloped Anglican beliefs had been shaken by rigorous academic skepticism, the preacher's claims of a living, relevant Christ were astounding and delicious. His messages, unadorned by flowery illustrations and manipulative badgering, drew students into faith.

The preacher, John Stott, had once been a student there too. He shared in their Anglican tradition. But he was like no Anglican they had ever heard.

In Short

Church of England minister and writer John Stott was rector of London's All Souls Church for twenty-five years, an evangelical in a denomination where such a thing was rare. His ministry as a pastor, writer, speaker, and evangelist continues to reach Christians throughout the world, both in and out of his denomination. In his best-known book, *Basic Christianity,* and dozens of others, Stott shows us that the oldest of church traditions—sharing the gospel—is the one most worth keeping.

Faith

John Robert Walmsley Stott was born in London on April 27, 1921. His father, Sir Arnold Stott, was an army physician, a man of reason, and a firm believer in education. His mother, Lilly, was a devout Lutheran who made sure John and his two older sisters said their prayers and attended church. As a boy John took on his father's interest in nature and bird-watching, which turned into a lifelong hobby.

At age eight John's parents sent him off to a boarding school in Kent. Later he entered Rugby, his father's old prep school, and there he met a man who changed his life. John attended a meeting where the Reverend E. J. H. Nash spoke to the students about Christ. As Timothy Dudley Smith writes in *John Stott: The Making of a Leader,* Stott later recalled, "He was nothing much to look at and certainly no ambassador for muscular Christianity. Yet as he spoke I was riveted. His text was Pilate's question: 'What then shall I do with Jesus, who is called the Christ?' That I needed to do anything with Jesus was an entirely novel idea to me, for I had imagined that somehow he had done whatever needed to be done and that my part was only to acquiesce. This Mr. Nash, however, was quietly but powerfully insisting that everybody had to do something about Jesus, and that nobody could remain neutral. Either we copy Pilate and weakly reject him, or we accept him personally and follow him."

After the meeting John asked Nash many questions. The teenager found in the man's answers the very thing he had been needing most. He realized that up to that point Christ had been only "mental furniture." John had often asked Jesus to guide him but had not been willing to give him complete control. In his dormitory room on a Sunday night Stott knelt by his bed to give Jesus that full control. Two days later he wrote in his journal: "I really have felt an immense and new joy throughout today. It is the joy of being at peace with the world and of being in touch with God. How well do I know now that he rules me and that I never really knew him before."

A few days later Nash sent John a booklet that gave instruction on how to grow in his new faith. For the next five years his mentor, whom John came to call "Bash," wrote him every week. Bash's letters varied in content, from pastoral guidance to theological or ethical principles to personal counsel. And sometimes they contained a rebuke. If John saw Bash's familiar handwriting among the envelopes in his letter stack, he would sometimes spend a half hour praying to prepare himself before he could open the letter. Bash had high expectations for his young disciple, and John lived to fulfill them. He began to underline verses in his Bible, started a new notebook filled not with bird sightings but sermon notes, and shared his faith with his school friends.

As the discipleship continued, Stott realized that God was leading him into a life of full-time ministry, and he prepared for that future at Cambridge University, graduated in 1945, and was ordained. World War II had called many of his peers into service, but Stott took a distinctly pacifist position, which he shared in letters to his parents. His army colonel father was so offended that he nearly cut off the financial support for his son's education.

FRUIT

Stott got an early taste of ministry life through his mentor, Bash, who brought John along on evangelistic missions. He also became involved in the Cambridge Inter-Collegiate Christian Union. Stott began to see his evangelistic and pastoral gifts and employed them in ministering to younger students. He was a workaholic and a perfectionist, amazingly efficient at administrative details, but these traits were complemented by his engaging cheerfulness and a mischievous sense of humor.

In 1945, following his ordination, Stott began work as a junior curate at All Souls Church, Langham Place, in the heart of London's West End. Among his favorite duties was youth ministry. Stott enjoyed taking his young people camping, where they could be separated for a while from life's distractions and think together about deeper things. The fruit of effective discipleship himself, Stott was committed to the discipleship of his students when they returned from these retreats with a new but untested faith.

In 1950 the rector, or head pastor, of All Souls Church died. King George VI appointed a replacement on the recommendation of church leaders. When the announcement came, it read: "His Majesty, the King, has been graciously pleased to appoint the Reverend J. R. W. Stott, M.A., to the living of All Souls Church, Langham Place." At age twenty-nine John Stott, an evangelical, became rector of one of London's most prominent Anglican churches.

Stott had shared his evangelical vision for the church in sermons before his appointment; now he set out to realize it. There were ten thousand people living within the borders of his parish, and it was the church's duty and privilege to reach out to all of them. In *John Stott: The Making of a Leader* he is quoted as telling the members of his congregation that they had "an unmistakable, inescapable responsibility towards [their] neighbors who are strangers to Christ and His gospel of grace. This responsibility is clearly shared by the whole congregation." That meant that members who had long been accustomed to simply sitting in the pews and dropping money in the collection plates were being called into active service.

Stott initiated a six-month evangelism training program for church members and then sent them out in pairs to go house to house. It was a biblical plan, and certainly one used in other denominations, but in an Anglican church it was strange indeed. Stott's evangelism plan, and many other ministry efforts that followed, revolutionized the church. In the fifties and sixties, All Souls Church saw tremendous growth, not just in attendance, but in the depth and breadth of its ministry: a community center, missions, ministries to storekeepers, and outreaches to students throughout Britain.

Meanwhile, Stott began to write books. His first, published in 1954, was *Men with a Message,* a simple introduction to the New Testament, its writers, and their message. The advance he received allowed him to purchase a cottage in Pembrokeshire, where he would write much of his later work. He has written dozens of books, nearly all of them focused on Christian living. His most famous is *Basic Christianity,* published in 1958.

Early in his pastorate Stott began to participate in many evangelical conferences and organizations, extending his reputation beyond Anglican circles. He and his church played a key role in Billy Graham's remarkable London crusade in 1954. During Graham's three-month stay, he and Stott became friends, and the rector served as a pastor to Graham's staff. The crusade's attendance topped two million, and more than thirty-six thousand turned in decision cards. Afterward, Stott helped to launch a magazine to support the new believers in the discipleship that he and Graham believed was essential.

As his reputation spread, Stott received offers from other churches and was asked to fill a bishop's position in Australia. But feeling called to continue the growing ministry at All Souls, he turned down all other offers—except one. In 1960 he was appointed chaplain to Her Majesty, Queen Elizabeth II. It involved no change in his work at his own church but simply required him to preach occasionally to the royal family at the chapel at St. James' Palace, an honor more than a duty.

For many in the Anglican church, Stott's evangelicalism was controversial. The denomination's leadership was becoming more and more liberal, making it tougher for the few evangelicals among them to retain a voice in important decisions. At the same time, some of his evangelical peers were leaving the denomination in protest. Like his colleague J. I. Packer, Stott encouraged Anglican evangelicals to stay in the church to carry out change from within, and he shared Packer's distress when in 1966 one of the most outspoken evangelicals in their denomination, David Martin Lloyd-Jones, encouraged Anglicans to forsake the denomination and start afresh elsewhere. This made both Stott's and Packer's jobs tougher—and all the more essential.

While Stott's evangelical fervor rankled many Anglicans, it was applauded by leaders in other churches and organizations. He received invitations to speak at churches, colleges, and conferences throughout the world. When he traveled, he left the congregation at All Souls in the capable hands of young ministers he considered his disciples. And he took with him his binoculars and camera, always eager to add new birds to his notebook of sightings. In 1975, after thirty years of abundantly fruitful ministry at All Souls, he became rector emeritus, thus expanding the borders of his parish from the London streets to the corners of the world.

Since his retirement from the church, Stott has continued to write and speak, providing a voice of evangelicalism in the Anglican church and a call to Christians everywhere to get on with the work of evangelism and discipleship.

LEGACY

As a young man John Stott met a minister who not only preached the gospel but took the time to "make disciples." Over a five-year period his mentor led him to Christ, then led him into ministry, a ministry in which Stott would duplicate this process thousands of times. He became a gifted expositor of the Bible, a prolific writer, and a mentor to ministers both in and out of his denomination. Turning down offers to take new churches and to leave his denomination, he chose instead to remain with a single flock for three decades and to see God use the fruit of this single labor to feed disciples around the world.

The underlying message of Stott's entire ministry is suggested in his popular book *Basic Christianity:* We are hopeless without Christ, we are redeemed by him alone—and we are compelled to tell this story to those who don't know it. To *not* tell it is a slap in the face of the Jesus who came to earth and died just to tell it the first time. But to share this gospel story and to serve as encouragers and mentors to those who accept it is to take part in a movement that predates all denominations, to join in the growing body of a far greater church.

[Jesus] asked them, "Who do you say I am?"

Simon Peter answered, "You are the Messiah, the Son of the living God."

Jesus replied, "You are blessed, Simon son of John, because my Father in heaven has revealed this to you. You did not learn this from any human being. Now I say to you that you are Peter, and upon this rock I will build my church, and all the powers of hell will not conquer it."

Matthew 16:15-18

BOOKS BY JOHN STOTT

1 & 2 Thessalonians: Living in the End Times (1998)
1 Timothy & Titus: Fighting the Good Fight (1998)
2 Timothy: Standing Firm in Truth (1998)
Acts: Seeing the Spirit at Work (1998)
Basic Christianity (1986)
Becoming a Christian (1984)
Being a Christian (1984)
Christian Basics: Beginnings, Beliefs and Behaviour (1992)
Ephesians: Building a Community in Christ (1998)
Evangelical Truth: A Personal Plea for Unity, Integrity and Faithfulness (1999)
Galatians: Experiencing the Grace of Christ (1998)
Human Rights and Human Wrongs: Major Issues for a New Century (1999)
Our Social and Sexual Revolution: Major Issues for a New Century (1999)
Romans: Experiencing the Gospel's Power (1998)
Same-Sex Partnerships? A Christian Perspective (1998)
The Beatitudes: Developing Spiritual Character (1998)
The Bible Speaks Today series (1997)
The Birds, Our Teachers: Biblical Lessons from a Bird-Watcher (1999)
Understanding the Bible (1999)
Your Mind Matters (1973)

1862 – 1935

BILLY SUNDAY

THE GOSPEL UNLEASHED

They play no favors in
Heaven. They shout and yell
for joy as loud in Heaven for
the hobo convert as they do
for the millionaire
conversion. They don't keep
a Dun and Bradstreet
on tap up there.

Preacher: Billy Sunday and Big-Time American Evangelism

Before radio, film, and television, a Billy Sunday revival was as entertaining as it was powerful. A crowd of thousands would converge in a field to fill a wooden tabernacle constructed especially for the occasion, seat themselves on benches above the sawdust-covered dirt floor, and watch the flamboyant evangelist with rapt attention.

Sunday was everything that a church preacher wasn't: He avoided religious language and spoke instead in the simple, common words of his listeners, seasoning his message with slang expressions he knew they would understand. Rather than stand stoically behind a pulpit, he would leap, dance, and slide across the stage, then pick up a chair and spin it over his head. And instead of inviting people to come forward to receive Christ, he told them to "hit the sawdust trail."

In Short

Evangelist Billy Sunday was the archetype of the traveling evangelist. His simple gospel message, delivered with startling theatrics and a booming voice, drew hundreds of thousands of Americans to consider the Christian faith. Many would follow in his footsteps, and Hollywood would try to capture his character on film, but in the first half of the twentieth century, none could match the personality and profound impact of the Billy who brought Sunday to every day of the week.

Faith

William Ashley Sunday was born in Ames, Iowa, on November 19, 1862. His father, William senior, who had fought with the

Union Army in the Civil War, died of pneumonia when Billy was born. Two years later the boy's widowed mother, Jennie, married an older man, an alcoholic who abandoned the family in 1871. Too poor to keep the family together, she relinquished eleven-year-old Billy and his older brother, Ed, to the Soldiers' Orphan Home. Billy held his own at the orphanage, hunting, playing baseball, and discovering that he could beat any other kid in a footrace.

When his brother was forced to leave the orphanage at age sixteen, Billy refused to stay without him. Both boys returned home, independent and stubborn from their orphanage career. Billy was fourteen at the time, and home was with his brother, mother, and grandfather. The reunion was short. After a vicious argument with his grandfather, the hot-tempered Billy left home for good. He found work as an errand boy for an army colonel and his wife, who sent the young man to public school.

Billy left high school without graduating, choosing instead to join the hose team of a fire brigade, where his remarkable running strength could earn him a wage. Billy also took an interest in a new sport catching on across the country: baseball. While playing for the local baseball team in 1882, Billy was discovered by Cap Anson, a famous player of the time, who happened to be visiting the town. Word got back to Chicago about Billy Sunday's "phenomenal" abilities, so the White Stockings invited him to try out for the team. He joined the team in 1883 as an outfielder, playing mostly right field and center, but he could step in as pitcher in a pinch because he had a good throwing arm. Billy was only a fair hitter, but when he did get a hit, he was an exceptional base runner.

In 1885 the young player became a Christian through Chicago's famous Pacific Garden Mission. Some have speculated that he did so to win the hand of a devout Presbyterian named Helen ("Nell") Thompson, the daughter of a wealthy Chicago businessman. Others, including Sunday's authorized biographers, say that he met Nell after his conversion but joined the Presbyterian church for her. Sunday himself admitted that had she been a Catholic, he would have become a Catholic. His growth in faith and involvement in the Presbyterian church grew after the two were married on September 5, 1888.

Earlier that year he had been sold to the Pittsburgh Alleghenies, but he considered Chicago his home and returned there in the off-seasons, teaching Bible studies and whetting his appetite for ministry. So when Pittsburgh sold Billy to the Philadelphia Phillies in 1890, he quit baseball for good to pursue ministry full-time. He took a position at the Young Men's Christian Association (YMCA) in Chicago, where he performed office duties, handed out tracts in saloons and on street corners, and led Sunday school classes.

In 1893 Sunday got his start in traveling ministry when he went to work for J. Wilbur Chapman, a traveling Presbyterian evangelist. Sunday served as Chapman's advance man, making arrangements for each stop on the tour before the meetings took place. He rented halls, recruited choir members from local churches, worked with the town's ministers, conducted prayer meetings, and set up committees to handle all the details. He often had to soothe the egos of pastors who saw the meetings as competition to their own church services. During the evangelistic meetings themselves, Sunday served as an usher, managed things backstage, and on occasion, preached.

FRUIT

When Chapman retired from the road in 1895, Sunday felt called to carry on his mentor's ministry. With Nell and their two kids and sermon outlines from Chapman, Sunday conducted his first revival meeting in Garner, Iowa. He would spend the rest of his life in this ministry.

Early on, Sunday developed his own style. He started with Chapman's messages but made them much simpler—ideal for the plain folk he encountered in the small, rural midwestern towns he visited. He added drama and volume, and newspaper reporters who witnessed his messages called them "fiery," "forcible," "clear," and "magnetic." The services drew crowds larger than anyone had ever seen in many of these towns. One reporter claimed, "largest congregation ever assembled"; another said, "church people aroused as never before."

As Sunday's style developed, so did his sophistication. After the tent collapsed on a meeting in 1905, Sunday's advance man made arrangements for the construction of a large temporary wooden hall at every town. The smallest of these structures seated fifteen hundred. The largest, used in Chicago and New York City, held twenty-two thousand. Sacks of sawdust were poured out on the dirt floor to keep down the dust. When converts came down the aisles, they "hit the sawdust trail," an expression that in America became synonymous with becoming a Christian.

In 1907 Sunday was ordained by the Chicago presbytery. Press accounts of his ministry passed from town to town, and his reputation grew with them. In some cities the papers published "box scores" of the baseball evangelist that showed the number of "trail hitters," or converts, at each night's meeting. The year Billy was ordained the average population of the towns he visited was ten thousand. Six years later, an "average town" had a population of seventy-six thousand. By this time Sunday was the most popular preacher in America, a national figure whose revivals were covered by every major newspaper.

Sunday was a preacher, but he was also a showman. He dressed stylishly, used contemporary language, and was never afraid to weave current social and political issues into his messages. In 1910 he was joined by choir director Homer Rodeheaver, who for the next twenty years directed choirs assembled from local churches in each town Sunday visited. As the meetings moved to larger cities, Sunday developed sophisticated systems for planning and conducting revivals. Each city was divided into districts, and each district was assigned a leader to coordinate all promotion efforts with its churches and businesses. At its peak, Sunday's tour included twenty professional staff members and hundreds of volunteers in each city. Later evangelists, including Billy Graham, implemented and expanded on Billy Sunday's innovative methods.

Of Sunday's many gifts, the most remarkable was not his animated stage presence but his resounding voice. Night after night he could preach to crowds numbering in excess of twenty thousand without amplification. His booming words filled every hall from the first row to the last. Before World War I those words often contained calls against alcohol as Sunday joined with the temperance preachers to help bring about the passage of the Prohibition Amendment. During the war he rallied audiences with patriotic fervor, encouraging them to support and pray for sons and husbands fighting for freedom in France.

Sunday's ministry reached its pinnacle of popularity in the war years; soon after it was over, attendance at his revivals declined. The press, which had done so much to make him popular, discovered that Billy Sunday headlines no longer sold papers, so they looked for other news to cover. When they did, Sunday lost one of his most valuable assets: free promotion.

Another factor leading to the decline of his popularity was the modernist debate. During the war Americans and their churches were largely united in a single patriotic cause, with little time for controversies such as theology, evolution, and the reliability and relevance of Scripture in the modern world. But after the war Christians turned their attention to those issues, and in doing so, they chose sides that split congregations and denominations. Sunday's message had not changed, but now that ministries tended to fit into either the modernist or the fundamentalist camp, Billy fell into the latter, which endeared him to like-minded churches but alienated him from those who embraced modernist teachings—and the press largely favored this new movement. To them, Sunday was a preacher of the "old time" religion and "the last of his line."

But the man who got started without news coverage was able to continue as in the old days, and Sunday carried on in his traveling ministry through the 1920s and halfway through the depression of the 1930s, drawing thousands to his meetings in the Midwest and the South. Indeed, because of the modernist debate, his fundamental faith drew fundamentalists in large numbers. Among those who heard him preach was a five-year-old boy named Billy Graham.

Billy Sunday was in his sixties and still traveling as an evangelist when he suffered his first heart attack. He died from another attack two years later on November 6, 1935. In his thirty-nine years as an itinerant evangelist he had conducted more than three hundred revivals and preached thousands of sermons, leading untold numbers of men and women to get out of their seats and "hit the sawdust trail" that led them to faith in Christ.

LEGACY

In these days of citywide Billy Graham crusades and stadium-filling Promise Keepers conferences, Billy Sunday's evangelistic meetings do not seem so extraordinary. But in many ways the former are the result of the latter. When Sunday toured America's dirt roads with his gospel message, he did so as a pioneer. Now and then a small town would have its small revival, and a big city might host an occasional evangelistic gathering, but neither had seen the likes of a Billy Sunday, a man who could ignite any small town or big city into a spiritual inferno.

He was among the first to unite a community's various and often competing churches into a common mission, to strategically organize all promotional and planning efforts, and to run an itinerant ministry with the efficiency of a business. The many evangelistic ministries that came after him can thank Sunday for blazing the trail.

But the ministry models he left us are just part of the story. The legions who attended his meetings were not there to marvel at his business strategy. They came to hear someone who was so passionate about his faith that he couldn't stand to see it locked behind church doors. They came to hear a gospel so relevant that it could be spoken in the earthy language they understood best. And they came in the hope of leaving with the same Jesus that could get an ex-baseball player to preach as well as he played.

Be strong with the Lord's mighty power. Put on all of God's armor so that you will be able to stand firm against all strategies and tricks of the Devil. Ephesians 6:10-11

BOOKS BY BILLY SUNDAY

Billy Sunday Speaks (Billy Sunday papers) (1981)
Sawdust Trail Preacher: The Story of Billy Sunday (with Betty S. Everett) (1987)

Too much of the preaching of today
is too nice; too pretty; too dainty. Lord save
us from off-handed, flabby-cheeked,
brittle-boned, weak-kneed, thin-skinned,
pliable, plastic, spineless, effeminate,
ossified three-karat Christianity.

From *Preacher: Billy Sunday and Big-Time
American Evangelism*

JONI EARECKSON TADA

HOPE IN ADVERSITY

As long as I can sit up in this chair and as long as my lungs hold out, I will echo Isaiah 12:5 and "sing to the Lord for he has done glorious things; let this be known to all the world." Come to think of it, even if I can't sit up in my chair, I'll avail myself of His grace.

Joni Eareckson Tada: Her Story

The writings of Corrie ten Boom had a profound effect on Joni Eareckson Tada. Corrie had lived through the horrors of Nazi imprisonment; Joni had survived an accident that would confine her to a wheelchair for life. Late in Corrie's life, she suffered a series of strokes that left her partially disabled and increasingly dependent on others to serve her—a tough blow to a woman who had spent her life in sacrificial service to others. But Corrie's situation became the grounds for a unique understanding between the two women.

They first met at a booksellers convention, where the two happened to be presenting their new books. As Joni described it, Corrie approached her, "hiked her cane on her elbow, reached for my hand with those strong hands that all survivors have, and announced in her thick Dutch accent, 'One day, my friend, we will be dancing together in heaven because of the Lord Jesus.'"

While attending this great Dutch woman's funeral in 1983, Joni recalled that first meeting, adding, "Today I can laugh and rejoice because Corrie is dancing now."

In Short

Artist, writer, and speaker Joni Eareckson Tada has called the world's attention to the needs of the disabled, influencing public law and social practice toward this long neglected segment of society. Her Wheels for the World program has brought new life to thousands previously imprisoned in their beds. Her art, books, speaking, and radio broadcasts have declared to millions that our greatest handicaps are spiritual, and therefore our only hope for wholeness comes in the power of Jesus Christ.

FAITH

Joni was born on October 15, 1949, in Baltimore, Maryland. Her parents, Johnny and Margaret "Lindy" Eareckson, were both energetic, athletic, and fond of sharing their love for the outdoors with Joni and her three older sisters. Joni inherited her father's name, his creativity, and his love for horses.

Although she attended an Episcopal church with the rest of her family and was active in the choir, Joni found little time for God in her teen years. She opted instead to spend time with her peers. But among her circle of friends were some who were involved in the Young Life ministry at her school. When she was fifteen, Joni joined these friends at a Young Life retreat, where she opened her heart to the gospel and committed her life to Christ.

The decision had an immediate effect on her, and she found new joy in her life and new energy for her church activities. But the fervor waned. Within two years, her faith was crowded out by her popularity, boyfriends, and a social calendar filled with parties, sports, and horseback riding. Not until after her high school graduation in 1967 did she pause again to reflect on the state of her spiritual life. One summer day after an especially invigorating ride on her horse, she recalled the joy she had experienced as a new Christian—joy that now eluded her, she realized. She prayed, "Lord, if you're really there, do something in my life that will change me and turn me around." A short time later, Joni got her answer.

On a hot July day that same summer, she decided to go for a late afternoon swim in the Chesapeake Bay. The moment she dove into the cool, murky water, her life changed forever. "I felt my head strike something hard and unyielding. At the same time, clumsily and crazily, my body sprawled out of control. I heard or felt a loud electric buzzing, an unexplainable inner sensation. It was something like an electric shock, combined with a vibration—like a heavy metal spring being suddenly and sharply uncoiled, its 'sprong' perhaps muffled by the water. Yet it wasn't really a sound or even a feeling—just a sensation. I felt no pain."

The impact of the dive severed Joni's spinal cord at the fourth and fifth cervical vertebrae. Before her eighteenth birthday she was a quadriplegic.

During the two years after the accident, Joni underwent surgery and rehabilitation. She worked and prayed for recovery, believing that she could regain the use of her arms and legs. When all efforts failed, she fell into depression and contemplated suicide on many occasions. Then she turned to philosophy, devouring existential writings and trying to convince herself that since God would not heal her, he had no business in her life.

Apparently, God disagreed. He heard the prayers of her friends and spoke through her mother, who read to Joni from C. S. Lewis's *Mere Christianity* during their visits. Eventually, Joni found hope again, and her eagerness to pursue God returned. She plunged into Scripture as well as the writings of Francis Shaeffer and other writings of C. S. Lewis. She began to realize that Jesus himself was with her in this trial. He had been "immobilized, helpless, paralyzed" when he was on the cross. "He did know what it was like not to be able to move—not to be able to scratch your nose, shift your weight, wipe your eyes." He knew exactly how she felt.

As Joni progressed in her rehabilitation, her faith was strengthened—not always through victory, but more often through trials and disappointments. Throughout her struggle, God patiently taught her to adapt. Her limitations brought her joy as well as pain.

Among the greatest pains were the social and emotional trials that confronted her daily. Before the accident, she had been resourceful and independent. Now she had to rely totally on others for her care. She had been admired and respected. Now she was stared at, treated with condescension, and made to suffer the attention of old ladies who would lean over her wheelchair, shake their heads, and say, "Oh, you poor thing. You brave, brave girl." The ignorance and insensitivity of others and the physical barriers to mobility in a world that had not yet addressed the needs of those with handicaps made every day a challenge—and every challenge an exercise in faith.

FRUIT

Confronted by all the things she couldn't do, Joni discovered two things that she had not lost in the accident. The first was her voice. A Christian friend invited her to attend a Bible study and to share her faith story. At these meetings, she could sit with other Christians, listen, and talk about her own struggles and victories. During these times, she could be lifted from her chair and for a few brief hours sit on a couch and feel as if she were just one of the crowd.

When she did tell her story, her listeners were moved and invited her to share it with others. Joni began receiving invitations to speak at churches and other Bible studies. Eventually, she became a Young Life leader, providing for high school students what she herself had received years earlier through this ministry.

The other gift she had not lost was her artistic creativity. She eventually learned to write again by holding a pen in her mouth, and a friend who had seen some of her drawings before the accident encouraged her to try drawing this way. Her first attempts were unimpressive, but Joni persisted and eventually mastered the technique. Her successes in speaking and drawing had a surprising result. For the first time since the accident, her disability had became an instrument of joy: It had forced her to discover abilities that most people never find in their lifetime.

As her art became more precise and the quality improved, Joni began giving her drawings as wedding presents and Christmas gifts. One day a visitor to her father's office spotted one of her drawings and remarked on its great detail and original style. He was even more impressed when Joni's dad told him how his daughter had drawn it. The admirer offered to put together an exhibition of Joni's work.

The day the exhibition opened in downtown Baltimore, Joni, her sister, and some friends got caught in a traffic jam trying to get there. The street had been blocked off for some kind of special event. As they attempted to maneuver down a side street, Joni spotted a brass band and a television crew in front of the building they were trying to get to. Stretched across the front of the building was a huge banner announcing: JONI EARECKSON DAY.

Her small collection of mouth-drawn art sold for fifty to seventy-five dollars apiece that day, bringing in one thousand dollars. But much more valuable to her was the experience itself. At the exhibition, total strangers regarded her as a talented, intelligent woman—a woman who just happened to be in a wheelchair. This response was a sharp contrast to attitudes Joni often faced—that because her legs and arms were damaged, her mind was also somehow injured. The event also opened up a new ministry for her. In the audience that day was a young fireman whose career had ended when his hands were lost in a fire. Joni met with him, telling him of her faith in Christ and restoring the man's hope in life. While many people could have told him the same thing, Joni was among the very few with the credibility to convince him. He went on to become a spokesman for the fire department.

The exhibition vaulted Joni into the public arena. She received invitations to speak at schools, churches, women's groups, and civic functions—even at the White House. Then came radio broadcasts and television appearances, including an interview with Barbara Walters.

To meet the demand for her work, the young artist launched a line of greeting cards and her own company, JoniPTL. The initials for "praise the Lord" were her expression of gratitude to God. "My art is a reflection of how God can empower someone like me to rise above the circumstances."

In 1976 Billy Graham invited Joni to speak at his Detroit crusade at the Silverdome, where he distributed free copies of her autobiography, *Joni*. A short time later Graham's film ministry, World Wide Pictures, made a movie of her story. It was released in 1979, made available in fifteen languages, and has been seen by fifty million people around the world. In the year of the film's release, Joni moved to southern California to launch her own ministry, Joni and Friends, now known as JAF Ministries. In 1982 she married Ken Tada, a high school history teacher, and together they travel the world, speaking and reaching out in ministry.

Among JAF's many efforts are workshops to teach people how to relate with disabled persons, ministry to those with handicaps, and a daily radio show, *Joni and Friends,* carried on stations nationwide. In 1993 JAF launched Wheels for the World, a campaign to provide wheelchairs to an estimated eighteen million disabled children and adults who need but cannot afford one. To date, this effort has distributed seventy thousand wheelchairs around the world.

Meanwhile, Joni's books, videos, and broadcasts in many translations reach a worldwide audience that stretches far beyond the disabled community. Her consistent message of hope in the face of adversity reminds all who hear it that Christ is the true healer of the spiritual deficiencies that handicap us all.

LEGACY

Joni Eareckson Tada's work on behalf of the disabled has been profound. Her name is known to countless members of the disabled community as well as to the friends and family members of those with disabilities. President Bush appointed her to the National Council on Disability, a group whose work shaped the Americans with Disabilities Act. This legislation changed American landscape and architecture and opened society's doors to millions of its neglected citizens.

Yet from the start, her ministry has not been confined to this community. Her message is so powerful and inspiring that most of her listeners and readers see her not merely as "a woman with a handicap" but as an eloquent, engaging communicator of the gospel. In the evangelical church, she stands with her hero Corrie ten Boom among the most influential and respected Christian women of the twentieth century.

For additional information about JAF, see appendix A.

We know that God causes everything to work together for the good of those who love God and are called according to his purpose for them.
Romans 8:28

BOOKS BY JONI EARECKSON TADA

A Christmas Longing (1996)
A Quiet Place in a Crazy World (1993)
Diamonds in the Dust (1993)
Glorious Intruder (1994)
God's Precious Love (1998)
Heaven (1997)
Holiness in Hidden Places (1999)
I'll Be with You Always (1998)
Joni (1997)
Joni Eareckson Tada: Her Story (1994)
Life and Death Dilemma (1995)
More Precious Than Silver (1998)
Secret Strength (1996)
When God Weeps: Why Our Sufferings Matter to the Almighty
   (with Steve Estes)(1997)
You've Got a Friend (1999)

MINISTRY INVOLVEMENT

Joni and Friends (JAF) Ministries is a nonprofit Christian organization dedicated to accelerating Christian ministry in the disability community . . .

- by advocating a biblical response toward disabilities, both visible and invisible.

- by providing opportunities for disability awareness.

- by educating the church community in practical ways of serving disabled persons.

- by assisting persons with disabilities in their progress toward independence and fulfillment.

KEN TAYLOR

THE LIVING WORD

God gives to some people the
gift of preaching; to some,
hospitality; to some, the
ability to do quality work
at a factory bench;
and to me, the ability
to paraphrase.

My Life: A Guided Tour

D uring a business trip to Israel in 1962 Ken Taylor received a package at his Jerusalem hotel. It contained the galley proofs of *Living Letters,* his painstaking paraphrasing of the New Testament epistles. As he held the sheets of paper in his hands, it occurred to him that he was in the very land where Jesus had once used five loaves and two fish to feed five thousand people. Taylor did the math. If five loaves fed five thousand, then two thousand *Living Letters* could feed two million.

IN SHORT
Ken Taylor paraphrased Bible verses so his children could understand them. Unable to find a publisher for his controversial work, he formed his own company, Tyndale House Publishers, and published it himself. The response was so strong that he continued paraphrasing and publishing until he had completed all of Scripture. *The Living Bible* immediately became the best-selling book in America. Taylor's passion to see God's Word come to life has led to immeasurable fruit through this Bible, the publishing company it spawned, and resources it has contributed to ministries around the world.

FAITH
Kenneth Nathaniel Taylor was born on May 8, 1917, in Portland, Oregon, the second son of George and Char-

lotte Taylor. His father was a pastor, and both parents raised their children so thoroughly in the Christian faith that Ken cannot recall a time when he did not consider himself a Christian. Ken excelled in high school, ran track, joined the debate team, and was speaker at his high school graduation. He and his brother Doug were strong competitors, and when Doug decided he wanted to go to Wheaton College, Ken made up his mind to go there too.

After graduating from Wheaton in 1938, Taylor planned to head to medical school but soon thought that biology, genetics, or even journalism might be a better fit for his talents. He entered Oregon State University and continued to court Margaret West, a teammate from his high school debating years. Sure of the woman but not of his educational plans, he proposed to her, then dropped out of school and joined the ministry of InterVarsity Christian Fellowship in Toronto. In 1940, halfway through his two-year stint in Canada, Ken and Margaret were married.

Ken entered Dallas Theological Seminary, and in 1943 the Taylors moved back to Chicago so Ken could complete his studies at Northern Baptist Theological Seminary. After graduation from seminary in 1944, he was ordained at Central Bible Church in Portland, his home church. During his seminary studies he had worked part-time at InterVarsity Press, and he continued there as editor of their magazine, *HIS,* until 1946. It was clear that God had chosen to use him in publishing.

FRUIT

In 1947 Taylor joined Moody Literature Mission, a division of Moody Bible Institute, and the following year became the director of Moody Press, where he stayed until 1963. Early in his tenure at Moody, he recognized what a sad shape the Christian bookstore industry was in. Stores were often in out-of-the-way locations, and few prospered. Ken joined with other publishers to form the Christian Booksellers Association. CBA sought to help store owners and managers share ideas that would build their businesses and brought publishers and wholesalers together to exhibit their products. The first CBA convention was held in 1950, and conventions have grown ever since.

Between 1942 and 1956 Margaret Taylor gave birth to ten children. After dinner each evening, Ken would read to them from the Bible. But the children had difficulty understanding the King James text. He searched for children's stories that covered the Bible, but finding few that met his needs, Taylor decided to write some himself.

He began by writing stories to accompany pictures the children brought home from Sunday school. That manuscript became *The Bible in Pictures for Little Eyes,* published in 1956.

This father's next endeavor to bring Scripture to life for his children was even more ambitious. It began one Saturday afternoon in 1955 as he sat at his desk in their Wheaton farmhouse. At random, Taylor took a King James Version Bible verse and rewrote it. The verse was 2 Timothy 2:3. When he was satisfied with the result, he went through the chapter, verse by verse, to make each section of Scripture understandable.

That evening he read the verses to his family, then began translating a few more verses for family devotions each evening. When he read his verses to the children, he usually received a positive response, but when he used the King James version, the children often seemed baffled.

As he prayed for God's leading, Taylor began to believe that God wanted him to translate the New Testament epistles into words that anyone could understand. The commuter train that he took each weekday between Wheaton and his downtown Chicago office at Moody Press became Taylor's office. As the swaying train bumped over the tracks, Taylor sat with a Bible on one knee and a writing pad on the other. Progress was slow, and the handwritten manuscript went through a half-dozen revisions until he thought it was ready for publication.

Living Letters was completed December 27, 1960. But finding a publisher was a problem. Taylor had the authority to publish the book at Moody Press, but he felt that doing so would put a strain on his friends there who were great fans of the King James version. He submitted it to another publisher, only to have it rejected. That's when he decided to publish it himself.

He found a Chicago printer who agreed to print two thousand

copies and let Taylor pay for them as the copies were sold. To ensure that he had orders for the book before it was printed, he arranged for an exhibit booth at the 1962 Chicago CBA convention, where he would display five hand-bound sample copies. Needing a name for his as yet nonexistent publishing company, he found it in the name of William Tyndale.

In the early sixteenth century, Tyndale had dared to do the unthinkable: He translated the New Testament from its original languages into English.

Alone in his tiny CBA exhibit booth, Taylor contrived a unique sales technique: He handed a copy of the book to passersby and asked them to find their favorite passage and read it. They were thrilled with what they found. He took eight hundred orders—enough to cover most of the printing costs of the first run of two thousand books. The next year the Billy Graham Evangelistic Association made arrangements to print *Living Letters*. Over Taylor's objections, they insisted on paying him royalties, so he received five cents a copy. Soon, over half a million copies were in print, and Taylor set up a foundation to receive the giant royalty checks and disburse the funds to Christian ministries.

The success of the book prompted Taylor to continue his work. From 1965 to 1970 he paraphrased additional Bible books and published them in various collections. In 1971 Taylor published the entire paraphrase of Scripture: *The Living Bible*. In the next two years it became the fastest-selling book in America. Mainstream bookstores clamored to get copies for their shelves, and soon such national chains as Waldenbooks and B. Dalton were stocking the book. By 1996 it had sold forty million copies.

While most readers of the paraphrased Scriptures found them refreshing and inspiring, some were ready to brand Taylor a heretic. But the positive responses far outweighed the negative. *The Living Bible* brought Scripture to life for believers new and old. It especially made the Bible accessible to teenagers and college students, thus fanning the flames of what became known as the Jesus People movement, an outpouring of evangelical fervor among young people that birthed new churches and a new style of contemporary Christian music.

Meanwhile, Taylor's work found admirers in an unexpected audience. Traditionally most Catholics received Scripture in the Mass rather than through personal study. That changed when the revolutionary Vatican Council II of the 1960s encouraged Catholics to read their Bibles. So when Tyndale House released a Catholic version of *The Living Bible,* it was received with open arms.

Flushed with the success of Taylor's paraphrases, the company expanded to publish other books as well. Titles by authors such as James Dobson, James Kennedy, and David Wilkerson were added to their book lists, and Tyndale House grew into a full-fledged publishing house.

Meanwhile, proceeds from sales of the *The Living Bible* continued to pour into Tyndale House Foundation, the organization Taylor had set up to receive all royalties. These funds have provided grants for food programs, equipment for missionaries, cancer research, child evangelism, literacy programs, and the development of Christian publishing overseas, the work that had touched Ken's heart long before. To date, the Foundation has distributed more than thirty million dollars to worthy causes.

Decades after its release *The Living Bible* was still selling well. But Taylor was compelled to see it updated, to make it as readable and relevant today as it was when it was first published. In 1996, exactly twenty-five years after *The Living Bible* was released, Tyndale House Publishers unveiled the *Holy Bible,* New Living Translation. Unlike Ken's earlier work, the NLT is a true translation, not a paraphrase. But its translators worked with the same vision, seeking to make God's Word clear and enjoyable to today's readers.

In 1984 Taylor retired as president of Tyndale House Publishers, the venture that became one of the largest Christian publishing houses in the world. His children, the inspiration for his life's work, are all grown up, as are many of his grandchildren. But when *their* children feel like hearing a Bible story told in words they can understand, they know just whose lap to sit on.

Legacy

The ministry of Ken Taylor was born of the frustration of finding Bible stories his own children could read. What began as a solution for his own family became a Bible accessible to the entire English-speaking world. Along the way, he encountered rejection and severe criticism, but he carried on with faith and determination.

Just as remarkable is the ministry born of this Bible. Its popularity drew countless newcomers to Scripture, including millions of Catholics. Other books released by the publishing house Taylor founded have reached millions more. The royalties received from *The Living Bible* and its predecessors have funded ministries the world over. And all because a father wanted his children to discover God through his Word.

Just tell me what to do and I will do it, Lord. As long as I live I'll wholeheartedly obey.

Psalm 119:33-34, TLB

BOOKS BY KEN TAYLOR

Almost 12 (1995)
Creation (1992)
Everything a Child Should Know about God (1996)
Family Devotions for Children (1999)
Giant Steps for Little People (1985)
Ken Taylor's Favorite Bible Stories (1995)
My First Bible in Pictures (1989)
My Life: A Guided Tour (with Virginia J. Muir) (1991)
My Little Bible in Pictures (1998)
Next Steps for New Christians (1989)
Right Choices (1998)
Small Talks about God (1995)
Stories about Jesus (1994)
The Bible in Pictures for Little Eyes (1997)
Wise Words for Little People (1987)
Words and Thoughts to Help You Grow (1998)

CORRIE TEN BOOM

FORGIVENESS

And so I discovered that it is
not on our forgiveness any
more than on our goodness
that the world's healing
hinges, but on His. When He
tells us to love our enemies,
He gives, along with the
command, the love itself.

The Hiding Place

When Cornelia ten Boom finished speaking at a church service in Munich, a balding, heavyset man walked toward her. In a flash, Corrie remembered him: The SS guard who had stood at the shower-room door of the Ravensbrück concentration camp years earlier. Suddenly, she was transported back to the horror—the mocking men, the lice-infested clothing, the cries of horror, her sister Betsie's pained face.

The church emptied as the man came toward her and spoke. "How grateful I am for your message, Fräulein. To think that, as you say, 'He has washed my sins away!'" He thrust his hand out. Corrie froze. She, who had preached so often about forgiveness, kept her hand at her side. Angry, vengeful thoughts boiled within her. Yet, she saw the sin of them.

"Jesus," she prayed silently, "I cannot forgive him. Give me your forgiveness." As she took his hand, a current rushed through her. Healing warmth flooded her being, bringing tears to her eyes. "I forgive you, brother!" she cried, "With all my heart!"

In Short
Dutch writer Corrie ten Boom survived the Holocaust and proceeded to tell the world of the God who carried her through. Her substantial library of writings have captivated and transformed readers for decades, making her one of the most recognized and beloved Christian writers of the twentieth century.

Faith
On April 15, 1892, Cornelia ten Boom was born into a loving Christian family in Haarlem, the Netherlands. She was the fifth

child of Casper and Cor ten Boom, who lived above a small jewelry store, where Casper worked as a watchmaker. The narrow house, called the Beje (pronounced bay-yay), was in the heart of the Jewish section of town. Devoted members of the Dutch Reformed church, the ten Booms were known for their faith and kindness. They had many Jewish friends and neighbors with whom they shared Jewish Sabbaths and feasts as well as Bible study of the Old Testament.

At age twenty-four, after graduating from a local Bible school, Corrie learned the craft of watchmaking and went to Basel, Switzerland, to serve her apprenticeship. When she returned home, she qualified as a watchmaker—the first woman in Holland to do so. Corrie continued to live and work at home—a home that had opened its doors to refugees and orphans. Corrie taught Bible classes in the public schools and led Sunday school classes at church. She also organized and ran a network of clubs for girls. Some of these groups later became Girl Guide clubs, an international organization equivalent to the American Girl Scouts.

FRUIT

In 1940 Holland was invaded by Nazi Germany. Because the ten Booms were known as charitable Christians, people came to them for help. In 1943 the ten Booms began to shelter Jewish neighbors who had been driven from their homes by the Gestapo. As the persecution intensified, so did Corrie's efforts to protect the Jews who sought her help. Corrie prayed for God's guidance with each new underground endeavor. And he provided everything she needed for her family's ministry—from safer hiding places in the Dutch countryside to ration cards that would feed her growing household.

Corrie soon found herself involved in the Dutch Resistance, which helped to coordinate the escape of her neighbors to homes outside of Haarlem. As soon as she found hiding places for those sequestered in her own home, more neighbors arrived on her doorstep. Before long, she had a builder construct a false wall in her bedroom, providing a safe place where she could hide Jews. Within eighteen months, the ten Boom home was the center of an underground ring that reached throughout the country. Corrie herself dealt with hundreds of stolen ration cards each month to feed the Jews hiding in homes all over Holland.

On February 28, 1944, a man came into the ten Boom watch shop and asked Corrie to help him. He told her that he and his wife had been hiding Jews and that his wife had been arrested. Corrie promised to help. But late that night the Gestapo stormed into her home, and Corrie and her family were arrested. Corrie was fifty-two at the time; her sister Betsie, who was also living in the Beje, was fifty-nine; Casper was eighty-four. The Gestapo stayed for two days, convinced that Jews were hiding in the house. When the agents left, Dutch underground members liberated the six Jewish refugees who had been stuck in Corrie's cramped hiding place the entire time.

Meanwhile, the ten Boom family was taken to prison. Casper ten Boom died within ten days of his arrest. Corrie and Betsie were transported to three different prisons and concentration camps, first in Holland and later in Germany. Through a miracle, Corrie was able to smuggle her Bible into Ravensbrück, the German concentration camp. She and her sister used the secreted Bible to hold worship services in their barracks. At first, they convened their meetings timidly because those who were found with a Bible often faced death. But when no guard ever came, Corrie and Betsie grew bolder. Each night they read from the Bible as women hung over the edges of the tightly stacked beds to listen.

A second service was added after evening roll call so more could join them. Their worship was as eclectic as their traditions. Roman Catholic women recited the Magnificat in Latin. Lutherans whispered their hymns. The Eastern Orthodox women softly spoke their chants. Then Corrie or Betsie read from their Dutch Bible, translating the text into German. Others passed on the Scriptures to their neighbors in French, Polish, Russian, Czech, and back to Dutch.

On one cold November day, the two sisters were sent to level a patch of rough ground outside the camp wall. Betsie was so weak that she could barely lift her shovel. The guard watching them grew angry and yelled at her. Impatiently, the guard snatched a leather whip from her belt and slashed Betsie across the chest. Seeing the welt rise on Betsie's neck, Corrie burst out in fury, raising her shovel and rushing at the guard. But Betsie, her eyes watering with pain, stood in Corrie's way. "Don't look at the whip mark, Corrie," she said. "Look at Jesus only."

Betsie died a month later, on December 16, 1944. Within days of her sister's death, Corrie was released from Ravensbrück—due to a clerical error. She later discovered that one week after her release, all women her age were taken to the gas chambers.

When Corrie returned to her father's watch shop in Haarlem, she knew she needed to write a letter. In the camp, she had learned who had betrayed her family. It was indeed the man who had come into the shop the day the family was arrested. She looked back on all that had happened since that day: the arrests of her entire family, her father's death ten days later, Betsie's suffering and death in the camp, the deaths of other family members, her own ten months of horrific imprisonment. Yet the letter she wrote to her betrayer was full of forgiveness: "I heard that most probably you are the one who betrayed me. . . . I have forgiven you everything. God will also forgive you everything, if you ask Him. . . . Never doubt the Lord Jesus' love. He is standing with His arms spread out to receive you. . . ."

When the war ended in the summer of 1945, Corrie purchased a house in Bloemendaal, taking in disabled people and former prisoners from the concentration camps. Later that same year Corrie sensed God calling her to tell her story. She traveled to the United States, where she met Christians who arranged for her to speak in churches, Bible studies, and conferences. In 1946 she returned to Europe, raising money for the purchase of the Darmstadt concentration camp, which was transformed into a home where people who suffered the traumas of the war could come for healing and recovery.

Corrie's war story and postwar ministry grabbed increasing attention among Christians worldwide. The authentic vitality of her faith had a profound effect on her audiences as well as on those she ministered to more personally. God opened doors to larger audiences each year. In 1948 she met Cliff Barrows at a Youth for Christ conference in Switzerland. Throughout the 1950s, Corrie traveled the globe on her own and with other ministries, speaking to audiences throughout Europe, North America, Africa, Asia, and the Pacific. And in 1960 she met Ruth and Billy Graham—the start of a long and cherished friendship for all three.

Corrie's writing also gained popularity, exposing millions of readers to her war and postwar work. The first of fifteen books was published in Dutch in 1946 and released in an English translation as *A Prisoner—and Yet!* the following year. Several of her subsequent books were written in German. Her last book, *A Tramp Finds a Home*, was released in 1978, after its road-weary author had finally retired in her new home in the United States. But certainly her most popular book is *The Hiding Place*, a retelling of her experiences during the war. In 1975 World Wide Pictures, the film ministry of the Billy Graham Evangelistic Association, released a film based on this book, providing millions of viewers worldwide with a glimpse of Corrie's remarkable journey of hope in the midst of darkness.

In 1977 Corrie was granted permanent residence in the United States. In the following year she suffered a stroke, which ended an exhausting traveling ministry that had spanned four decades. The stroke left her without speech and most movement, but she continued, with assistance, to respond to the flood of letters she received from friends and admirers. Corrie died five years later, on April 15, 1983. It was her ninety-first birthday.

Outside the Holocaust Memorial in Jerusalem stands a grove of trees dedicated to the non-Jewish men and women who risked life and liberty to save Jews from the Nazi campaign of death. Corrie ten Boom hid and fed Jews in her bedroom hiding place, led many to safety beyond the reach of the Gestapo, and went to prison for her efforts. One of the trees in this grove is dedicated to her—a living memorial to the fearless faith of a Dutch watchmaker.

LEGACY
Corrie's long ministry is filled with lessons. While God undoubtedly used her before the war as she taught her students, led her

girls clubs, and ministered to her Jewish neighbors, her most significant ministry did not begin until after the war, when she was in her *fifties*. And her most fruitful efforts were carried out when she was in her sixties and seventies, even her eighties—long past the time when most people retire. In this century Corrie engaged a greater Christian audience in her *old* age than any other Christian woman of *any* age. And in the twentieth-century church, where women have had few opportunities to rise to national, much less international, stature, this watchmaker's ministry was unsurpassed in its impact and continues even after her death.

Of course, it was her experiences during the war that gave Corrie a voice. After World War II, the world was exposed to many accounts of the Nazi atrocities and the men and women who sacrificed their freedom and even their lives to save the Jews. *Anne Frank: The Diary of a Young Girl* and more recently the movie *Schindler's List* have captured our hearts, reminding us of what once was—and what must never be again.

While the story of Corrie ten Boom serves us in a similar way, it adds something else just as important—and harder to contend with: *forgiveness*. We can hardly grasp the extent of the horrors she endured, the heartsickness she suffered. But even from the small portion we *can* grasp, we're filled with a rage that makes such forgiveness seem impossible. Yet Corrie, who suffered not vicariously but in person, forgave her betrayer, her captors, her tormentors. Not with a cheap grace, a blind faith, a repression of her true feelings, but with the boundless love that she truly found in Christ.

Her remarkable, seemingly impossible act of forgiveness reminds us that forgiveness is not just a part of our faith; forgiveness is *essential* to it. We cannot accurately reflect to others the love of Christ without demonstrating in our own lives the one act that makes our faith matter at all: Christ's forgiveness of our own sins. Corrie ten Boom discovered this truth in the middle of a war, in the greatest of tests, and spent the rest of her life making sure we would discover it too.

When you are praying, first forgive anyone you are holding a grudge against, so that your Father in heaven will forgive your sins, too. Mark 11:25

BOOKS BY CORRIE TEN BOOM

Amazing Love (1953)
A Prisoner—And Yet! (1947)
A Tramp Finds a Home (1978)
Anywhere He Leads Me (1997)
Common Sense Not Needed: Some Thoughts about an Unappreciated Work among Neglected People (1968)
Corrie ten Boom: Her Story: A Collection Consisting of The Hiding Place, Tramp for the Lord, *and* Jesus Is Victor (1995)
Corrie ten Boom's Prison Letters (1975) (out of print)
Defeated Enemies (1983)
He Cares for You (1998)
In My Father's House: The Years before the Hiding Place (1976)
Marching Orders for the End Battle (1970)
Not Good If Detached (1963)
Not I, but Christ (1997)
Plenty for Everyone (1967)
Prayers & Promises for Every Day: From the Living Bible (1997)
Reflections of God's Glory: Newly Discovered Meditations by the Author of The Hiding Place (1999)
The End Battle (1997)
The Hiding Place (1972)
The One Year Book of Personal Prayer (1998)
This Day Is the Lord's (1999)
Tramp for the Lord (1974)

1910–1997

MOTHER TERESA

LOVE IN ACTION

Love begins at home;
it is not how much we do,
but how much love we put
in the action that we do.
To God Almighty how much
we do does not matter,
but how much love we put
in that action.

From Mother Teresa's acceptance speech after receiving the Nobel Peace Prize in 1979,
quoted in *Bright Legacy: Portraits of Outstanding Christian Women*

Atiny woman in a white sari peered over a podium across a sea of influential leaders who had come to the National Prayer Breakfast in Washington, D.C. "It is not enough for us to say, 'I love God,' but I also have to love my neighbor. St. John says that you are a liar if you say you love God and you don't love your neighbor. How can you love God whom you do not see, if you do not love your neighbor whom you see, whom you touch, with whom you live? It is also very important for us to realize that love, to be true, has to hurt. I must be willing to give whatever it takes not to harm other people and, in fact, to do good to them. This requires that I be willing to give until it hurts. Otherwise, there is no true love in me, and I bring injustice, not peace, to those around me."

In these few words spoken in 1994, Mother Teresa preached what she had spent a lifetime living.

IN SHORT

Catholic nun, missionary, and Nobel Peace Prize recipient Mother Teresa gathered into her arms the despised and discarded of the world. In God's name, she treated the wounds and healed the hurts of thousands in India, formed a missionary society whose workers have touched tens of thousands more, and became a living symbol to the entire world of the Father's love for his children.

FAITH

Agnes Gonxha Bojaxhiu was born in 1910, in Skopje, Yugoslavia, in what is now Macedonia. Her parents, Nikola and Drana, were Albanians who settled in Skopje shortly after the beginning of the century. Her father was demanding yet affectionate, a committed Catholic and a successful businessman. He was also an Albanian patriot and active civic leader in the politically troubled times following World War I. When Agnes was nine, he attended a political meeting in Belgrade. He returned home deathly ill—poisoning was suspected—and died soon afterward. To make matters worse, his business partner ran off with the company's funds, leaving Agnes's family devastated both emotionally and financially.

At age twelve, Agnes told her family that she wanted to belong wholly to God. She became more deeply involved in her church and through it met Franjo Jambrenkovic, a Jesuit priest who opened her eyes to mission work. He introduced her to Jesuit missionaries who had served around the world, and by age thirteen Agnes was going out of her way to meet with them, hear their stories, and organize concerts to raise money for their work. At age eighteen, after much prayer and counsel, Agnes told her mother that she believed God was calling her to be a nun.

Agnes told Father Jambrenkovic that she wanted to serve in Calcutta, India. He recommended that she pursue joining the order of the Sisters of the Institute of the Blessed Virgin Mary, also known as the Sisters of Loretto, which had a mission there. After studying at their convent in Dublin, Ireland, for less than a year, Agnes sailed to India to enter the Loretto convent in the city of Darjeeling at the foot of the Himalayas. She arrived in January, 1929. A year and a half later, she took on the name Teresa, in honor of St. Teresa of Avila, a sixteenth-century Spanish nun.

FRUIT

During Teresa's training in India, she studied languages (including English, Bengali, and Hindi), taught Indian children in a one-room schoolhouse, and served in a hospital. As she was completing the eight-year process of becoming a full Sister of Loretto, she was assigned to teach in a high school in Calcutta. Teresa loved teaching, and she was well liked by her students, who called her

Ma. In 1937 she made her final vows in a ceremony presided over by the archbishop of Calcutta and took on the title of Mother. Her first appointment as Mother Teresa was as principal of the school where she taught.

In 1943 a famine swept through India as a result of World War II, killing two million people. The streets of Calcutta were crowded with beggars, lepers, and homeless people. Unwanted infants were left to die on the streets or in garbage bins. The British, fearing an attack on Bengal, took over the city and installed order temporarily. Immediately after the war, the long-simmering tensions between Hindus and Muslims boiled over, causing more turmoil. Breaking the Sisters' rules, Mother Teresa walked out of the compound alone, only to encounter the horror of disemboweled, beaten, stabbed, and putrefied bodies.

After witnessing the carnage from both the famine and the fighting, Mother Teresa heard what she described as a "call within a call"—a firm leading from God to leave her position at the school to care for the needy in the slums of Calcutta. "I realized that I had the call to take care of the sick and the dying, the hungry, the naked, the homeless—to be God's love in action to the poorest of the poor." In 1948 Mother Teresa received permission from the archbishop to answer this call, and she soon left the school to begin what would become her life's work.

Working on her own, Mother Teresa focused her efforts on the poor children in Calcutta's streets, teaching them to read and to care for themselves. In 1949 her first recruit, a young girl from Bengal, joined her in the streets. A year later Mother Teresa founded a new order, the Missionaries of Charity, and chose a simple habit for the sisters to wear: a plain white sari with a blue border and a simple cross pinned to the left shoulder. Each recruit to her new order was required to devote her life to serving the poor without accepting any material reward. Over the next few years many of her own former students joined Mother Teresa in her work.

The Missionaries of Charity grew quickly. The sisters opened the Kalighat Home for the Dying in an abandoned Hindu temple, bringing to it those who were dying on the streets so they could be loved and cared for in their final days. They also opened a colony on a thirty-two-acre plot that the government gave them to provide a community for those suffering from leprosy. As the work in Calcutta expanded, the sisters opened new missions in other parts of India. And in 1965 Mother Teresa received permission from the pope to expand the order beyond India. Centers to treat lepers, the blind, the disabled, the aged, and the dying began opening worldwide, and the Brothers of Charity, associated with Mother Teresa's order, was formed to run the homes for the dying.

Mother Teresa and her spreading ministry caught the attention of Indian, Catholic, and world leaders, who honored her with high awards. In 1979 she received the Nobel Peace Prize. Mother Teresa accepted all of her awards on behalf of the poor, using any money that accompanied the awards to fund her missions. By 1990 more than three thousand nuns belonged to the Missionaries of Charity, running centers in twenty-five countries.

In 1983, while visiting Pope John Paul II, Mother Teresa suffered a heart attack. After another near-fatal attack a few years later, she began wearing a pacemaker. In 1996 she passed through another dangerous period, but her recovery was not complete, and on September 5, 1997, Mother Teresa died at the age of eighty-seven. Just months before her death, a new leader was selected to head the global ministry of the Missionaries of Charity, ensuring that its work would continue in the spirit of its founder.

LEGACY

Like any well-known person, Mother Teresa was given a public image shaped largely by the media. They saw her as the peacemaker, servant, and saint. While her life was worthy of these titles, there was much more to Mother Teresa than the headlines proclaimed. Many world leaders who met her came expecting to be blessed, but they got a lecture instead. In her passionate love for God's children, she spoke boldly against policies that persecuted those children—violence, oppression, abortion. To some people, this judgmental side seemed incongruous with Mother Teresa's message of love and compassion. But the truth was that her judgment was evidence of her integrity. Deep love fosters deep conviction; righteous actions are the electors of true authority. Mother Teresa could say what she said because she had lived it first.

This tiny woman profoundly changed the twentieth-century world, but when one studies her life, it becomes clear that her story was written in the first century. She comforted the dying and was comforted herself in the mourning. She sought no power, fortune, or fame, yet in her meekness she inherited the prayers of the world and the awed respect of its most powerful leaders. She counted the immense cost of following Jesus and then did so with her whole being, leading thousands of men and women to do the same.

Above all things, Mother Teresa loved God. We don't have to read her own words to know that. We have pictures to prove it—photographs of this remarkable servant of God as she held dying children, hugged lepers, caressed tired and weary faces with broken teeth and wrinkled cheeks, and walked through the steamy, rotting streets of Calcutta to greet others in God's name. The world caught Mother Teresa in the act of loving God—loving in action, loving until it hurt.

For more information about Mother Teresa's Missionaries of Charity, see appendix A.

"Teacher, which is the most important commandment in the law of Moses?"

Jesus replied, "'You must love the Lord your God with all your heart, all your soul, and all your mind.' This is the first and greatest commandment. A second is equally important: 'Love your neighbor as yourself.'" Matthew 22:36-39

BOOKS BY MOTHER TERESA

A Gift for God: Prayers and Meditations (1996)
A Simple Path (1995)
In the Heart of the World: Thoughts, Stories and Prayers (1997)
Jesus, the Word to Be Spoken: Prayers and Meditations for Every Day of the Year
    (1999)
Joy in Loving: A Guide to Daily Living with Mother Teresa (1997)
Loving Jesus (1991)
Meditations from a Simple Path (1996)
Mother Teresa: In My Own Words (1997)
No Greater Love (1997)
The Best Gift Is Love: Meditations by Mother Teresa (1993)
The Blessings of Love (1996)
Total Surrender (1993)
Words to Love By (1989)

1896–1982

CAMERON TOWNSEND

GOD'S WORD FOR ALL PEOPLE

Only a person's
mother tongue truly
speaks to the heart.

From *Uncle Cam*, a Wycliffe Bible Translators ministry brochure

I n the fourteenth century John Wycliffe translated the Latin
edition of the Bible into English so that his countrymen could
read God's Word in their own tongue. Two centuries later
William Tyndale, following in Wycliffe's footsteps, translated the
Bible into English from the original Hebrew and Greek.

In 1929 another translator completed his work, taking God's
Word on its first leap from English to Cakchiquel, the previously
unwritten language of a tribe of Guatemalan Indians. Although
Cameron Townsend's translation would reach far fewer people
than those of his famous predecessors, it would inspire him to lead
an army of linguistic missionaries across the globe to show people
everywhere that God cares enough to speak to them in their own
language.

In Short

Missionary and Bible translator Cam Townsend spent a decade
translating the New Testament into an obscure Central American
tribal language. Then he founded the Summer Institute of Linguistics (SIL) and Wycliffe Bible Translators to give the people from
every other tribe on earth the same thing: their own Bible, in their
own tongue. Townsend stands with John Wycliffe and William
Tyndale among the most influential Bible translators of all time.

Faith

William Cameron Townsend was born July 9, 1896, on a farm in
Downey, California, just east of Los Angeles. His parents, Will and

Molly Townsend, were poor farmers, but they were rich in faith. They raised their children—Cam, his four older sisters, and one younger brother—to work hard on the farm and to trust God to provide the rest. Their mother was witty and cheerful; their father, who had lost his hearing in a farming accident, was strict yet kind. His parents' faith had a profound effect on Cam, and he shaped his to be like theirs.

Cam's boyhood was filled with adventures. After hearing a Sunday school lesson about Jacob shearing his sheep, Cam got out his mother's sewing scissors and attempted the same thing on his little brother. When Cam's prized calf ate his first store-bought necktie, it choked, bringing both calf and tie to an inglorious end. Cam even exhumed his brother Paul's dead bunny so it would have enough air to breathe in case Jesus brought it back to life.

At age twelve Cam went through confirmation class and joined the family's Presbyterian church. For most of his teenage years he had been planning to become a teacher, but upon graduating he began to think about entering the ministry. After working to save for school, he entered Occidental College, a Presbyterian liberal arts school in Los Angeles. The famous missionary advocate John Mott came to speak at the school, and Cam was inspired by the man's vision. He was also moved by the life of Hudson Taylor, the founder of the China Inland Mission who adapted to the Chinese culture to win the Chinese people to Christ. Cam began to set his heart on missions.

But in his junior year in 1916 Cam enlisted in the Coast Guard, figuring that if the United States entered World War I, he would be drafted anyway. He also applied for a ministry position with the Bible House of Los Angeles, which was looking for Bible salesmen to go to Latin America. He was accepted and made plans to go to Guatemala. But in the spring of 1917 the U.S. declared war on Germany. It looked as if Cam's mission plans would have to be postponed. He had never heard of an able-bodied man being discharged from the service during a time of war, but he asked his Guard captain anyway. To Cam's surprise, he got the discharge, and in August of that year he sailed for Guatemala.

FRUIT

Soon after his arrival in Guatemala City, Townsend received his assigned territory: two Cakchiquel Indian villages. Some of the Indians were Christians, so Cam went hut to hut, trying to sell his Bibles. As he discovered, the Spanish Bibles were a tough sell. Most of the Indians didn't speak Spanish, and among the minority who could speak Spanish, few could read it. But Cam also conducted church services, which went better than the sales work, and soon he had helped a villager find Christ. It was the first time he had ever played such a role in a person's life, and the experience gave him new excitement for mission work.

After spending Christmas with other missionaries who took turns sharing their stories, Townsend spent the next eleven months traveling through El Salvador, Honduras, and Nicaragua. Then he met Elvira Malmstrom. She was a first-term missionary from Moody Church in Chicago, and she shared his excitement for working among the Indians. He proposed, she accepted, and they were married on July 9, 1919.

The couple soon opened a mission school to Cakchiquel Indians. The Cakchiquels were descendants of the mighty Mayas. Townsend was fascinated by their ancient, never-written language and its strange popping consonants. Convinced that the Cakchiquels needed to have the Scriptures in their own tongue, he began to build a notebook of Cakchiquel expressions—the first time anyone had ever done so. After figuring out the structure of the grammar, he set about translating four chapters from the Gospel of Mark. When it was completed, he heard the Cakchiquels say, "God talks in our language."

The work, though rewarding, was toilsome, and the Townsends returned to the U.S. for a much needed rest. In Los Angeles Cam became a member of the Church of the Open Door, which provided a generous gift for his work, and met radio preacher Charles Fuller, who pledged to support two Cakchiquel pastors. But the Townsends had an even more important goal for their furlough: Elvira had begun to suffer from extreme mood swings. They had hoped that the rest back home would alleviate the problem, but it didn't help. A psychiatrist who examined Elvira told her to get back to the mission field. So they returned to Guatemala to continue their work on the Cakchiquel New Testament.

By 1928, with other concerns in the village frequently interrupting the painstaking translation work, the Townsends made arrangements to return to California with two Indian assistants so that they could concentrate on the translation work alone. On October 15, 1929, after ten years of toil, the Cakchiquel New Testament was completed. Elvira typed all but the last two words. At a dedication ceremony at First Presbyterian Church of Santa Ana, Cam gave an emotion-filled speech. When he finished, he asked his parents to join him. He let them fill in the last two words of the book of Revelation.

Cam and Elvira returned to Guatemala with the printed New Testaments and began literacy programs among the Indians using this wonderful new book as a reader. They returned to California when Cam's mother died, and it was then that Cam learned that he had tuberculosis and Elvira had a serious heart condition. While convalescing, Townsend began mapping out his future. Hundreds of tribes in Latin America had no written language and therefore no Bible in their own tongue. To give them their own Bible he would need an army of translators. So he established a boot camp.

The first Summer Institute of Linguistics was held in 1934 in an Arkansas farmhouse. There were two students. They named the place Camp Wycliffe in honor of the daring fourteenth-century translator. In 1936, in response to an invitation from Mexican president Lazaro Cardenas, who had heard of Cam's work with an Aztec tribe the previous year, Cam and Elvira, accompanied by ten students, went to Mexico to work among the native tribes. Impressed with Townsend's literacy program, Cardenas met with Cam, and the two began a friendship. Two years later thirty-two SIL members were in Mexico. In 1942 Townsend incorporated the ministry as Wycliffe Bible Translators, and that year they saw 122 students enrolled in the Summer Institute of Linguistics.

But as the ministry grew, Townsend's dear circle of family and friends diminished. In a four-year span he lost his father, then his

SIL friend and partner, Leonard Livingston Legters, and in 1943 his wife. The following year Cam married Elaine Mielke, a teacher to the children of Bible translators in Mexico. Cam and Elaine would have four children.

Wycliffe embarked on Bible translation projects throughout Latin America and in the fifties and sixties to countries in Asia and Africa. By 1965 there were sixteen hundred ministry members working on 350 languages in sixteen countries. Meanwhile, to serve Wycliffe's growing ranks of translators in remote jungles, Townsend developed an aviation ministry. Raising money for planes and recruiting missionary pilots, he formed the Jungle Aviation and Radio Service (JAARS).

In 1965 Townsend settled in North Carolina. He was sixty-nine. But two years after his "retirement" from the field, Townsend heard the call again to go overseas. On October 3, 1968, exactly fifty-one years since he first set foot in the mission field of Guatemala, Cam and Elaine arrived in the USSR to meet with government officials there about translation work. Over the next decade Townsend returned there eleven times, pulling a house trailer through eight Soviet republics and persuading the government to translate a single book of the Bible, 1 John, into five languages that had no Bible.

In 1982, after hearing that his friend Billy Graham had received an invitation to speak in the USSR, Townsend wrote to him, pleading with Graham to go. Now eighty-five, Cam was fighting a losing battle with leukemia and told Graham that he and Elaine would not be able to accompany him. On April 23, ten days after Graham received the letter, Cam died. Graham accepted the Soviet invitation. He later wrote: "I thought of Uncle Cam often during my trip to the Soviet Union two weeks later. As usual, he had been there first, pioneering the way."

LEGACY

Cameron Townsend often said, "Only a person's mother tongue truly speaks to the heart." It was with this belief that he set about translating the New Testament into the unwritten language of a forgotten Guatemalan Indian tribe, and it was the same belief that launched him on a global campaign to bring God's Word to the eyes and ears of thousands more people groups. The ministries he founded, Wycliffe Bible Translators, the Summer Institute of Linguistics, and the Jungle Aviation and Radio Service, continue this colossal mission.

To date, these ministries have seen the completion of the New Testament in 432 languages spoken by over 30 million people. Wycliffe's ministry team includes over five thousand people from more than forty countries, making its mission nearly as international as the field it reaches. Yet the task before them is still great: 440 million people on the planet speak a language for which there is no Bible translation.

The task of reaching all these people with God's Word in their own tongue is daunting. But as Cam himself proved, it's not impossible. Armed with no formal training, he learned an obscure Indian language, invented its alphabet, and gave its speakers the New Testament. But most of all he immersed himself in their culture, became their humble servant and teacher, and revealed God's Word to them in flesh and blood long before he handed it to them in paper and ink.

For additional information about Wycliffe Bible Translators and the Summer Institute of Linguistics, see appendix A.

After this I looked and there before me was a great multitude that no one could count, from every nation, tribe, people and language, standing before the throne and in front of the Lamb. They were wearing white robes and were holding palm branches in their hands. And they cried out in a loud voice: "Salvation belongs to our God, who sits on the throne, and to the Lamb."

Revelation 7:9-10, NIV

Sötiepa nequejtac, hua oyejyeya lalebes meyactie giente, hasta que abele öque quemates intlapoal. Huölajque de noche naciones hua noche tribus hua noche puieblos, hua noche tlajtulte. Ijijcataya ixtla trono hua tieixtla Calnielo. Quepejpeaya intlaquie istöc, hua quepejpeaya ipa inmöhua ixejyo suyotl. Tzajtzajtzeya checöhuac, que-jejtoöya:

Ye tiechenmöquextejque yejuantzetzi toDeus öque yehualuteca ipa trono hua inu Calnielo.

Apocalipsis 7:9-10 (from the Nahautl language, courtesy of Wycliffe Bible Translators)

BOOKS BY CAMERON TOWNSEND

They Found a Common Language: Community through Bilingual Education (out of print)

Tolo, the Volcano's Son: A Novel (out of print)

1897 – 1963

A. W. TOZER

IN PURSUIT OF GOD

Worship is to feel in your heart
and express in some appropriate
manner a humbling but delightful
sense of admiring awe and
astonished wonder and
overwhelming love in the presence
of that most ancient Mystery, that
majesty which philosophers call
the First Cause, but which we call
Our Father in Heaven.

In Pursuit of God: The Life of A. W. Tozer

In 1948 A. W. Tozer received an invitation to preach in McAllen, Texas. When he boarded the Pullman car for his long train ride from Chicago, he set Bible and paper before him. Then he began to write. All night long the words came to him as quickly as he could put them down. Approximately a thousand miles later, as the train pulled into the McAllen station the next morning, Tozer had completed the first draft of *The Pursuit of God*.

In Short

The words of A. W. Tozer flowed from his soul. To him, writing was a form of worship with pen in hand. While it took one long train ride to write his most famous book, Tozer spent a lifetime in the pursuit the book describes. For half a century readers have found in the works of this tenacious pursuer guidance and direction for their own quests to find and marvel in the presence of God.

Faith

Aiden Wilson Tozer was born in rural western Pennsylvania on April 21, 1897. As a child he was small for his age, and he made up for what he lacked in stature through mischief, discord, and a sharp wit. His formal education ended with grammar school, as did the use of his formal name, which he shortened to "A. W." Later on he preferred that others simply use his last name.

While he was still a boy, his family's house was destroyed in a fire, and his father suffered the first of several nervous breakdowns. When Tozer was a teen, his family moved to Akron, Ohio, where Tozer was first confronted with the question of his faith. A neighbor asked him if he was a Christian, and Tozer replied that he would have to think about it. That neighbor had planted a tiny seed in the young man who would soon begin a lifetime of thinking about that very thing.

The seed sprouted a year later when Tozer stumbled upon a small crowd of people gathered in the street. He moved in for a closer look and spotted an old man in the heart of the circle. He was preaching. Tozer was struck by the strangeness of the idea— preaching in the *street*. But the old preacher's words struck him even more strangely. The moment Tozer got home he climbed into the attic, where he could grapple with God in privacy. When he emerged, he knew he was a Christian.

Tozer was overcome by a desire to get to know this new Lord of his and immediately sought out a quiet place in his crowded household to make further acquaintance. While his faith started in the attic, it grew up in the cellar. There he found a space behind the furnace, claimed it, cleaned it, and began spending hours in his quiet place to pray, study, and meditate. Tozer's early ritual of spending long hours with God grew into a lifelong habit.

He became active in a local church, where he met his future bride, Ada Pfautz. Ada's deeply spiritual mother took an immediate liking to Tozer and eventually convinced him of his need to be filled with the Holy Spirit. One evening in her home the two prayed together. *In Pursuit of God: The Life of A. W. Tozer* relates Tozer's description of what happened that night: "I was baptized with a mighty infusion of the Holy Spirit. I know with assurance what God did for me and within me. At that point, nothing on the outside held any important meaning for me. In desperation and in faith I took a leap away from everything that was unimportant to that which was most important: to be possessed by the Spirit of the living God. . . . Any tiny work that God has ever done through me and through my ministry for Him dates back to that hour when I was filled with the Spirit."

FRUIT

On April 26, 1918, three years after they had met, Tozer and Ada were married. The groom had gone on a missions trip to West Virginia before they were married, and he returned there with Ada soon after the wedding. They held tent meetings and prayer services and went door-to-door to share the gospel. The two saw firsthand both the trials and the victories of ministry life, and they liked what they saw. That same year Tozer was drafted into the military, but World War I ended within months, bringing him home by Christmas. Soon after, Tozer was preaching occasionally at a local church and, to his own church's dismay, delivering sermons in the street.

So Tozer found some other street preachers and followed them back to *their* church. It was a Christian and Missionary Alliance fellowship, and he and Ada decided that they had found their home. The pastor befriended Tozer, lending him books from his own library and letting him preach in his pulpit. He also opened the young man's eyes to the idea of becoming a pastor. Tozer received a call from a West Virginia church and took it. It was the first of several Alliance churches he would serve in.

In those days many Alliance congregations embraced a "walk by faith" philosophy in regard to the pastor's pay. Simply put, there *was* no pay, just the gifts the members offered. The Tozer family, now with a new baby, had to pray and trust God for food to eat. God provided for them in creative and faith-testing ways, convincing Tozer that as long as he was doing what God called him to do, he had no need to worry about material things.

Indeed, in later years, as he enjoyed success in his many pursuits, he never deviated from this. If a church board brought up the subject of his pay, he would excuse himself and leave the room. If he got an honorarium for speaking, he gave it away. And although his books sold in great quantities, he signed away much of what he received in royalties to those he deemed more needy.

After serving in two churches in West Virginia, Tozer accepted the pastorate at an Alliance church in Toledo, Ohio, where he witnessed his father's conversion following one of his sermons. In 1924 Tozer took the call to a large church in Indianapolis, whose

members were more educated and had higher expectations for
their pastor than did those in his previous churches. Tozer,
conscious of his own lack of education, began a regimen of intense
study.

Every Monday and Wednesday he could be seen walking from
the library, his arms filled with books. He read voraciously and
contemplated everything he read, and he also began to write. The
church's newsletter expected him to submit a pastoral sermon
each month, which forced him to labor intensely over messages
that were easily spoken but harder to write. Word by word he
honed his writing for maximum impact.

After four years in Indianapolis Tozer received an invitation to
become pastor of Chicago's Southside Gospel Tabernacle, which
later became Southside Alliance Church. Initially he turned down
the invitation, but eventually he agreed to go on the condition that
he would not be a "visitation pastor"—that is, he would not be
expected to spend his days meeting members, greeting visitors,
and comforting the sick. Instead, he would spend hours each day
in study, prayer, and meditation, preparing his own heart as he
prepared his messages. The church board agreed, and the Tozers
moved to Chicago, where they stayed for thirty-one years.

The church grew quickly, and Tozer's reputation grew with it,
resulting in invitations to speak at many churches, camps, and
Bible conferences. His family expanded too. Nine years after the
birth of their sixth son the Tozers finally got a daughter. Tozer
hosted a Saturday-morning radio program on Moody Bible Institute's station WMBI. During the broadcast, called *Talks from a
Pastor's Study,* Tozer would stand—never sit—in his study, delivering his message to an unseen audience on the other end of the
radio microphone.

In 1946 he was elected vice president of the Christian and
Missionary Alliance. At the end of his four-year term, he became
editor of the Alliance's official weekly magazine.

To find the critical inspiration he desired, Tozer would read
from the Bible and read or softly sing hymns. Soon he would be
enveloped in God's presence. Ideas would begin to come, and he

would pick up the pencil and write as fast as he could to keep up with what was being poured into his soul.

The Alliance magazine gave him a much-watched platform from which to address the issues confronting Christians. But the stress of producing weekly editorials nearly cost him his life. In 1952, just two years into his editorship, he suffered a heart attack. Tozer recovered and tendered his resignation to his leaders. At the next council meeting, however, he allowed himself to be reelected, and he continued as editor until his death.

In the late 1950s Tozer decided to bring to a close his long tenure at Southside Alliance to concentrate on writing and conference speaking. But he got a call from Avenue Road Alliance Church in Toronto, and under his standard condition that he could focus on his messages, he became their preaching pastor. This was to be Tozer's final church. He died four years later, on May 12, 1963, at the age of sixty-six. His body was laid to rest in a small cemetery in Akron. The epitaph inscribed on his stone is the title once given to Moses, David, Elijah, and other faithful pursuers: A Man of God.

LEGACY

Although we know him best for his writing, A. W. Tozer was first a preacher. He covered hundreds of topics in over four decades of preaching, but he spoke best of what he cherished most: the work of the Holy Spirit, purity of heart, the indwelling Christ, the importance of worship.

In prayer Tozer would discover that God was entrusting him with a particular message. It would become a "burden" and often find its way into a series of sermons. If the burden intensified, he knew it was time to take pen in hand.

Most pastors must serve in a wide variety of often conflicting roles, from preacher to shepherd, evangelist to counselor, administrator to comforter. God called Tozer to a very specific ministry and blessed him with churches that permitted him to stick to his call to preach. Some might question the prudence of investing hours each day, every day, in preparing a single Sunday sermon. Tozer couldn't see it any other way. A. W. Tozer spent his life in pursuit of God. The words he wrote along the way are meant to spur us into joining the pursuit.

When Moses came down the mountain . . . he wasn't aware that his face glowed because he had spoken to the Lord face to face. Exodus 34:29

BOOKS BY A. W. TOZER

How to Be Filled with the Holy Spirit (1992)
Let My People Go: The Life of Robert A. Jaffray (1990)
Of God and Men (1995)
Prayer Warriors: Powerful Portraits of Soldier Saints on God's Front Lines (1998)
Success and the Christian: The Cost and Criteria of Spiritual Maturity (1994)
The Attributes of God: A Journey into the Father's Heart (1998)
The Best of A. W. Tozer, vol. 2 (1995)
The Best of Tozer (1995)
The Divine Conquest (1995)
The Early Tozer: A Word in Season (1998)
The Knowledge of the Holy: The Attributes of God: Their Meaning in the Christian Life (1997)
The Pursuit of God (1998)
The Pursuit of God/The Pursuit of Man (1999)
The Pursuit of Man: The Divine Conquest of the Human Heart (1998)
The Tozer Pulpit: Selections from His Pulpit Ministry (1994)
The Tozer Topical Reader (1999)
Tozer on Entertainment and Worship: Selected Excerpts (1998)
Tozer Speaks to Students (1998)
Who Put Jesus on the Cross? And Other Messages on Christian Integrity (1996)

1931–

DESMOND TUTU

NOT POWER BUT AUTHORITY

Humans are of infinite worth
intrinsically because they
are created in God's image.
Apartheid, injustice,
oppression, exploitation are
not only wrong; they are
positively blasphemous
because they treat the
children of God as if they are
less than His.

The Words of Desmond Tutu

On a February day in 1988 a group of ministers representing nearly every denomination in South Africa gathered in a cathedral in Cape Town. After praying, they linked arms and marched toward the government building to deliver a petition to the prime minister. They didn't get far. Outside the cathedral a line of riot police blocked their path and ordered them to disperse.

Instead, the ministers knelt at the policemen's feet. Under orders, the police arrested them and dragged them away. One of these robed criminals was Desmond Tutu. Like Moses before Pharaoh, his petition was refused. And like the Hebrew story, this one would get much worse before it ever got better.

IN SHORT

Archbishop Desmond Tutu, Nobel Peace laureate and leader of the Anglican church in South Africa, is arguably the most respected Christian on the African continent. As Moses had done three millennia earlier at the opposite end of the continent, Tutu led his people to freedom. His life's story is largely the story of South Africa's hard-won release from the slavery of apartheid, a freedom won not through power but in the authority of Jesus Christ.

FAITH

Desmond Mpilo Tutu was born "in exile" on October 7, 1931. Like the Jews in ancient Egypt, most blacks in South Africa had few rights and no say in their destiny. Tutu grew up surrounded by poverty and injustice in a world starving for social and spiritual freedom.

The Tutu family was very poor. Desmond's mother worked as a domestic servant for a white family, and his father was a respected schoolteacher, but even these good jobs paid poorly in a land where whites had all the wealth—and the power to keep it that way. One day, while walking with his mother, the young Desmond saw a priest do something unheard of for a white man in South Africa: He smiled at Mrs. Tutu and tipped his hat. The Anglican priest was Father Trevor Huddleston.

At fourteen Desmond contracted tuberculosis. For two years he lay in a hospital filled with dying men, at one point nearly dying himself. During his long illness Father Huddleston visited him daily. The priest brought him books and inspired Desmond to a lifelong commitment to Christ.

In 1948, while Desmond was still in high school, South Africa's white voters elected the National Party to leadership. Their campaign slogan was "apartheid," an Afrikaans word meaning "apartness." Their objective was to separate South Africa's races, both socially and geographically. The Party outlawed mixed-race marriages and divided communities and public services according to race. Blacks who lived near white neighborhoods were forced to move. Black Africans, who had long been forced to live as marginal citizens, were now exiles in their own country.

Tutu was one of the fortunate few. He graduated from high school with distinction and was able to enter the university. He followed his father's path and studied to become a teacher.

In 1955 Tutu married Leah Nomalizo Shenxane. They named their first child Trevor, after Desmond's mentor. One other life-changing event happened that year. The government passed the Bantu Education Act, which federalized the church schools and severely restricted the quantity and quality of education provided to black children.

Tutu could not tolerate being a teacher under the Act's conditions, so in 1958 he resigned his teaching position and entered a seminary. Three years later he was ordained in the Anglican church. In 1962, at age thirty-one, he moved his family to London, where he would study theology at King's College and work as an assistant curate in a parish. Life in London came as a delightful shock. In South Africa, every police officer was a potential enemy, empowered to detain a black person for any reason. But at Speaker's Corner in London's Hyde Park, anyone could speak on any issue, no matter how outrageous, while the police stood by to protect the speakers!

Tutu excelled at King's College, earning a bachelor's degree in 1965 and a master's degree a year later. During his studies he worked in several London churches. His powerful, heart-lifting sermons and casual, outgoing nature won him many friends among the congregations. By the time he left England to return to Africa, Tutu was convinced that blacks and whites could live and work together easily if they chose to. Unfortunately, his own country had chosen another path.

While he was away, things in South Africa had worsened. Opponents of apartheid were imprisoned without trial and often tortured. Nelson Mandela, the leader of the African National Congress (ANC), had received a life sentence. Blacks were forced from their homes and neighborhoods and were exiled to "homelands," bleak patches of low-value land that quickly became slums.

Tutu's first appointment was as a lecturer in the Federal Theological Seminary in the Cape Province. He also served as chaplain at Fort Hare University, one of only three universities for black students. In 1968, as campus protests in the United States and Europe made the news worldwide, the Fort Hare students held their own sit-in. About five hundred students were sitting quietly on a lawn when the riot police arrived. The protesters were told to disperse or face expulsion. When they refused to leave, the police came at them with armored cars, dogs, and tear gas. Many were expelled. In South Africa that meant they could never attend college again.

The violent incident shook Tutu to the soul. He was a man with three degrees, the respect of the church, and many friends. But he was a black man, without a vote, without a voice, without the power to change things. Or so it seemed. Tutu continued in his spiritual growth, setting aside regular times for prayer, meditation, and fasting.

FRUIT

Tutu took his first bold political action in 1976. After witnessing firsthand the growing poverty, despair, and anger among his neighbors, especially the young, Tutu sent an open letter to the new prime minister, John Vorster, appealing to him as a fellow Christian to heed the fact that Jesus Christ "has broken down all that separates us irrelevantly—such as race, sex, culture, status, etc."

In his reply to the letter Prime Minister Vorster suggested that the white opposition in parliament had put Tutu up to writing it. Within six weeks of the letter the police had gunned down a thirteen-year-old high school student in a protest. In the resulting riots, the death toll ran to 140. What started as a student protest in Soweto quickly became a national uprising, with school children across South Africa joining in calls for change.

But Tutu was not among them. The Anglican church had elected him bishop of Lesotho, so he and his family moved back to the tiny nation for two years.

In 1978 Tutu was called back to South Africa, this time to serve as the first black general secretary of the South African Council of Churches (SACC). Meanwhile, the unrest of the past few years had led the government to begin easing some of the apartheid laws.

However, the rising tide of angry black young people demanded more. Violence escalated on both sides, and Tutu found himself in the middle. He pleaded for peace and reconciliation with each side, but his views on the key issue were clear: In every speech, sermon, article, and interview, he denounced apartheid.

To Tutu, apartheid and oppression and violence were moral and spiritual concerns. But to most white South Africans, apartheid was a political policy, and Tutu, a clergyman, had crossed the line. They attacked him with a vengeance.

To the degree that he was hated in his own country, Tutu was becoming loved in the rest of the world. In his travels abroad Tutu began to call on the heads of countries and corporations to stop buying South African exports and divest themselves of investments in his country. That got the world's attention. The South African government also took note. They could control his messages in South African media, but overseas he was beyond censorship.

In October 1984 Tutu received the Nobel Peace Prize. South African blacks went wild in celebration. Congratulations poured in from world leaders, among them Pope John Paul II, President Ronald Reagan, Poland's Lech Walesa, and Indira Gandhi of India. To Tutu's great regret and sadness, South Africa's leaders were silent.

In 1986 Tutu was elected archbishop of Cape Town, the highest position in South Africa's Anglican church. He was now the most respected black leader in the world and one of the most important people in South Africa.

In 1988, after President Botha banned all antiapartheid groups, Tutu and other church leaders led the petition-delivery march that got them arrested. On March 16, 1988, Tutu was granted an interview with President Botha. Botha questioned Tutu and his followers on their faith, asking if they were acting on behalf of the kingdom of God or the kingdom promised by the outlawed African National Congress and the Communist Party.

In Tutu's written reply he defended his biblical authority to speak out against the "political issue" of apartheid.

In May the churches of the SACC launched a nonviolent campaign under the banner "Standing for the Truth." Then on August 31, a bomb destroyed the SACC headquarters in Johannesburg. Over the next year church leaders would hold many marches and services. There would be strikes and rallies and arrests and murders. Tutu spoke at countless churches, meetings, and rallies.

Finally, in September 1989, after an election-day bloodbath in Cape Town, public opinion among white voters began to turn. Tutu scheduled an illegal march, the first challenge to the newly elected president, F. W. de Klerk. The march was allowed to go forth, and a crowd of thirty thousand people moved triumphantly through the streets of Cape Town. On the balcony of City Hall Tutu invited the new president to "come and see the new South Africa!" Within weeks de Klerk removed the ban on outlawed opposition groups and released Nelson Mandela from twenty-seven years of political imprisonment.

In 1991 the key segregation laws were repealed, and the following year de Klerk won a mandate for constitutional reforms to be negotiated with Mandela and others.

In 1994, after many near-disasters and dead ends, black South Africans voted in their first national elections. On May 9 Tutu led another parade to Cape Town's City Hall. Before a crowd of seventy thousand Tutu introduced the new executive deputy president, F. W. de Klerk, the man he had invited to join them five years earlier on the same spot. Then he introduced their new president, Nelson Mandela. Tutu had prayed countless prayers in the eighteen years between his first humble letter to the leader of the old South Africa and this introduction. He finally had his answer.

Legacy

Archbishop Desmond Tutu's role in South Africa and the world has not changed since the 1994 victory. A country whose people have been born and bred to racism and violence does not change overnight. Tutu continues to pray, speak, plead, and counsel for justice in his country, always holding up Jesus as the model and maker of what is right. And he continues to work as Christ's emissary in other parts of the world, persuading governments and their people that peace is the only road to prosperity.

It is tempting for those who have seen only the glorious results of Tutu's work to label him a charismatic political leader who just happens to be a Christian. But Tutu's victories were not his own. They were the fruit of his faith, the products of a God at work in an obedient servant. He never sought or held political office, never counted upon the power of the State to carry out his mission. Instead, he called upon Christ as the source of authority over power, good over evil. He calls us to do the same.

You are all children of God through faith in Christ Jesus. And all who have been united with Christ in baptism have been made like him. There is no longer Jew or Gentile, slave or free, male or female. For you are all Christians—you are one in Christ Jesus. Galatians 3:26-28

BOOKS BY DESMOND TUTU

Crying in the Wilderness (1982)
Cry Justice! (1986)
The Vision of Peace (1999)
Exploring Forgiveness (1998)
Reconciliation (1997)
The Rainbow People of God (1996)
Christianity amidst Apartheid (1990)
The Words of Desmond Tutu (1989)
Hope and Suffering (1984) (out of print)
South Africa (with Francis Norton) (1986) (out of print)

Appendix A:
Information about
Organizations and Ministries

Brother Andrew
Open Doors International
Open Doors USA
P.O. Box 27001
Santa Ana, CA 92799
phone: (949) 752-6600
fax: (949) 752-6442
Web site: http://www.solcon.nl/odi

Booth
The Salvation Army (locations in virtually
  every city in the U.S.)
phone: (800) SAL-ARMY (725-2769)
Web site: http://www.salvationarmyusa.org

Bright
André Kole Productions
325 W. Southern
Tempe, AZ 85282
phone: (480) 968-8625
E-mail: ak@andrekole.org
Web site: http://www.andrekole.org

Athletes in Action
P.O. Box 588
Lebanon, OH 45036
phone: (513) 933-2421
Web site: http://www.aiasports.org

Campus Ministry (national office)
100 Lake Hart Drive, Dept. 2500
Orlando, FL 32832
phone: (407) 826-2500
Web site: http://www.uscm.org

Family Life
P.O. Box 23840
Little Rock, AR 72221-3840
phone: 1-800-FL TODAY (1-800-358-6329)
Web site: http://www.familylife.com

Here's Life Inner City
142 W. 36th Street
New York, NY 10018
phone: (212) 494-0321
Web site: http://home.ccci.org/hlic/home.htm

JESUS Video Project
275 W. Hospitality Lane, Suite 315
San Bernardino, CA 92408
phone: 1-800-29-JESUS
Web site: http://www.jesusvideo.org

Josh McDowell Ministry
P.O. Box 1000
Dallas, TX 75313-1000
phone: (972) 907-1000
Web site: http://www.josh.org

Student Venture
100 Lake Hart Drive, Suite 3200
Orlando, FL 32832
phone: 1-800-699-4678
Web site: http://www.ccci.org/
  student_venture

Colson
Prison Fellowship
P.O. Box 17500
Washington, DC 20041-0500
phone: (703) 478-0100
Web site: http://www.prisonfellowship.org

Dobson
Focus on the Family
8605 Explorer
Colorado Springs, CO 80920
phone: (719) 531-3400
resource orders: 1-800-232-6459
Web site: http://www.FOTF.org

Falwell
Thomas Road Baptist Church
701 Thomas Road
Lynchburg, VA 24502
phone: (804) 239-9281
E-mail: jerryfalwell@trbc.org
Web site: http://www.falwell.com
    http://www.trbc.org

Liberty University
1971 University Boulevard
Lynchburg, VA 24502
phone: (804) 582-2000

Graham
The Billy Graham Evangelistic Association
1300 Harmon Place
Minneapolis, MN 55403
phone: (toll-free response number)
    (877) 247-2426
(general information) (612) 338-0500
Web site: http://www.graham-assn.org

The Billy Graham Center Museum Home
    Page
Web site: http://www.wheaton.edu/bgc/
    museum

Hybels
Willow Creek Community Church
61 East Algonquin Road
South Barrington, IL 60010-6143
Contact: Jean Blount
phone: (847) 765-5000
Web site: http://www.willowcreek.org

John Paul II
Web site: http://ww.vatican.va

Johnson
YFC National Headquarters
Youth for Christ/USA
P.O. Box 228822
Denver, CO 80222
phone: (303) 843-9000
fax: (303) 843-9002
E-mail: yfc@gospelcom.net
Web site: http://www.gospelcom.net/yfc

King
The Martin Luther King Jr. Center
    for Nonviolent Social Change, Inc.
The King Center
449 Auburn Avenue, NE

Atlanta, GA 30312
phone: (404) 524-1956
Web site: http://www.thekingcenter.com

The Martin Luther King Jr. Web site at
    Stanford University:
http://www.stanford.edu/group/King

Machen
Westminster Theological Seminary
P.O. Box 27009
Philadelphia, PA 19118
phone:(215) 887-5511
Web site: http://www.wts.edu

McPherson
The International Church of the Foursquare
    Gospel
1910 West Sunset Boulevard
Los Angeles, CA 90026
phone: (213) 989-4242
Web site: http://www.foursquare.org

Mears
Gospel Literature International
P.O. Box 4060
Ontario, CA 91761-1003
phone: (909) 481-5222
fax: (909) 481-5216

If you are in the neighborhood and would
like to visit GLINT, the street address is:
Gospel Literature International
2910 Inland Empire Boulevard, Suite 104
Ontario, CA 91764-4896
Web site: http://www.glint.org

Mott
YMCA of the USA
101 North Wacker Drive
Chicago, IL 60606
phone: (312) 977-0031
fax: (312) 977-9063
Web site: http://www.ymca.net

YWCA of the USA
Empire State Building
350 Fifth Avenue, Suite 301
New York, NY 10118
phone: (212) 273-7800
fax: (212) 465-2281
Web site: http://www.ywca.org

Palau

Luis Palau Evangelistic Association
P.O. Box 1173
Portland, OR 97207
phone: (503) 614-1500
Web site: http://www.lpea.org

Perkins

Christian Community Development
   Association (CCDA)
3827 W. Ogden Avenue
Chicago, IL 60623
phone: (773) 762-0994
fax: (773) 762-5772
Web site: http://www.ccda.org

Pierce

World Vision
Partnership Offices
800 West Chestnut Avenue
Monrovia, CA 91016-3198
phone: (626) 303-8811
fax: (626) 301-7710
Web site: http://www.wvi.xc.org

Samaritan's Purse
P.O. Box 3000
Boone, NC 28607
phone: (828) 266-1980
fax: (828) 266-1053
E-mail: usa@samaritan.org
Web site: http://www.samaritan.org

Tada

JAF Ministries
P.O. Box 3333
Agoura Hills, CA 91301
phone: (818) 707-5664
TDD: (818) 707-7006
Web site: http://www.jafministries.com

Mother Teresa

Missionaries of Charity
335 East 145th Street
Bronx, NY 10451
phone: (718) 665-3054

Townsend

Wycliffe Bible Translators street address:
100 Sunport Lane
Orlando, FL 32809
phone: (407) 852-3600
fax: (407) 852-3601
E-mail: info.usa@wycliffe.org

Calvin Hibbard Townsend Archives
Summer Institute of Linguistics
Box 248
Waxhaw, NC 28173
phone: (704) 843-6000
E-mail: info@jaars.org.

Appendix B:
For Further Reading

Books about Oswald Chambers
Oswald Chambers, Abandoned to God: The Life Story of the Author of My Utmost For His Highest
   by David McCasland (1993)
Oswald Chambers, An Unbribed Soul by David Willoughby Lambert (out of print)

Books about G. K. Chesterton
As I Was Saying: A Chesterton Reader edited by Robert Knille (out of print)
Gilbert Keith Chesterton by Maisie Ward (out of print)
G. K. Chesterton by Michael Finch (out of print)
The Man Who Was Chesterton by E. Raymond Bond

Books about Jim Elliot
Shadow of the Almighty: The Life and Testament of Jim Elliot by Elisabeth Elliot (1989)
Through Gates of Splendor by Elisabeth Elliot (1986)

Books about Jerry Falwell
Jerry Falwell: Aflame for God by Gerald S. Strober (out of print)
Jerry Falwell and the Jews by Merrill Simon (1984)

Books about Charles E. Fuller
A Voice for God: The Life of Charles E. Fuller by Wilbur M. Smith (out of print)
Give the Winds a Mighty Voice: The Story of Charles E. Fuller by Daniel P. Fuller (out of print)

Books about John R. Mott
History of the World's Alliance of Young Men's Christian Associations by Clarence Prouty Shedd
   et al., with a foreword by John R. Mott
John R. Mott: Architect of Cooperation and Unity by Galen M. Fisher
John R. Mott: World Citizen by Basil Joseph Matthews
Layman Extraordinary: John R. Mott, 1865–1955 by Robert C. Mackie and others.

Books about J. B. Phillips
J. B. Phillips: The Wounded Healer by Vera Phillips and Edwin Robertson (out of print)

Books about Bob Pierce
Bob Pierce: This One Thing I Do by Franklin Graham and Jeanette Lockerbie (out of print)
Days of Glory, Seasons of Night by Marilee P. Dunker (out of print)
Man of Vision, Woman of Prayer by Marilee Pierce Dunker (out of print)

Books about Dorothy L. Sayers
Dorothy L. Sayers by Mary Brian Durkin
Dorothy L. Sayers: The Life of a Courageous Woman by James Brabazon
Such a Strange Lady: An Introduction to Dorothy L. Sayers (1893–1957) by Janet Hitchman (out
    of print)
The Letters of Dorothy L. Sayers by Barbara Reynolds
The Remarkable Case of Dorothy L. Sayers by Catherine Kenney (1991)

Books about Mother Teresa
Mother Teresa by Joan Graff Clucas (1988)
Mother Teresa by Linda Carlson Johnson (1991)
Mother Teresa by Caroline Evenson Lazo (1993)
Mother Teresa by Richard Tames (1989)
Mother Teresa of Calcutta: A Biography by Edward Le Joly (1985)
Teresa of Calcutta: A Pencil in God's Hand by Franca Zambonini (1993)

BIBLIOGRAPHY

In addition to many of the books listed at the end of each chapter and the titles listed in appendix B, the authors have consulted the following sources:

Aikman, David. *Great Souls: Six Who Changed the Century.* Nashville, Tennessee: Word, 1998.

Bailey, J. Martin, and Douglas Gilbert. *The Steps of Bonhoeffer: A Pictorial Album.* New York: MacMillan, 1969.

Baldwin, Ethel May, and David V. Benson. *Henrietta Mears and How She Did It!* Glendale, California: Regal Books Division/Gospel Light Publications, 1966.

Barker, Dudley. *G. K. Chesterton: A Biography.* New York: Stein and Day, 1973.

Berk, Stephen E. *A Time to Heal: John Perkins, Community Development and Racial Reconciliation.* Grand Rapids, Michigan: Baker, 1997.

Bethge, Eberhard, ed. *Dietrich Bonhoeffer: Letters & Papers from Prison.* New York: MacMillan, 1953.

Bowden, John. *Karl Barth.* London: SCM Press Ltd., 1971.

Bruns, Roger A. *Preacher: Billy Sunday & Big-Time American Evangelism.* New York: W. W. Norton, 1992.

Callahan, Annice. *Spiritual Guides for Today.* New York: Crossroad Publishing Company, 1992.

Campus Crusade for Christ International. "Bill Bright Wins 1996 Templeton Prize." [Online]. Available: http://www.ccci.org/news/pressrelease1.html [no date].

Canton Baptist Temple. "Christian Hall of Fame." [Online]. Available: http://www.bbfi.org/hof/portraits/html [no date].

Canton Baptist Temple. "Christian Hall of Fame." [Online]. Available: http://www.bbfi.org/hof/ironside/html [no date].

Canton Baptist Temple. "Christian Hall of Fame." [Online]. Available: http://www.bbfi.org/hof/fuller/html [no date].

Casalis, Georges. *Portrait of Karl Barth.* Garden City, New York: Doubleday, 1963.

Christian History Institute. "January 31, 1955—The Death of John R. Mott." [Online]. Available: http://www1.gospelcom.net/chi/calendar/jan31.html [no date].

Coomes, David. *Dorothy L. Sayers: A Careless Rage for Life*. Oxford: Lion, 1982.

D'Souza, Dinesh. *Falwell before the Millennium: A Critical Biography*. Chicago: Regnery Gateway, 1984.

Dale, Alzina Stone. *Maker and Craftsman: The Story of Dorothy Sayers*. Grand Rapids, Michigan: Eerdmans, 1978.

————. *The Outline of Sanity: A Life of G. K. Chesterton*. Grand Rapids, Michigan: Eerdmans, 1982.

Du Boulay, Shirley. *Tutu: Voice of the Voiceless*. Grand Rapids, Michigan: Eerdmans, 1988.

Dudley-Smith, Timothy. *John Stott: The Making of a Leader*. Leicester, England: InterVarsity Press, 1999.

Eden, Martyn, and David F. Wells, eds. *The Gospel in the Modern World: A Tribute to John Stott*. Leicester, England: InterVarsity Press, 1991.

Elliot, Elisabeth. *Passion and Purity*. Old Tappan, New Jersey: Revell, 1984.

————. *A Chance to Die: The Life and Legacy of Amy Carmichael*. Grand Rapids, Michigan: Revell, 1987.

English, E. Schuyler. *Ordained of the Lord: H. A. Ironside, A Biography*. Neptune, New Jersey: Loizeaux Brothers, 1976.

Fellows, Lawrence. *A Gentle War*. New York: Macmillan, 1979.

Finley, James. *Merton's Palace of Nowhere*. Notre Dame, Indiana: Ave Maria Press, 1978.

Focus on the Family [Online]. Available: http://www.family.org

Fuller, Daniel P. *Give the Winds a Mighty Voice: The Story of Charles E. Fuller*. Waco, Texas: Word, 1972.

Furlong, Monica. *Merton: A Biography*. San Francisco, California: Harper & Row, 1980.

Gehman, Richard. *Let My Heart Be Broken with the Things That Break the Heart of God*. New York: McGraw, 1960.

Gjergji, Lush. *Mother Teresa: Her Life, Her Works*. New Rochelle, New York: New City Press, 1991.

Graham, Franklin. *Rebel with a Cause*. Nashville, Tennessee: Nelson, 1995.

Greene, Carol. *Desmond Tutu, Bishop of Peace*. Chicago: Children's Press, 1986.

Hart, D. G. *Defending the Faith: J. Gresham Machen and the Crisis of Conservative Protestantism in Modern America*. Baltimore, Maryland: Johns Hopkins University Press, 1994.

Hefley, James, and Marti Hefley. *Uncle Cam: The Story of William Cameron Townsend, Founder of the Wycliffe Bible Translators and the Summer Institute of Linguistics*. Waco, Texas: Word, 1974.

Hibbard, Calvin T. *Significant Events in the Life of William Cameron Townsend and the Organizations He Founded*. Waxhaw, North Carolina: Summer Institute of Linguistics, 1995.

Hopkins, C. Howard. *John R. Mott: 1865–1955, A Biography*. Grand Rapids, Michigan: Eerdmans, 1979.

Houghton, Frank. *Amy Carmichael of Dohnavur: The Story of a Lover and Her Beloved*. London: S.P.C.K., 1953.

In Touch Ministries. "Spiritual Journeys of Great Christians." [Online]. Available: http://www.intouch.org/INTOUCH/portraits/amy_carmichael.html [no date].

In Touch Ministries. "Spiritual Journeys of Great Christians." [Online]. Available: http://www.intouch.org/INTOUCH/portraits/aw_tozer.html [no date].

In Touch Ministries. "Spiritual Journeys of Great Christians." [Online]. Available: http://www.intouch.org/INTOUCH/portraits/francis_schaeffer.html [no date].

In Touch Ministries. "Spiritual Journeys of Great Christians." [Online]. Available: http://www.intouch.org/INTOUCH/portraits/corrie_ten_boom.html [no date].

In Touch Ministries. "Spiritual Journeys of Great Christians." [Online]. Available: http://www.intouch.org/INTOUCH/portraits/henrietta_mears.html [no date].

In Touch Ministries. "Spiritual Journeys of Great Christians." [Online]. Available: http://www.intouch.org/INTOUCH/portraits/oswald_chambers.html [no date].

In Touch Ministries. "Spiritual Journeys of Great Christians." [Online]. Available: http://www.intouch.org/INTOUCH/portraits/jim_elliot.html [no date].

In Touch Ministries. "Spiritual Journeys of Great Christians." [Online]. Available: http://www.intouch.org/INTOUCH/portraits/peter_marshall.html [no date].

JAF Ministries. [Online]. Available: http://www.joniandfriends.org [no date].

King, Coretta Scott. *My Life with Martin Luther King, Jr.* New York: Holt, Rinehart and Winston, 1969.

Larson, Mel. *Young Man on Fire: The Story of Torrey Johnson and Youth for Christ*. Chicago, Illinois: Youth Publications, Inc., 1945.

Lawler, Ronald O. *The Christian Personalism of John Paul II: The John Paul Synthesis—A Trinity College Symposium I*. Chicago, Illinois: Franciscan Herald Press, 1982.

Livingston, J. "An Introduction to Karl Barth." [Online]. Available: http://www.faithquest.com/frames.html [no date].

Longfield, Bradley J. *The Presbyterian Controversy: Fundamentalists, Modernists & Moderates*. New York: Oxford University Press, 1991.

"Luis Palau Evangelistic Association." [Online]. Available: http://www.lpea.org [no date]. Press kit supplied by Mike Umlandt, LPEA, (503) 614-1500.

Malinski, Mieczyslaw. *Pope John Paul II: The Life of Karol Wojtyla*. New York: The Seabury Press, 1979.

Marshall, Catherine. *A Man Called Peter*. New York: Avon Books, 1994.

————. *His Name Is Peter: The Story of Peter Marshall*. New York: McGraw, 1951.

McGrath, Alister. *J. I. Packer: A Biography*. Grand Rapids, Michigan: Baker, 1997.

McKim, Donald K., ed. *How Karl Barth Changed My Mind*. Grand Rapids, Michigan: Eerdmans, 1986.

McKinley, Edward H. *Marching to Glory*. San Francisco: Harper & Row, 1980.

Minus, Paul M. *Walter Rauschenbusch: American Reformer*. New York: MacMillan, 1988.

Mott, John R. "The Pastor and Modern Missions—A Plea for Leadership in the World." Ed. Dick Cotton. Mission Frontiers, Jan/Feb 1995. [Online] Available: http://www.uscwm.org/mf/95/MF95.01-02.14-Mott.html [no date].

Mott, Michael. *The Seven Mountains of Thomas Merton*. Boston: Houghton Mifflin Company, 1984.

Murdock, Norman. *Origins of the Salvation Army*. Knoxville, Tennessee: University of Tennessee Press, 1994.

"Nobel Lectures." Amsterdam: Elsevier Publishing Company, 1964–1970. [Online]. Available: http://www.ee.nobel.se/laureates/peace-1946-2-press.html [no date].

Oates, Stephen B. *Let the Trumpet Sound: The Life of Martin Luther King, Jr*. New York: Harper & Row, 1982.

Piper, John. "Brothers, Read Christian Biography." [Online]. Available: http://wwwdesiringgod.org/resources/brothers_biography.html [no date].

Poletto, John M. *Modernity and the Schaefferian Legacy: Evangelicalism at the End of the 20th Century*. South Hamilton, Massachusetts: Gordon-Conwell Theological Seminary, 1994.

Quebedeaux, Richard. *I Found It! The Story of Bill Bright and Campus Crusade*. San Francisco, California: Harper & Row, 1979.

Reddick, L. D. *Crusader without Violence: A Biography of Martin Luther King Jr*. New York: Harper & Brothers, 1959.

Reynolds, Barbara, ed. *The Letters of Dorothy L. Sayers: 1899–1936: The Making of a Detective Novelist*. New York: St. Martin's Press, 1995.

Rian, Edwin H. *The Presbyterian Conflict*. Grand Rapids, Michigan: Eerdmans, 1940.

Schaeffer, Edith. *The Tapestry: The Life and Times of Francis and Edith Schaeffer*. Waco, Texas: Word, 1981.

Schulke, Flip. "Martin Luther King, Jr. Biography." In *King Remembered*. [Online]. Available: http://members.aol.com/Steph2110/MLK/mainpage.html [no date].

Sharpe, Dores Robinson. *Walter Rauschenbusch*. New York: MacMillan, 1942.

Sheen, Fulton J. *On Being Human: Reflections on Life and Living*. Garden City, New York: Doubleday, 1982.

———. *The Divine Romance*. Washington, D.C.: National Council of Catholic Men, 1938.

Simpson, J. F. Minor. *The True View of Dr. J. Gresham Machen*. Booklet—no other information available.

Sister Marie Virginia. *G. K. Chesterton Evangel*. New York: Benziger Brothers, 1937.

Smith, Wilbur M. *A Voice for God: The Life of Charles E. Fuller*. Boston: W. A. Wilde, 1949.

Snyder, James L. *In Pursuit of God: The Life of A. W. Tozer*. Camp Hill, Pennsylvania: Christian Publications, 1991.

Spanger, Ann, ed. *Bright Legacy: Portraits of Ten Outstanding Christian Women.* Ann Arbor, Michigan: Servant Books, 1983.

Stonehouse, Ned B. *J. Gresham Machen: A Biographical Memoir.* Grand Rapids, Michigan: Eerdmans, 1954.

Strober, Gerald, and Ruth Tomczak. *Jerry Falwell: Aflame for God.* Nashville, Tennessee: Nelson, 1979.

Supremacy of God Ministries. "Christian Biography." [Online]. Available: http://www.wp.com/griffith&books/1/2/sfe/sf.html [no date].

Sussman, Cornelia, and Irving Sussman. *Thomas Merton.* Garden City, New York: Image Books, 1980.

The Dorothy L. Sayers Society. "Dorothy Leigh Sayers." [Online]. Available: http://www.sayers.org.uk/dorothy.html [no date].

"The History of Wycliffe Bible Translators." [Online]. Available: http://www.wbt.org/wbt-usa/WBT-hist.htm [no date].

"The Holy Father." [Online] Available: http://www.vatican.net/holy_father/john_paul_ii/index.html [no date].

The Museum Home Page. [Online]. Available: http://www.wheaton.edu/bgc/museum [no date].

Tischler, Nancy M. *Dorothy L. Sayers: A Pilgrim Soul.* Atlanta, Georgia: John Knox Press, 1980.

Von Bismark, Ruth-Alice, and Ulrich Kabitz, eds. *Love Letters from Cell 92.* Nashville, Tennessee: Abingdon Press, 1995.

Wilson, Philip Whitwell. *General Evangeline Booth of The Salvation Army.* New York: Scribner, 1948.

Winner, David. *Desmond Tutu: The Courageous and Eloquent Archbishop Struggling against Apartheid.* Milwaukee, Wisconsin: G. Stevens Publishing, 1989.

Yancey, Philip, ed. *The Classics We've Read, the Difference They've Made.* New York: McCracken Press, 1993.

Young, Dinsdale T., ed. *Oswald Chambers: His Life and Work.* London: Simpkin Marshall Ltd., 1933.

Zellweger-Barth, Max. *My Father-in-Law: Memories of Karl Barth.* Allison Park, Pennsylvania: Pickwick Publications, 1986.

Zettersten, Rolf. *Dr. Dobson: Turning Hearts toward Home.* Nashville, Tennessee: Word, 1989.

Zoba, Wendy Murray. "Bill Bright's Wonderful Plan for the World." *Christianity Today,* 14 July 1997.

ABOUT THE AUTHORS

Writer and producer **Todd Temple**'s passion is to introduce teenagers to the excitement of living for Christ. His writing projects and other productions are the fruit of seventeen years of youth work on both local and national levels. He is the founder of 10 TO 20, an organization that writes, produces, and presents events for teens both on its own and for other national youth ministries, including Josh McDowell Ministry, Youth for Christ/USA, and Promise Keepers, as well as for several denominations.

Todd has written eighteen books for teenagers and adults and dozens of articles for magazines such as Focus on the Family's *Breakaway* and *Brio* and Youth Specialties' *Youthworker.* He has a bachelor's degree from the University of California, Irvine, and makes his home in Del Mar, California, where he is an "occasional" surfer.

Kim Twitchell studied magazine journalism and English at Syracuse University. She has been on staff with Campus Crusade for eleven years, nine of those working with Josh McDowell Ministry, where she has most recently directed the writing department. Kim has traveled to Russia twice with Josh McDowell Ministry, leading groups and serving on the media team.

She has also worked on special projects with the chaplain for the New England Patriots and the Boston Red Sox. Kim is a student at Westminster Theological Seminary in Philadelphia, where she is pursuing a master of arts in religion.